the Eunuch and the Virgin

the Eunuch

and the Virgin

A STUDY OF CURIOUS CUSTOMS BY

PETER TOMPKINS

Bramhall House, New York

NEW YORK

Library of Congress Catalog Card Number: 62-19289

Manufactured in the United States of America
First Edition

This edition is published by Bramhall House,
a division of Clarkson N. Potter, Inc.

(A)

To UGK who had the courage to put up with its conception; to HBT who had the courage to support it; and to CNP who had the courage not to try to abort it, this volume is timorously dedicated.

ACKNOWLEDGMENTS

The author wishes to acknowledge the use of information from the following sources:

Hans S. Bellamy, *Moons, Myths and Man,* 1936; *The Book of Revelation Is History,* 1942; and *In the Beginning God,* 1945, all published by Faber & Faber Ltd. and quoted by permission of the author and Faber & Faber Ltd.; Robert Briffault's essay on "Sex In Religion" is from *Reasons For Anger,* published by Simon & Schuster, New York, 1936; *The Mothers,* Macmillan & Co., New York, 1927; and *Sin and Sex,* The Macaulay Co., New York, 1931; Francois Fejto, *Behind the Rape of Hungary,* David McKay Co., New York, 1957; Sigmund Freud, *Totem and Taboo,* W. W. Norton & Co., New York, 1952; *Collected Papers,* Volumes II and V, Basic Books, Inc., New York, 1959; *Modern Sexual Morality* and *Modern Nervousness,* Eugenics Publishing Co., 1931; Sir James Frazer, *The Golden Bough,* twelve volumes, published by Macmillan & Co., New York, 1936; Robert Frazier, *Malenkov,* Lion Books, Inc., New York; Robert Graves, *The Nazarene Gospel,* Doubleday & Co., Inc., Garden City, 1954; E. M. Harding, *Woman's Mysteries,* published by Longmans Green & Co., New York, 1935; Professor Edwin Oliver James, *The Cult of the Mother-Goddess,* Barnes & Noble, New York, 1959; John A. MacCulloch, *Religion of the Ancient Celts,* T. T. Clark, Edinburgh, 1911; Barnette Miller, *Beyond the Sublime Porte,* Yale University Press, 1931; and *The Palace School of Muhammad the Conqueror,* Harvard University Press, 1941; Norman Mosley Penzer, *The Harem,* G. G. Harrap & Co., London, 1936; Petronius, *The Satyricon,* translated by William Arrowsmith, The University of Michigan Press, 1959. Copyright by William Arrowsmith. The poetry on page 27 is used with the permission of The University of Michigan Press and appears on page 22 of their edition; Wilhelm Reich, *The Function of the Orgasm,* 1961, and *Selected Writings,* 1960, published by Farrar, Straus & Cudahy, New York. Bulletins of the Orgone Institute Press are quoted by permission of the Wilhelm Reich Infant Trust Fund; as are excerpts from *Character Analysis,* 1949; *The Sexual Revolution,* 1962; *Cosmic Superimposition,* 1951; and *The Oranur Experiment,* 1951; Steven Runciman, *Byzantine Civilization,* Longmans, Green & Co., Inc., New York, 1933; Vincent Starrett, *Oriental Encounters,* Normandie House, Chicago, 1938; Budu Svanidze, *Georgiy Malenkov,* Allan Wingate, London, 1954; Immanuel Velikovsky, *Ages in Chaos,* 1952, and *World's in Collision,* 1950, Doubleday & Co., Inc., Garden City, N. Y., by permission of Immanuel Velikovsky and Doubleday & Co., Inc.; John Sebastian Marlowe Ward, *Who Was Hiram Abiff?,* Baskerville Press, London, 1925; Jessie L. Weston, *The Quest for the Holy Grail,* G. Bell, London, 1913; Merton S. Yewdale, *The Origin of the Human Race,* American Book-Stratford Press, New York, 1939.

CONTENTS

I
ON LUI COUPA "LE" ET "LES"

This book was to have started with a bang!—with the description of the castration of a ten-year-old boy by Coptic monks in the Upper Nile valley at the beginning of the twentieth century.

But the pathos with which my publisher pleaded that the general public, unable to stomach such details, would read the book no further, led me to desist.

Indeed the operation is a bloody and a gruesome one; its purpose, in this case, to provide eunuchs as guards for Moslem seraglios—units, like the Western family, of a social structure.

Still, I would not have desisted, even after I understood the publisher to be willing to include the material later on—when, as he put it, "the reader won't mind so much: he'll be used to the subject"—unless I had realized that, at the very outset, he had gone to the heart of the subject, to the point and purpose of the book.

With his squeamishness he had bared a psychological substratum in human beings, and especially males, of a great touchiness about sex and castration—more deadly even than the operation itself.

What's more, his attitude was proof of the contention of modern psychologists that fear of sex is unnatural in human beings, that it is an implanted phenomenon, held down to a large extent, as in brainwashing, by the very horror of castration!

I realized too that he might well have bared the motivating energy of my own years of research into what has turned out to be one of the most hidden and glossed-over questions: why human beings desecrate the human organism by castrating each other—and themselves?

Some force had urged me on.

Why else—apart from the fact that no such study exists in the English language, or in any other that I could find after a decade or more of research in the major libraries of Europe and America—should I struggle with a history of eunuchs and virgins?

As I pieced together the story of castration, tracing it through historic times, both in Occident and Orient, analyzing the various purposes to which it has been put, tracing it through the convolutions of religion and mythology, I found myself in possession of a reversed Ariadne's thread, which, as I fingered it into corners—sometimes fascinating, sometimes nauseous, sometimes far afield from the apparent goal—led, at last, to the very depths of the maze, face to face with a minotaurish monster the facets of which were made up of life and death and sex and the future of the race.

Sigmund Freud, and especially his early follower, Wilhelm Reich, have all along maintained that castration is a phenomenon primarily of the patriarchal era, designed to control human beings, to make them submissive, to mold them, in fact, into the precise opposite of that ideal of the democratic world, the self-determined, genitally uninhibited, free man, enjoying the fruit of his own labor.

It is a theory with far-reaching connotations.

At the beginning of the period of authoritarian patriarchy —which has lasted some four to six thousand years—the sexuality of children and adolescents was fought, says Reich, by direct castration or genital mutilation of one kind or another. Later, and more effectively, psychic castration, by way of implanting sexual anxiety and guilt feelings, became the accepted method.

But why castration? And what great power or series of events initiated the patriarchal era?

In Reich's theory, the basic function of sex repression was and is to keep humans more easily in a state of submissiveness, just as castration of stallions and bulls serves that of securing willing beasts of burden. With this theory Sigmund Freud—who seems to have graduated from the class of revolutionary to that of elder statesman—was in thorough agreement.

But to facts before figurings. It subenters at this point that the reader—or some of the readers—may not know exactly what takes place in the operation of castration, so that, after all, to postpone the details would hardly serve his interest, any more than to avoid the subject would alter the fact that in the Middle East it is still being done today very much as it was at the turn of the century when small boys, torn from their families, were dragged across the hot Sahara to the present site of the Aswan dam and there castrated.

It was a pretty bloody procedure.

But let us take the plunge.

Attached to a horizontal table by means of leather straps across his arms, waist and legs, a thin ligament was knotted tightly around the boy's genitals, then the lot sliced off with a very sharp razor.

To cauterize the wound a red poker or hot tar was applied; whereupon the mutilated youngster was buried to the waist in hot sand, or in the mud of the Nile, there to suffer for five or six days without food or water to impede micturition and prevent death from hemorrhage.

If lucky enough to survive—and the mortality rate was about eight in ten—the freshly made eunuch was unearthed, bandaged with aromatic oil, nursed on milk and water for another eight days.

If within three months cicatrization did not occur, improper healing and infection might last indefinitely, causing the victim great pain with each micturition.

An alternative method—rarely used because its results, if anything, were even less satisfactory—was to twist and tear off the entire array of organs as was formerly done with horses.

Thus, in this civilized world, young boys between the ages of seven and ten were, and still are, castrated to serve as slaves for their fellow human beings. But there is nothing new about the system.

The operation, usually partial, of the testes only, but often complete, has been performed from earliest times, and for the oddest reasons.

Not only by conquerors has it been done as a means of subduing the vanquished, but by doctors as a supposed cure for masturbation, by the Church (or enterprising impresarios) to produce the greatest soprani that have ever graced *bel canto*, by Roman matrons—and in this case the operation was only partial—to obtain a lover without unwanted children, by husbands as revenge against importunate lovers, by old men to spite their overdemanding younger wives, by soldiers as a means of avoiding military service, by slothful Chinese to obtain a pension, and—most extraordinarily—by Puritan Christian sects as a key to the gates of heaven.

Throughout history, and very likely earlier, eunuchs have played the most diverse roles, from cooks and chamberlains to dukes and admirals, from fathers of the Church to transvestite wives of Roman emperors.

In the twentieth century there have been, and in many cases still are, eunuchs scattered across the globe from the Politburo to the Porte, from Pernambuco to the Palace of Peking.

The Bible—that is to say, the New Testament in the King James version—gives three basic types of eunuchs: those so born from their mother's wombs, those made eunuchs by men, and those who do it to themselves "for the kingdom of Heaven's sake."

An extraordinary passage, which appears only in Matthew, much disputed, possibly itself emasculated by some editor, and the cause of many a Christian hacking off his private parts, it has been so cleaned up in the Revised English Bible as to be unrecognizable; neither the word eunuch nor any euphemism for it any longer appears.

Nevertheless, as the text originally stood, it drew the fundamental difference among the three main categories; among those to whom it happened by birth, those who did it to themselves, and those who, for what might be classed generically as political reasons, did it, or do it, unto others.

Of the latter sort, the Egyptians, Persians, Assyrians, Ethiopians, Medes, and the Hebrews all castrated, as a means of subduing them, their vanquished enemies. So did the Chinese. Among the American Indians, it was the women who did it to their captured prisoners.

Ancient monuments show conquerors cutting off the phalli of the vanquished in sign of servitude, their right hand that they might no longer bear arms.

In the inventory of trophies taken by the Egyptian King Meneptah from the invading Libyans, thirteen centuries before Christ, there are included a total of 13,230 penises, six of which belonged to generals. No worse, I suppose, than the Nuremberg trials.

A Theban relief shows the victorious Egyptians throwing trophies into a pit, with the inscription: "Prisoners brought before the king, 1000; phalli, 3000."

Nebuchadnezzar II of Babylon thus mutilated his Jewish prisoners of war, whereas the Biblical David, to prove that he was worthy of becoming Saul's son-in-law, brought him, so it tells us in I Samuel 18:27, two hundred foreskins of conquered Philistines.

The most fantastic of such tales is the one told by a nineteenth-century historian of the Seldjuk sultans in which after a great victory over the last of the Khwarazmians, Key Coubad I ordered the testicles or scrotums of thirty thousand slain enemy soldiers joined together to produce three hundred tents—a task which apparently occupied the greater part of the army for five whole days, but produced what was described as a memorable memento of the battle!

Soon the practice developed of seeking out the smartest-looking children of a conquered enemy, castrating them, bringing them up with care in the palace, usually by other eunuchs, to form a sort of palace civil service.

Herodotus flatly maintained that it was the Assyrians who were the first to make use of eunuchs for other than religious purposes. He tells how Persian generals in their campaigns against the Greeks no sooner got possession of a town "than they chose out all the best favored boys and made them eunuchs, while the most beautiful girls they tore from their homes and sent as presents to the king. . . ."

Xenophon gives the first truly analytic description of their use. When Cyrus was about to rule an empire he became suddenly worried for his own security, realizing that "men are nowhere an easier prey to violence than when at meals or at wine, in the bath, or in bed and asleep."

Looking about to see who were the most faithful men to have around him at such a time, he concluded that no man was likely to be absolutely faithful to his master so long as he was tied by love of life, sweetheart or child. As eunuchs had none of these attachments, nor could they have any, "he selected eunuchs for every post of personal service to him, from doorkeepers up."

Not that it helped him in the end: a eunuch with the odd

name of Masabetes, was to sever his head from his dead body, as a reward for which—such was the tenuous temper of the times—he, in turn, was flayed alive.

In the Persian empire many eunuchs rose to high positions: Bagoas, one of the generals of Artaxerxes III, helped him conquer Egypt in the fourth century B.C., though his reliability can be judged by the fact that he poisoned Artaxerxes, and was then put to death by Darius.

That the Persians had long made use of eunuchs is indicated by the carvings on the walls of Nineveh. On the walls of Assyrian palaces dating 1000 B.C. or earlier there are bearded, jowled chamberlains with double chins, strongly in contrast with the bearded males. They appear also as musicians, bread-bakers, cooks, military intendants or high civil servants.

Some historians maintain that the Egyptians borrowed the use of eunuchs from the Persians. If so, say the archeologists, it must have been at an early date, for there are representations of dancing women guarded by eunuchs on the walls of Egyptian tombs as early as 4450 B.C.

Other historians maintain that the Persians and Babylonians adopted the custom after their early incursions onto the shores of the Nile.

Ammianus Marcellinus, in whose works history and mythology are pleasantly confused, maintained that it was the legendary Semiramis of Babylon—of whose irresistible charms and sexual excesses Lucian gives such a pretty picture—who, after murdering her husband, originally had the idea of surrounding herself with eunuchs to protect her "nonexistent reputation for virtue." Supposedly of a jealous disposition she is reputed to have had her lovers emasculated as soon as she was through with them so they could not enjoy the embraces of other women—a subtlety for which she in turn was said to have been murdered by one of her own emasculated victims.

Later historians who set her down as Summuramat gave her a far less interesting sex life; still others attribute to her genocide, accusing her of having castrated weaklings and the infirm so they would not weaken the race.

Unlike the Persians and the Assyrians, the Greeks did not go in for castrating prisoners of war, though Herodotus does tell a tale of retribution which befell a certain Pannovius of the island of Chios, who made a practice of castrating small boys whom he sold to the Persians for profit. Of this habit he was cured by one of his victims, Hermontinus the Pedasian, when the latter, having become a favorite at Xerxes' court, took advantage of a campaign against Greece to lure four of Pannovius' sons into a trap where he emasculated them and forced them to do likewise to their father.

What eunuchs there were in Greece were attributed to the Phoenicians who passed the custom westward; though in Greece they appear to have been despised by the people and only esteemed by the aristocracy as instructors for their children. Legally, castration was used only against rapists and where a husband caught a lover *in flagrante*.

As a form of punishment for "sex crimes" castration has as long a history as it does for political control.

In ancient Egypt rape was punished by the total ablation of the male's sexual organs. The women involved had their noses cut off, presumably to make them unattractive enough not to be desired by further prospective adulterers.

In India, castration was the punishment for rape and adultery.

In China it was used against what the Chinese considered the worst of crimes: parricide.

Herodotus mentions an extraordinary punishment for rapists and adulterers devised by some wandering tribesmen called Sarmatians, about five centuries before Christ, who would hang their victim by his sexual organs and put a blade near at hand, so that, if he chose, he could free himself. The Poles, many years later, reinstituted the device by nailing the guilty man to a beam and putting a razor in his hand.

In Gaul slaves guilty of adultery were mutilated in their sexual organs, as were some thieves. Among the Huns, adulterous women were cut in half, while the man had his genitals torn off.

The historian Herbert says that in the England of Henry II castration was reserved for refractory priests who refused to follow the edict against Thomas à Becket.

On this Hume elaborates, in his *History of England,* saying that Geoffrey, the father of Henry II "being master of Normandy, the Chapter of Suez presumed, without his authority, to proceed to the election of a bishop, upon which he ordered the whole of them to be castrated, and caused all their testicles to be brought to him on a platter." At which Hume remarks: "Of the pain and danger they, the monks, might justly complain, yet since they had vowed chastity, he deprived them of a superfluous treasure."

A poignant tale is told of Theobold, Marquis of Spoleto, who, having captured several Byzantines sent them back with a notice: "As your Emperor loves eunuchs, every cock he sends me I'll return a capon."

This threat he would have carried out, so the story goes,

had not a Greek woman come to his camp to complain it was not the men he was thus mutilating, but the women; depriving them of that which made for "health, pleasure and children." To which she added that if he wished, Theobold could take their noses, eyes, hands, or feet, but not what "was theirs."

Moved by her naïveté, Theobold is said to have returned her husband intact.

In the Middle Ages, according to a French surgeon, Dr. Millant, in a rare book on eunuchs, castration was the usual pain for *libertinage*, and he quotes one of Froissart's chronicles as saying of some poor sodomist that *"on lui coupa le et les."*

Such punishment was formally ended in French territory by the Code Napoleon when penalties for venery were applied to the exchequer. Lifting a woman's skirt to the knee was then fined six sols (about 35 francs at the turn of the century) the sum being raised in proportion to the height of the skirt, reaching double for exposure of a thigh. If adultery was proved, the whole of 200 francs was required.

Before the Code went into effect, several noted Frenchmen are said to have suffered the penalty of castration, among them the brothers Launay, accused of seducing the daughters of King Philippe le Bel, and Roger de Mortimer for his liaison with Isabel of France.

To Admiral Coligny, head of the Protestants, it was done on St. Bartholomew's night. Not to be outdone, the Calvinists did it to seventeen Catholic priests at Beltreme and Metz.

And to illustrate how dreadfully human beings can behave in wars of religion, Herbert recounts that one of these priests, an old man, had his testicles cooked before his eyes, was made to eat them, then had his stomach cut open so the crowd could witness the degree to which he had digested them.

After the Sicilian vespers it is said that there were shipped from Palermo tons of phalli mixed with salt tunny.

The Serbs and Montenegrans practiced castration as late as the end of the nineteenth century. The Turks did likewise in the Armenian vespers of 1893.

Up till recently, central African tribes cut the phalli of conquered enemies and wore them around their necks as trophies—which is said to have made them a great success with the ladies.

In the Atlas Mountains, Berbers still brought to their prospective fathers-in-law the members of beaten enemies to show their prowess; though a handier method might have seemed more to the point.

As late as 1935 the Abyssinians—famed, or ill-famed, in antiquity as able emasculators—did it to Italian invaders of Ethiopia. An idea of their method can be gained from a chronicle about earlier Abyssinian victims: "Each was stripped, held down by four or five others while one took a sort of yatagan or sword, made a crease in the skin of the victim just below the navel, and cut down towards his goal in the shape of a thong which got wider as it went, then cut the whole off neatly. Hemorrhage was rapid and copious, but it was discovered that it could be stopped by pouring hot butter on the wounds." Of the victims some 40 per cent appear, by this antidote, to have been saved to go home, though, as the author of the above description, Dr. Dermarquay, puts it with somewhat gruesome Gallic humor, only to find "their beds occupied by brother-in-law"—such being the custom in the country.

Thucydides, describing an Athenean plague through which he lived, said people trying to avoid the disease when it had descended "to those parts of their anatomy" resorted to castration, as they did when struck by elephantiasis, so as not to pass it on.

During the Renaissance and up to the time of Amboise Paré, castration was almost invariably a concomitant operation for hernia; children were even castrated as a means of preventing hernia, on the theory that eunuchs were never known to have suffered from the ailment.

Paré, known to the French as the father of modern surgery, inveighed against the practice, urging that men should not be deprived of *"ce qui fait la paix du menage."*

Undaunted, charlatans continued to wield the knife, and one eighteenth-century character, armed with a razor, is accused of having mutilated two hundred males in the town of Breslay alone. Pierre Dronis, surgeon to Marie Thérèse, tells of one castrator who was able to keep a huge dog alive on the testicles of the young men he castrated.

Finally the French Royal Society of Medicine took steps to stop the practice, especially after receiving complaints from the provinces of a great number of young men rendered incapable by the operation of performing not their marital but their martial services.

A report of the committee tells how several "surgeons," arriving in town to the blasts of trumpets, proclaimed a surefire cure for hernia for a mere £35.

So successful were they in convincing the patients, that five hundred children were castrated in his diocese, according to reports of the Bishop of St. Papoul, though usually only of one testicle.

Louis XIII forbade the operation by any but "reputable" surgeons. Yet the practice lasted clandestinely into the first half of the nineteenth century, when Millant quotes a man called Delpeck as saying that a woman in the Ardennes had for twenty years been removing the testicles of children as soon as they appeared in the scrotum as a preventive against hernia.

Boethius, in his history of Scotland, states that if any person were visited with madness, epilepsy, gout, leprosy, or any other such dangerous disease, which was likely to propagate from father to son, he was, according to the ancient law of Scotland, to be castrated; if a woman were so afflicted she was to be carefully secluded from all company of men, and, if, by chance, having some such disease she was found pregnant, she, with her offspring, was to be buried alive.

But that is nothing to the subtlety of the twentieth century in which castration has been used as a cure—only a touch more radical than insulin and electric shock—for all sorts of "mental" ailments, the theory being that eunuchs were as free from such derangements as eunuchs in antiquity had been "known" to be free of hernia!

British doctors, leaning to the theory that epileptics were mostly onanists, permanently excited sexually, figured castration as an obvious cure—with varying degrees of success. One patient, having heard of their theory, seized a razor and succeeded in slicing his genitals, of which wound the doctors managed to cure him, but not of his fits.

A Dr. Bacon advocated castration indiscriminately for *all* epileptic males.

In the United States, just catching up with Semiramis at the end of the last century, castration was advocated as a means of preventing the procreation of criminals, and a Dr. Agnew seriously proposed it as a cure for erotic maniacs, further suggesting it for cretins and even alcoholics!

In February of 1888 a doctor with the appropriate name of Orpheus Everts read a long paper before the Academy of Medicine in Cincinnati in which he indicated that castration could constitute the most important factor in social renovation.

Eventually, such is the madness of those who try to attribute madness, the idea was incorporated into the statutes of most of the states of the Union, the method of castration being diminished only to cutting or strangulating the seminal ducts. In California, laws were passed allowing surgeons to castrate even for seduction. In New York, Connecticut, Indiana, Iowa, Kansas, Michigan and North Dakota it was stipulated that "such operations shall be performed in a safe and humane manner."

In Nevada and Washington it was the punishment for "knowledge" of a female under ten years of age, even *with* her consent. *Addio* Lolitas!

In New Jersey and Wisconsin epileptics can still be castrated!

Full circle back to the ancients!—except for one practice, largely attributed to the Romans, not so current in modern times.

In Imperial Rome the principal use for young eunuchs—best summed up by the onomatopoeically descriptive word "voluptas"—caused some wag to point out that Amor backwards spelled Roma.

Tarquin is said to have castrated children to enjoy his "*gouts hors nature*."

Octavius, Tiberius, and Caligula all made spectacles of themselves with orgies of eunuchs.

Hadrian's favorite, *il bell' Antonio*, became world celebrated not only as a eunuch but as a statue.

Lucian, speaking of the "*vice grec*," says that "in the final degradation of this abject life some went so far as to remove with a hot iron those parts which qualified them men," adding that no sort of voluptuousness was foreign to them. Being fatter, softer, hairless, but with a certain part of their anatomy firmer than women, eunuchs were most popular because they could be used in either role without impregnating or being impregnated.

It was through eunuchs, *on dit,* that pederasty spread across the empire and into every class. According to Livy, during the Bacchanales men gave themselves up to debauch more amongst themselves than with women.

In the capital city of the empire a whole street, known as the Via de Toscani, became inhabited by perverts designated *pathici* or *paedicones.*

Dressed usually in a toga and semitransparent clothes, Rome's young eunuchs are described by Seneca as having long hair and bodies completely depilated. The job of emasculating them—as was to be the case many centuries later in the Kingdom of the Two Sicilies—was done by barbers or *tonsores.*

By the end of the second century one could buy an emasculated youth for about a talent, though Domitian, emperor from 81 to 96 A.D., ordered that no boy should be prostituted before he was seven years old.

The eunuch Halotus was supposed to have helped Agrippina poison Claudius with a dish of mushrooms so that her son Nero might succeed as emperor.

Thereafter, Nero, whose tastes were more anal than banal, enjoyed the use of as many as sixty eunuchs in his orgies, even having one of them, Sporus, decked out in female clothing, whom he proceeded publicly to marry, with considerable pomp, and, as Juvenal put it, "was not afraid to appear on the Via Flaminia with this castrated spouse whom he publicly caressed," rumor being that by a second operation the eunuch had been made as much as possible to resemble the fairer sex.

One Roman emperor is said to have become a eunuch himself, but as the historians who make the claim were evidently paid to give him as bad a press as possible the fact is doubtful. Heliogabalus, the young successor to Caracalla, who, two hundred years before Constantine, tried to unite the Roman world in the monotheistic worship of his Sun God, is said by Lampridius to have cut off his genitalia so as to officiate as a priest of his own imported Phrygian religion; however, according to others he did not have the courage to amputate his organ and was content with having it infibulated—a practice current at the time, especially to keep gladiators fit for the arena, of piercing the prepuce with a ring to prevent erection, but which, such is the wantonness of woman, seems to have made them the more in demand as the more sensational.

In fact, the great ladies of Rome, not to be outdone in the pastimes of their spouses, used half-eunuchs, or *spadones*, from whom the testes but not the verge had been gelded, for purposes of their own. As St. Jerome complained, patrician matrons could thus give themselves up to libidinous pastimes in absolute security.

Martial, in one of his epigrams, summed up the reason: "Do you ask, Pannychus, why your Caelia only consorts with eunuchs? Caelia wants the flower of marriage—not the fruit."

Juvenal thundered against this degeneration from the old Roman standard of manliness, and described the method in detail: "Some women always delight in soft eunuchs and tender kisses, and in the absence of beard, and the fact that the use of abortives is unnecessary. The height of their enjoyment, however, is when the lads have been led to the doctor in the heat and first flush of youth with a bush of dark hairs already visible; and the testicles they have waited for and encouraged to grow, in early stages, as soon as they reach a couple of pounds [sic], the surgeon, Heliodorus, seizes and scores just that much over the barber. Made a eunuch by his mistress, conspicuous from afar, he enters the bath the cynosure of all eyes. . . ."

Castrated after puberty, males could apparently perform as required, though some authorities maintain they ceased to be useful after about the first eighteen months.

As for the matrons, Seneca says they counted the time of day by the number of adulteries they could accomplish, and that one day was not sufficient to visit all their lovers.

An essential part of a lady's retinue, eunuchs accompanied their mistresses to the baths—rather like the blackamoors of Venetian ladies some fifteen hundred years later—and lounged about with them on their litters: the elegance of a woman was counted by the number of her attendant eunuchs.

A sufficiently scabrous picture of these Roman eunuchs is painted by Petronius in his *Satyricon* of which the following short passage should be sufficient: "As the crowning touch to our miseries, in waddled a eunuch dressed in a robe of myrtle-green bound up with a sash . . . springing at us again and again, he slobbered our faces with filthy kisses and ground away at us with his buttocks until Quartilla, holding her dress up above her knees, drove him off with a whale-bone-cane. . . .At this point a second eunuch arrived, so incredibly insipid that he seemed a fitting representative of the whole menage. Clapping his hands for attention, he cleared his throat, grunted, and gave vent to the following (in the translation of William Arrowsmith):

O fairies, O buggers
  O eunuchs exotic!
Come running, come running,
  ye anal-erotic!

With soft little hands,
  with flexible bums
Come, O castrati
  unnatural ones!

"Having finished his effusion, he promptly started to slobber me with loathsome kisses, and before I knew it, he had straddled me on the couch and, despite my resistance, pulled off my clothes. Then, for what seemed hours, he worked on me but without the slightest success. Meanwhile a river of sweat and perfume was streaming down his face, leaving his wrinkled cheeks so creviced with powder that he looked like some cracked wall standing desolate under a pelting rain. . . ."

And so on, *ad nauseam*.

Constantine made a stab at limiting the process when he ordered capital punishment for castrators; but as the decree was applicable only within the empire, castrates continued to be imported from the East.

When Constantine moved his court to Byzantium eunuchs were relegated to monasteries mostly in the Taurus mountains. One such, called Topos, was exclusively for emasculates.

But under Constantine's successors eunuchs became thoroughly established at court and soon gained such power that Gibbon in his *Decline and Fall* was led to complain that after Constantine's death ". . . they multiplied in the palaces of his degenerate sons, and insensibly acquired the knowledge, and at length the direction of the secret councils. . . ."

Taking a view diametrically opposed to that of Cyrus, Gibbon insisted that "some particular instances may occur of eunuchs distinguished by their fidelity, their valour and their abilities; but if we examine the general history of Persia, India, and China, we shall find that the power of the eunuch has uniformly marked the decline and fall of every dynasty."

With this the modern historian Steven Runciman disagrees, saying there is no evidence of their physical limitations having warped their characters. Throughout Byzantine history, says he, eunuchs appeared "no more corrupt nor intriguing, no less vigorous or patriotic than their completer fellows . . . providing for the Emperor a governing class which he could trust."

Under Constantius II when the eunuch Eusebius filled the palace with his co-castrates, young patricians subjected themselves to the operation in order to obtain higher places at court.

"Even the noblest parents," says Runciman, "were not above mutilating their sons to help their advancement, nor was there any disgrace in it."

Several eunuchs rose to high rank in the army and the navy. Narses, one of the most renowned, named Chamberlain by the Empress Theodora, put down an insurrection with such cool-headedness that he received the generalship of the armies with which he managed to throw the Goths out of Italy—then live to be almost a hundred.

In the tenth century Nicephorus Urason became a brilliant general, Eustachius Cymnineanus an admiral, and after the Manikert campaign Nicephoros the Logothete was a bold reformer of the army.

In the civil service, where eunuchs were encouraged, the castrated bearer of a title "took precedence of his unmutilated compeer" and many of the higher ranks were reserved for eunuchs alone.

A few posts, such as the prefecture of the city, says Runciman, were traditionally closed to eunuchs, but the strong bureaucracy they developed was a balance against power being concentrated in the hands of the hereditary nobility, a problem which plagued the annals of the West.

Though in Byzantium a eunuch could not be emperor, nor pass his powers to his heirs, this was considered an advantage, as those *too* close to the throne risked losing not their testes but their *têtes*.

Some, like Phocas, lost both in turn: when the fleet of Heraclius, exarch of Africa, appeared before the city to unseat him, he was dragged by women from a hole in which he had hid, mutilated, and executed on the scaffold.

The history of Byzantium reads from one castration to the next.

Nicetas, the young son of Michael I, was castrated when his father fell from power, but later rose to be the patriarch Ignatius.

Romanus I castrated not only his bastard son Basil, who then ruled the empire for several years as Grand Chamberlain, but also his youngest son, whom he intended to make patriarch.

The Empress Irene, who tried unsuccessfully to marry Charlemagne, tried a new variant for keeping one of her sons from succeeding to the throne: she deprived him not of his testes but of his eyes. The Emperor Leo, finding her in bed with his equerry, promptly had the lover castrated.

When Leo was deposed, his four sons suffered a similar fate.

In 1078 when the Comneni took over as a new dynasty the son of Michael Ducas, known as Parapinakes, was made a eunuch: and so it went, till the fall of the empire.

When, in 1453, the Ottoman Turks took over Byzantium and its institutions, they took over the palace eunuchs and maintained them in office to the present century, developing a system from which it is possible to see in detail the mechanics of an authoritarian state in which sexual repression—as described by Freud and Reich—helped one man maintain a dictatorship through the control of a hierarchy of caponized and sadistic males.

European travelers, diplomats, and historians have left a fascinating picture of the intricacies of this system. However, on closer study, it reveals strong similarities with another and much older civilization farther to the east.

2

THE MOST PRECIOUS CHINESE POSSESSION

The central character of the most common Chinese word for eunuch means both "palace" and "castration," yet the earliest record in Chinese history of the use of eunuchs appears to have been about the twelfth century before Christ.

This is no doubt attributable to the destruction of original sources by the Emperor Ch'in shih huang Ti (246-209 B.C.) when, as scholars have pointed out, he ordered all books on history and astronomy as well as works of classical literature, to be burned. Yet China—now once more the seat of an authoritarian dictatorship—has the longest uninterrupted history of the use of eunuchs.

Carter Stent, a Victorian Englishman, who made a painstaking survey of the subject about a hundred years ago (the results of which he published in the *Journal of the Royal Asiatic Society*), maintains he could find no mention of the use of eunuchs in China before the Chow dynasty—which began in 1122 B.C.—when Chow Kung, the younger brother of the first monarch, prescribed castration as a punishment slightly greater than amputation of the hands and feet, slightly lesser than decapitation.

Prisoners thus treated were placed in the service of the imperial family, mostly to guard the emperor's concubines and wives, a practice which continued throughout succeeding Chinese history right to the present century.

As late as 1879 the *Times* correspondent from Shanghai reported that the son and the grandsons of the executed Central Asian rebel chief Yakoob Beg had been castrated and delivered into the hands of the Imperial household as eunuchs because of their father's crime of treason—though the victims were less than ten years old. And this is but one of a series of such reports.

Although Ch'in shih huang Ti may have managed to destroy the records of what preceded him he has left a pretty description of the institution as it flourished in his own reign recorded in the book of Lien-kuo.

There the emperor is said to have kept three thousand concubines attended by innumerable female servants, so that once he had dismissed his court, "he could enjoy their society, drinking with them, listening to their music and strolling with them through his beautiful gardens."

To maintain his privacy this emperor built a palace the walls of which were recorded as being fifteen *li* in circumference, with a tower every fifth step and an enclosed pavilion every tenth. Within these walls were gardens filled with rare flowers and plants, through which, to add beauty to the scene, meandered "a crystal stream, spanned here and there by marble bridges."

However—or so says the book of Lien-kuo—as it was impossible to keep so immense a place in order with women only, and fearing "the ladies would give way to licentiousness were he to employ *men* to do the necessary work, the emperor selected a great number of lads who were made eunuchs for this purpose."

The emperor thus came to be the only male resident of the Palace of Peking, causing Carter Stent to remark: "What a life for the ladies!"

Gradually the system became formalized; the number of eunuchs who served members of the royal family residing in their own palaces became stabilized: the emperor was entitled to three thousand eunuchs; princes and sons of the emperor, to thirty; imperial princesses, daughters of the emperor who married high officials, also to thirty; nephews and young sons (and, in later history, the descendants of the eight Manchu chiefs who assisted in establishing the Manchu dynasty) twenty; grandsons of the emperor, ten; great-grandsons, six; and great-great-grandsons, four. As the court grew in size and luxury, the number of prisoners grew insufficient and recruits had to be sought from volunteers.

Among the reasons which induced Chinese men or boys to become eunuchs Carter Stent enumerates three primary ones: compulsion, poverty, choice. Boys in China were compelled to obey their parents' word as law and would therefore have to submit to castration if the parents, or whatever relative was in authority, decided they needed the money derived from the sale of such a boy, or believed the boy could thus best be provided for in later life.

Grownups, with no means of obtaining an honest livelihood, would choose to become eunuchs rather than beggars, others did so out of laziness because of the good board and lodging and the certainty of provision in old age as well as the possibility of rising to high position (otherwise excluded by birth). There were even cases of middle-aged men becoming eunuchs, some of them after they had been married and had families, induced to it either by poverty, or, as Carter Stent puts it, "the tongues of their better-halves."

As an instance he quotes the case of a poor man in 1853 who entered a pawnshop to dispose of a coat for a small sum. Seeing that the coat was worthless, the pawnbroker refused to advance anything on it, whereupon the man, in a rage, pulled out a knife, emasculated himself, threw the parts emasculated onto the counter, and insisted on pledging them for about four dollars.

The manner in which young boys or men were made eunuchs in China differs only slightly from that practiced in the upper Nile, but appears to have been well systematized and far less dangerous to the patient.

All eunuchs being for the use of the imperial family, the operation was performed within the walls of the imperial palace in a "mean-looking building" near the main gates known as "the shed" and by men known as "knifers."

Recognized by the government, even as late as the twentieth century, these knifers (whose job by then had become hereditary) had the duty of emasculating "those desirous of, or sent to them for the purpose of, becoming eunuchs"; but for this service they were not officially remunerated. A fixed sum—about a guinea and a half of English money—they received from the victim or his parents which was to cover the operation, the victim's convalescence, and the upkeep of the knifers.

Grown-up men who were too poor to pay such a fee could make a sort of installment arrangement with the knifers to pay them a certain percentage of their future salaries as eunuchs, though, as elsewhere in the business world, the knifers appear to have demanded security from their clients and someone to vouch for their credit rating.

When the operation was about to take place the candidate or victim—as the case might be—was placed on a sort of camp bed in a sitting or semireclining position. One man supported him round the waist, while the others separated his legs, holding them firmly down to prevent any movement.

The operating knifer then stood in front of the man, knife in hand, and inquired if he would ever repent. Boys were not asked the question, the consent of their friends being considered sufficient. At the last moment, were a grown victim to demur, even in the slightest, the knifer would not perform the operation, but if he expressed his willingness, "with one sweep of the knife he is made a eunuch."

To prevent too much hemorrhage, white ligatures were bound tightly round the lower part of the belly and the upper part of the thighs. The parts about to be operated on were then bathed three times with hot pepper-water—a recipe normally used to revivify, but in this case obviously intended to have some such effect as the warm milk used in the upper Nile—whereupon the whole, both testicles and penis, were cut off as close as possible with a small curved knife somewhat in the shape of a sickle.

The emasculation being effected, a pewter needle or spigot was carefully thrust into the main orifice at the root of the penis; the wound was then covered with paper saturated in cold water and carefully bound. After the wound was dressed the patient was induced—according to the tenets of the modern school of therapy—to walk about the room for two or three hours, supported by two of the knifers, before being allowed to lie down.

For three days the patient was forbidden liquids, during which time he is said to have suffered great agony, not only from thirst, but from the intense pain of not being able to relieve himself.

At the end of three days when at last the bandage was removed, and the spigot pulled out, the victim obtained "relief from the copious flow of urine which spurts out like a fountain."

If this took place satisfactorily, the patient was considered out of danger, and congratulated; if, on the other hand, he could not make water, he was "doomed to a death of agony, for the passages have become swollen and nothing can save him."

Despite this rough mode of operating, deaths appear to have been rare, and when thoroughly cured, which was generally in about a hundred days, the eunuch was sent to the palace of one of the princes, there to learn his duties.

At the end of about a year, he was transferred to the imperial palace for appointment to whatever services might be required of him. If a number of eunuchs were available at one time, "the ladies who required additional eunuchs, selected from them according to their rank."

From then on the eunuchs began to acquire rank of their own. To rise in the hierarchy each eunuch was required always to be in possession of what was euphemistically called his "precious." To this end, the knifers developed a recipe for pickling the emasculated parts and preserving them in hermetically sealed pint measures.

Upon each promotion the chief eunuch would "inspect the precious" of the candidate and if any had lost it, or had it stolen, he was obliged to buy another from the knifers or borrow or hire one from a eunuch friend.

The "precious" was also prized by a Chinese eunuch because it was placed in his coffin when he died so as to avert the Chinese dread of presenting oneself in another world in any way mutilated, it being the belief that the "King of Hades" was inclined to turn into she-asses men who arrived unpossessed of their manhood!

Naturally, only a few of the three thousand eunuchs in the emperor's employ could reach positions of importance—the "eunuchs of the presence," as they were called; the rest in various grades, were distributed in forty-eight departments, the lowest performing such menial jobs as watchmen, water carriers, chair bearers, gardeners, cooks, and the Chinese equivalent of "tweenies."

Certain "eunuchs of the presence" rose to very high positions, the chief eunuch normally holding the rank of third-degree mandarin.

The Emperor Long had ten favorite eunuchs who managed not only the affairs of the palace, but the more important business of state.

Chinese historians maintain that without scruple they

made use of their influence and power to extort wealth from all ranks and classes. "Those who failed to comply with their rapacious demands, were invariably made to feel the power of the eunuchs by being stripped of office and honors as well as having their wealth squeezed out of them."

Discipline among the palace eunuchs was administered in a manner very similar to that later employed in the Ottoman Empire.

Punishment ran from the bastinado for trifling offenses such as laziness and neglect of duty, to imprisonment or banishment for a number of years in more serious cases. The bastinado was administered by fellow eunuchs from each of the forty-eight departments, each being armed with "a baton made by gluing together two strips of bamboo with the rough side outwards."

As many as eighty to a hundred blows were then administered. When the beating was finished the victim was sent to a surgery and rubbed with ointment, only to be subjected to a repeat performance three days later "to render the punishment more severe." This second flogging, in true Chinese style, was known as "raising the scabs."

Boys, made eunuchs under the age of ten, termed "thoroughly pure" (because they were supposed to be free from the least licentiousness, even in thought), were especially prized, and employed by ladies of the palace with as much freedom as if they were girls, performing, as Carter Stent puts it, "such offices as ought only to be done by women—some of them of a nature that it would be impossible to describe."

Among the duties of the eunuchs in the palace was, of course, that of escorting concubines to the emperor's bed:

"When the emperor wishes for the presence of any particular concubine in his bed chamber he gives a label or tally, on which he has written the name of the lady, to the eunuch in waiting, who takes it to the lady in question, and she is borne in a chair by eunuchs to the emperor's sleeping apartment, which is named the Yang-hsin-tien."

So precisely do the details in this ceremony match those practiced by the sultans of the Ottoman Empire, as will be seen later, it is hard to believe they could have developed independently.

"On retiring to rest the lady does not dare get into the emperor's bed in the usual manner—that is, from the head, or rather, side—but it is etiquette for her to crawl in from the foot till she comes in a line with her imperial bedfellow."

Outside the door two eunuchs kept a tantalizing watch, and before break of day they would arouse the concubine who was then borne back to her own apartment.

As in the Ottoman Empire, the circumstances of the concubine's having slept with the emperor were recorded in a book, with the name of the lady, and the date of the visit. The entry was signed by the emperor and the book referred to in order to substantiate legitimacy of any fruit of that particular encounter. But in harems as large as this it was hardly possible for every inmate to get a chance at mating.

Of the emperor Yang of the Sui dynasty, who reigned about 600 A.D., Chinese historians relate a poignantly pathetic tale. A very licentious type, he selected three thousand women as concubines in his various palaces whom he put under the charge of a chief eunuch named Hsu-yuan, who, being "covetous and avaricious," let himself be bribed by the women with money and presents to induce him to recommend them to the emperor.

But among the women there was one who was so poor she did not have enough with which to bribe the eunuch; unable ever to see the emperor she became so melancholy she committed suicide by hanging.

When the eunuch in charge reported the death to his master the emperor took it into his head to look at the corpse. To his surprise he found it more beautiful than any of the bodies of the women he had possessed and promptly reproached the eunuch for not having brought the lovely creature to his bed while she was still living.

Hearing this, some of the other concubines gathered courage enough to inform the emperor of the reason the girl had never managed to buy her way to her master's favor. So enraged was the emperor he ordered the eunuch instantly beheaded.

And, adds Carter Stent, so smitten was the emperor with the charms of the lovely corpse, "that he wept over it and embraced it, regretting that he had never had an opportunity of doing so while she was living" till, tired out with "unavailing lamentations and caresses," he fell asleep with the corpse of the beautiful concubine still in his arms.

As no outsiders were allowed within the palace walls, one of the special employments of the eunuchs was to entertain the ladies with theatricals. For this purpose a dramatic corps of over three hundred eunuchs was maintained in a special building and on a permanent footing, having no other duties than the rehearsing and performing of plays, at least once a month, and more often when so requested by the emperor or his ladies.

Also, as the ladies could see no man other than the

emperor, a group of eighteen lama priests was recruited from the eunuchs to minister to the spiritual welfare of the ladies of the palace. Apparently it was a job much sought after, if only because lamas received double pay—as eunuchs *and* as priests.

The obvious drawbacks of choosing pastors from such a limited flock are emphasized by Carter Stent: "When a vacancy occurs in the eighteen it is speedily filled up by selecting a eunuch who has either a desire to become a priest, or fancies he has a vocation that way; so that, independent of not having been trained for the priesthood from childhood—as were the regular lamas—many of them know nothing whatever pertaining to their craft when they join; some of them, too, can neither read nor write, and we can readily imagine the amount of ignorance and superstition to be found among these eunuch priests, and the spiritual benefit likely to accrue to the employers of their service."

Vincent Starrett, an American diplomat in China during the 1930's, did some research into Chinese eunuchs which he incorporated into a small book privately printed in Chicago entitled *Oriental Encounters.* After looking into their history "in odd records, sometimes difficult of access" this diplomat came to the conclusion, much like Gibbon's, that "on the whole they have been as vicious and unscrupulous an influence, down the years, as any other herd of jackals one can mention."

Of their function in history he says: "Like politics it became a profession that promised the unscrupulous rogue high office, great power, and vast emoluments; and not a few such rascals adopted it by choice, becoming ministers of state and commanders of armies."

Claiming that in all generations they were the object

of the utmost hatred and fear, this American diplomat also reflected the opinion of some earlier scholar in the following scathing passage: "Compensated for their emasculation perhaps by an increased talent for statecraft and perversion, they became the confidential advisers of emperors and the companions of their most undignified moments. Down the centuries by their craftiness and corruption, their ambitions and their tireless intrigue, the creatures came to exercise so pernicious an influence upon government that several successive dynasties were ruined by their machinations."

So arrogant and overbearing were they in the reign of Ch'ien Lung, and so generally detested, that they were made to suffer for it by one of the Emperor's ministers, whom the chief eunuch had badly insulted.

To revenge himself the minister informed the emperor of a rumor that during the Ming Dynasty there had been considerable licentiousness in the palace between the ladies and certain eunuchs whose mutilated organs had, in the course of time, "grown to some extent," and that he was afraid the situation might be repeating itself.

To prevent any scandal the minister suggested that all the palace eunuchs be inspected and that those whose organs might have partially grown have them "swept clean."

Of a jealous nature, the emperor had the order carried out and many of the eunuchs were forced to undergo a second operation, several of them dying, or, as the Chinese put it, being "swept dead" instead of "clean"—a cruelty for which even the emperor was said to have repented.

One of the more gruesome tales about Chinese eunuchs was told of one who ranked as a prince about five hundred years ago. Having tried all possible means to find a way to regain his manhood, and being advised by an eminent physician that this might be done if he consumed the brains of seven living men, he proceeded, with the help of a battle axe, and seven criminals, to obtain and devour the required prescription, with results that are not recorded.

Certainly the most valorous tale of all is that told of Kang Ping, a favorite and faithful general of the Ming emperor Young Lo.

Being entrusted with the emperor's palace while the emperor went on a journey, and afraid the jealous ministers would accuse him of having taken liberties with the ladies of the palace Kang Ping took steps to preclude any possible disgrace.

When the emperor returned, and, as was expected, falsely accused him, Kang Ping advised his sovereign to look into the hollow of the saddle upon which the emperor had ridden away.

On discovering its contents the emperor promptly raised Kang Ping to the position of Chief Eunuch, and, upon his death "deified" him, which, in China, means a form of sanctification, building a temple to his memory, and creating a patron saint of eunuchs who was venerated "ever after."

The story, of course, is almost identical with that told by Lucian of Combabus and the Assyrian queen Stratonice-Semiramis, more than a thousand years earlier. Combabus, ordered by the king to accompany the queen to Hierapolis and build a temple to Hera, rightly suspected the king would grow jealous of their intimacy, so he secretly castrated himself and placed the results in a sealed coffer which he entrusted to the king.

Sure enough, three years later, when the temple was

built, the king, in a jealous fury, ordered Combabus killed and was dissuaded only at the last minute when Combabus requested the coffer, the contents of which returned him to favor.

Tradition adds that many of Combabus' friends, hearing of his noble gesture, did likewise to keep him company in his affliction, originating, so goes the tale, an order of castrate priests; but the tale, as will later be seen, serves to cover a deeper reality, as does the explanation that Combabus decided to wear only female clothing after a foreign girl, who had come to assist at the ceremony, seeing him so handsome and manly, fell in love with him so deeply that when she discovered their love could not be consumated she killed herself, prompting Combabus, so the story goes, forthwith to dress as a woman to avoid the repetition of such a sad occurrence.

Had Kang Ping, one wonders, heard the story of Combabus?

In the 1930's, when foreign diplomats could still play a leisurely game of golf on the outskirts of Peking, Vincent Starrett, the American envoy, had occasion to visit a nearby temple and interview and even photograph the last of thirty-odd surviving eunuchs from the imperial palace who, at that time, ranged in age between sixty and eighty, and whom he found to be "thin, hairless, fat-lipped and bejowled old men with shrill voices and hair which hung down to their necks."

No longer cringing and servile—as they were supposed to have been under the empire—the American diplomat found them "fellows of a certain spirit and address," one still wearing the velvet pants of the days of former splendor whereas most of the others were dressed in coolie cloth.

In an untidy garden, separated from the graves of some seventeen hundred other eunuchs, mostly of the Ming and Ch'ing dynasties, Starrett found what was marked as the grave of Kang Ping, patron saint of the Chinese eunuch—known to those who revered him as the "Iron Duke"!

For those who wish to satisfy their curiosity further there is an excellent photographic portrait by Cartier-Bresson of one of the very last of these eunuchs taken in the 1950's; and for those who wish to go even further, there is a photograph in one of Dr. Millant's books of such a Chinese eunuch taken in the nude.

Summing up his work, Carter Stent was led to conclude that if it weren't for one word—eunuchs in China might be as scarce as unicorns: the word, of course, was "jealousy."

But what, one may ask, brought jealousy into the world?

3

SCHOOL OF THE WHITE EUNUCHS

Islamic historians claim that the practice of having eunuchs to guard women was unknown among the Ottoman Turks until they took over, in the middle of the fifteenth century, the Byzantine Empire, along with some of its pomp and splendor.

The early sultans, little more than nomad chieftains, were, they say, as unacquainted with the institution of eunuchs as they were with that of keeping a harem. The beginning of the custom is generally attributed to the Calif Muawiyah, founder of the Ommiad dynasty.

Before the advent of Mohammed, Arabs castrated escaped prisoners of war or leading members of tribes who succumbed to them in battle. Mohammed forbade the practice. Later commentators of the Koran were definitely against it.

However, as the Ottomans piled up victories in the Balkans, Middle East and along the coast of Africa, and an ever increasing booty of slaves—male, female and eunuch—poured in on the sultan and his top officers, some system had to be devised to cope with the bonanza. The system was to be the seraglio: a place in which male and female slaves were reared and guarded by eunuchs.

With the increasing need for eunuchs, the Ottomans, avoiding the letter of Islamic law, had the operation performed by non-Moslems.

The word "seraglio," a Westernization of the Persian *serai* (which at first meant simply palace or building—as in caravanserai: a hostel for caravans) came to mean the whole of the palace of the sultan, not only the women's quarters but the central apparatus of government included within its walls, consisting of a cabinet of ministers, a supreme court of justice, the most extraordinary military and civil academy in history, and all the personnel required to service it.

At the height of the system, a corps of eunuchs—well over a thousand in number—not only guarded the royal harem, but were in charge of its academy for training of young executives to run the empire, and, if possible, perpetuate the system.

The social, political, economic, military and educational system developed round the King Bee, the sultan, with his harem of females, ministered by a corps of eunuchs and sexually inhibited young men, is such an extraordinary phenomenon, has left such strong marks on the rest of Europe, and so perfectly illustrates the authoritarian patriarchy analyzed by Freud and Reich, it is worth seeing how it came into being.

To catch the nuances of the system (not far removed from that strange world of bees so carefully described by Maeterlinck) it must be seen in its own peculiar setting.

Not only in Constantinople but in other former capitals of the Ottoman Empire such as Brusa, Adrianople and Salonika, seraglios were built; but the one designed by Suleiman the Magnificent, which came to be known—though erroneously—as the Sublime Porte, was to be the pearl of the diadem. Nor could the Ottomans have chosen a grander setting for this precious ornament which those who have seen it cannot forbear from labeling "a truly Grand Seraglio."

On a narrow point of land where the Dorians first laid the foundations of the great city of Byzantium (named after their leader Byzas), and where Constantine set the capital of his Eastern Roman Empire, this greatest of Turkish seraglios was founded in 1465 on the furthest outpost of Europe, separated from Asia by the swirling waters of the Bosphorus.

Here, cut off from Constantinople and the cupolas and minarets of St. Sophia by a massive wall, and from the water by dentelated sea walls, a strange congeries of buildings, courtyards, and gardens, surmounted by the pointed tower of the Divan, became the seat of one of the most extraordinary and powerful empires in history, the keys to which, literally and figuratively, were in the hands of a corps of eunuchs who are themselves imprisoned within its walls, often for a lifetime.

The first eunuchs to be introduced into the seraglio at the beginning of the fifteenth century were all white and it was not till the latter part of the century that black ones made an appearance.

The first white eunuchs were captured Circassians or Balkans, or whatever the fortunes of war brought to hand. The black, who proved to be more enduring, were introduced from Africa primarily to guard the women of the harem who, with the flow of Christian virgins also captured in war or sent as gifts to the sultan from outlying provinces, kept growing in number.

The theory behind the use of black eunuchs was the hope they would prove so unattractive to the women there would be little chance of dallying: the more ugly or disfigured the eunuch the greater he was prized. For, it must be remembered, the loss of their sexual organs did not necessarily mean loss of sexuality.

Jean-Baptiste Tavernier, Baron of Aubonne, who traveled through Turkey before Shakespeare had written *Venus and Adonis,* and who produced a description of the Grand Signor's Seraglio "containing several remarkable particulars never before exposed to publick view" explained the system thus:

"The most deformed yield the greatest price, their extreme ugliness being look'd on as beauty in their kind. A Flat Nose, a frightful Aspect, a large Mouth, thick Lips, and Teeth black, and standing at a distance one from another (for ordinarily the Moors have fair Teeth) are so many advantages for the Merchants who sell them. . . . The Black, or Negro-Eunuchs, are appointed to guard the Apartment of the Women, and they make choice, for that Office, of the most deform'd and most Aesopical, that can be found."

White eunuchs came to be used solely as chamberlains

to the sultan and to run the various parts of the palace other than the women's quarters—or *haremlik*.

The primary difference between the black and the white eunuchs—apart from color—was that the first were spadones and the latter not.

Tavernier tells an amusing tale about how the black eunuchs got that way: "They are all cut even with the Belly, ever since the time of Solyman the Second, who being one day in the fields, and seeing a Gelding offering to leap a Mare, inferr'd thence, that the Eunuchs who Kept his Wives might likewise endeavor to satisfie their passions; for which he bethought himself of a present remedy, by ordering them to have all cut off; and his Successors have since observ'd the Rule."

During the reign of Sultan Mohammed II the number of white eunuchs in the grand seraglio was twenty-three and the entire number employed by the sultan some forty-odd. After the introduction of black eunuchs as guards for the royal harem, the number increased. By the early sixteenth century there were forty black eunuchs to guard some three hundred women. Under Murad III, who had as many as twelve hundred women, the number of black eunuchs increased accordingly. At the height of the institution there may have been as many as nine hundred of them.

At first the white eunuchs reigned supreme in the hierarchy, but gradually the black eunuchs took over more of the duties of their white brethren so that by the twentieth century not only the harem but the whole seraglio, and thus the whole Ottoman Empire, came under their control.

The functions of the eunuchs is more easily grasped if they are seen in their actual physical surroundings, every detail of which was designed to bolster an atmosphere of absolute authority.

Access to the small point of land known as Seraglio Point was obtainable only through a huge gate in the massive outer wall which separated the sultan's palace from the city, and on either side of which, in appropriate niches, were exhibited the heads of executed victims as a sign to the inhabitants of Constantinople, the empire, and the world at large, of the power of the sultan.

Guarded by day by fifty gatekeepers with guns, bows, and scimitars, and reinforced at night by janissaries (the famed foot soldiers of the empire) in little movable sentry boxes on wheels, this gate of gleaming white marble opened onto an unpaved courtyard about a quarter of a mile long with cobbled paths leading to its various surrounding buildings. Around part of the court was a colonnade to protect horses and servants if the weather was wet.

Known as the first court, or Court of the Janissaries, anyone, of whatever rank, race, color or creed, might enter it freely; but already the atmosphere of absolute power was evident.

This atmosphere was caught in print by another French traveler, Monsieur de Tournefort, who visited Constantinople at the end of the seventeenth century: "Everything is so still, the Motion of a Fly might be heard in a manner; and if anyone should presume to raise his voice ever so little, or shew the least want of Respect to the Mansion-place of their Emperor he would instantly have the Bastinado by the Officers who go the rounds; nay, the very Horses seem to know where they are, and no doubt they are taught to tread softer than in the streets."

Facing onto the court were the infirmary, the imperial bakery and water works, the mint (which employed as many as 580 craftsmen, fifty-eight of them goldsmiths), the private treasury, the palace storehouse, two pavilions for members of the outer service, and, in the corner, the famous Janissary tree, under which until they were mass-murdered almost to a man, the Janissaries had originally dared to overturn their soup cauldrons in a sign of revolt. In another corner stood the fount of execution at which the chief executioner and his assistant washed their hands of blood.

The next court, or Court of the Divan, was separated from the first court by another strongly built wall in the middle of which was the central gate, or Gate of Salutation, again guarded by fifty gatekeepers part of whose duties it was to see that absolute silence was maintained within.

Foreign ambassadors who were allowed to ride through the first court now had to dismount. By the guardrooms was the gate of the executioner, and underneath it dungeons into which prisoners were thrown, pending execution. In the case of high officials it was above this gate that their heads were placed on a row of iron spikes "slowly to blacken in the sun."

A quiet and reposeful court, with boxed hedges lining its radiating paths, it was described by the Venetian Bailo (or consul general) Ottoviano Bon as he saw it in the first decade of the seventeenth century as "a little smaller than the first court but much more beautiful, owing to its variety of elegant fountains, avenues flanked by very tall cypresses, and the presence of certain stretches of lawn where the growing grass provides pasture for a number of gazelles which breed and are regarded with pleasure."

Known as the Court of the Divan because of the small

building at the far end where the "divan" or council of state met four times a week, it was here that the sultan would dispense justice for the empire and give audience to the world.

Next to it, the grand vizier, who, with the sultan, officially governed the empire, had his office.

The purpose of the ceremonies in the Court of the Divan was clearly to impress whoever witnessed them. Norman Mosley Penzer, a modern English historian who spent a great deal of time in the seraglio to write a scholarly book on the subject, called *The Harem*, to which this chapter is indebted, and who may justly claim to have seen more of it than any living man, envisages the scene: ". . . the pageantry of Court Ceremonial, the brilliancy and variety of costumes, the flashing of jewels from turban and scimitar, the silent and almost grim background afforded by the double line of Janissaries, all contributed to attest the power of the Sultan and impress the foreigner with the might and majesty of the Ottoman Empire."

Around the courtyard, as well as the Hall of the Divan, were, *to one side*: a double row of ten kitchens with suites of rooms for the chief kitchen functionaries, two mosques, baths, storerooms, offices and pantries, quarters for the cooks, confectioners, scullions, woodcutters, ice collectors, water carriers, a school of cookery, a musicians' room, tinning shops and the dormitories and washrooms for 150 cooks; *to the other side*: the great stables which housed from two- to four thousand horses in charge of the master of the royal horse, who commanded three thousand or more grooms, stablemen, saddlers and apprentices.

From this court one moved closer to the private domain of the sultan.

At the end of the Court of the Divan was yet another

wall with a third gate known as the Gate of Felicity, or sometimes as the Gate of the White Eunuchs, because of the thirty white eunuchs who guarded it. This was the closed gate, "sacred to majesty," beyond which nothing officially was supposed to be known, but about which sufficient reports have leaked out to be able to form a pretty picture.

Here in the third court, at the height of the Ottoman Empire, the White Eunuchs reigned supreme, and the power they wielded, indirectly, can be seen through the positions they held and the duties they performed, even greater than in China or Byzantium.

Not only were their leaders the confidants of the sultan, but it was they who personally selected, trained and appointed all the leading officials of the Ottoman Empire.

The basic institution they governed was known as the Palace School.

Tayyar Zadeh Ata Bey, the only Turkish historian to have made a thorough study of the palace school system wrote of Murad II:

"Impressed by the great loyalty of the pages and convinced that it would be impossible to find more faithful servants and friends to help him preserve his throne against the attacks of outside enemies and of the Janissaries, the Sultan conceived the idea of rearing and educating in adequate numbers in a general school in his Royal Palace the type of valiant soldier and scholarly official which was so badly needed for all the functions of an empire."

Barnette Miller, an American historian who lived in Turkey during World War I, and who did a great deal of careful research in the Turkish language to produce in the 1930's two extraordinary works on the subject, *Beyond the Sublime Porte* and *The Palace School of Muhammad the Conqueror*, to both of which this chapter is also much in debt, says of the system: "The development of the Palace School from the embryo school of princes in the reign of Murad II into a military school of state for the powerful Ottoman Empire which continued to exist and to function effectively along the same general lines for three and a half centuries, takes rank in the history of education as an achievement of a very high order. So perfect an instrument did it prove of the purpose for which it was designed, that its perpetuation and development became one of the most conscious policies and one of the most powerful traditions of his successors."

The result of this system, as the Venetian diplomat Marcantonio Barbaro was to remark as early as 1584, was that the "Wealth, the military power, and the government, in a word the whole Ottoman state, is founded upon Moslem slaves born in the Christian faith."

And Baron Wenceslas Wratislaw, a Bohemian nobleman who was in Constantinople seven years after Barbaro, noted: "Never, therefore, did I hear it said of any pasha, or observe either in Constantinople or in the whole of Turkey, that any pasha was a natural born Turk; on the contrary, kidnapped, or captured, or turned Turk."

What then was the role of the Turk in Turkey?

Richard Knolles, who wrote a general history of the Turks during the reign of Elizabeth of England, says they gave themselves "wholly unto the Trade of Merchandise, and other their Mechanical Occupations; or else to the feeding of Cattel their most ancient and natural Vocation, not intermeddling at all with matters of Government or State."

Knowledge of the Palace School and of its inmates was for many years extremely scant. For the entire period of their studies—which lasted normally from twelve to fourteen years—the former Christian slaves were cut off entirely from the world, and upon leaving the palace they were bound by vows of secrecy, betrayal of which meant ruin and death.

Upon admission they were given new Turkish names and all connection with their past was severed. They were forbidden communication with their former families and many lost track completely of their original identity and nationality.

Within the palace, conversation except for what was necessary with the officers of the hall was permitted only on stated intervals, and there was no communication between the different halls. Errands were executed in the city by official messengers who were required to obey the slightest of the pages' commands, providing it did not infringe on school regulations. Only on very special occasions was a visitor permitted to visit a page, and always in the presence of two or more white eunuchs.

"It is popularly believed," says Barnette Miller, "that the majority of the student body never saw a woman from the time they entered the Grand Seraglio as young men till they left it as mature men, and that some of them did not remember what a woman looked like!"

Not that this seclusion from women meant they were any more sexually abstemious than the English public school boy. Their "abominable vices against nature" are thus described by the historian Habesci. "The vilest passions of the pages, and their shameful amours with those placed about the person of the monarch, would sometimes occasion commotions that might lead to very dangerous consequences, if fire and sword were not employed to restore tranquility. Yet notwithstanding the utmost vigilance of the eunuchs and governors, they cannot eradicate this unnatural vice. But what can be expected, when it is well known that the Sultans themselves have been almost all of them guilty of the same crime?"

When the Palace School was at its height the course of training for the pages lasted a full fourteen years—a novitiate of seven or eight years in one of the auxiliary schools, then promotion to either the Great or the Small Hall, or else permission to leave the auxiliary schools with the rank of Sipahi, or reserve corps cavalryman. A very small portion of the students completed the entire course, the majority being sent to inferior posts in the army or government upon completion of preparatory school.

The curriculum of the school was planned with a view to promotion from one to the other of the halls in hierarchical order, and also with a view of appointment to military or civilian posts of corresponding grades.

Those who know something of the English public school system and of what has been copied from it by American prep schools, may be amused to find much of the original pattern in the school of the Ottoman pages.

The buildings of the Palace School in the Third Court of the Seraglio at the height of its development consisted of six separate halls or joint dormitories and recitation buildings for six separate schools, plus a conservatory of music, a special mosque for the Palace School, a smaller mosque for the students, a common room for the faculty and staff, four separate apartments for the higher officials of the school administration, and a field of archery. The school infirmary and kitchens were outside the third court.

The halls, about eighty feet in length, each had a gallery sometimes used as dormitory space and sometimes to stow away the coffers in which the pages kept their clothing and personal belongings. According to Tavernier, every page had but "four feet in breadth for his reposing place and as well as by day as by night." They were permitted only one woolen coverlet, four times doubled which served as a quilt and over that they ordinarily had a gold or silver piece of brocade or other rich material. They were not permitted to have coverlets of wool, which would have been much warmer, because they would not afford a decent sight for the grand signor when "he comes ever and anon in the night time pretending indeed as if he would surprise them to see how they demean themselves, in fact sometimes to cover lewd designs."

Those set aside for the Palace service were again separated into two classes, the comeliest and cleverest, those in whom "besides the accomplishments of body they discovered noble genius fit for higher education" were designated as student pages capable of serving the prince.

From this group the cream was again skimmed for the Palace School of the Grand Seraglio; the remaining pages were distributed among the three auxiliary schools and some reserved for high officials in the capital and provinces.

The training of the pages combined in almost equal proportions instruction in the humanities of Islam and physical training in the art of war and government, along with some sort of manual training. It was believed among the Turks that every man up to and including the sultan should be able at any time to earn his living if he chose.

From the day of his admission until his graduation, a student was meticulously drilled in Turkish etiquette and the ceremonies of Moslem religion, especially the prescribed manner of saying the five daily prayers and the reading of the Koran.

Jean Claude Flachat—an eighteenth-century French manufacturer who, together with the French ambassador, the Comte de Castellane, got themselves into the seraglio while the sultan was momentarily away by disguising themselves as workmen delivering some mirrors sent by Louis XV, and of whom more later—reported that the dispositions and inclinations of the students were carefully consulted, the only absolutely required subjects being the Turkish language and the Koran. Languages, grammar, syntax, Moslem theology, jurisprudence and law, Turkish history, mathematics, and music were also taught—instruction being offered in military music and in chamber music, the latter being almost entirely vocal.

Exercises in composition consisted of writing poetry or translating books from Arabic and Persian.

Physical training was begun with gymnastic exercises, and from these progressed to sport of various kinds, cavalry exercises, and other "arts of war."

Initial exercises were archery, wrestling, and sword-practice. The favorite games were *chomaq,* a game played with a ball attached to a cord, and *jerid,* an early oriental form of polo. As they were mostly destined for the cavalry not only did the pages become skilled cavalrymen, but they were also noted for extraordinary feats of riding.

While running their horses at full speed they could unsaddle or resaddle them without slackening their pace, ride standing on the seat of the saddle, ride two horses at a time with one foot on each; whereas two pages, while riding at top speed, could exchange horses, or slide under the bellies of their horses and remount from the other side.

The essential aim of training—apart from the acquisition of the accomplishments believed necessary for men who were to marshal an army or govern a nation—was to instill "a deep loyalty and reverence for the Sultan whose person they were destined to attend, and whose chief ministers they were to become."

Along with general education they were taught good manners, accuracy, honesty and modesty. When addressed by a superior they kept silence, lowered eyes, and arms folded across the breast.

Professor Lybyer in his book on the Empire in the time of Suleiman, suggests that certain elements of the curriculum such as the early division into intellectuals and artisans, the freedom allowed in the choice of subjects, the systematic training of the body, and the emphasis on music, especially choral music, would seem to have been derived from Plato's *Republic*.

In any case it was the object of the training to discover and give further training to youths of exceptional ability for leadership in the state.

Promotions from one hall to another, appointments to student offices, and later to military and administrative positions were all based strictly on the merit system, and pages were "rewarded for the smallest service to their lord, and punished for the smallest fault." The discipline by all accounts must have been comparable to a U.S. Army stockade in time of war. So rigorous was it that many a student after years of hardship and within a few months of graduation and promotion to a high position would throw in the sponge, do anything to get out of the institution, though it meant having to accept lower rank, if not almost a menial position.

Additional incentive to merit was provided in the form of scholarships and allowances, and punishment for failures of duty or accomplishment were frequent and severe, being scolding, fasting, deprivation of the more popular physical exercises and flogging with a long slender lash or stick on the soles of the feet. Anyone who exceeded the limits was expelled from the school, or if the offense were really flagrant suffered the loss of one of his hands.

As one historian put it: "Sour and crabbed eunuchs as preceptors applied the bastinado upon the soles of their feet sometimes until they could not walk for days, or, occasionally even died."

At the height of its development the six halls of the Palace School were the Great and Small Halls in which students usually spent a novitiate of six or seven years; from these they graduated into one of three vocational halls known as the Hall of the Expeditionary Force, the Hall of the Commissariat or the Hall of the Treasury. The few that survived the years of training in one or other of these halls, and were especially able, graduated to the last and highest Hall of the Royal Bedchamber where they were trained for close attendance on the Sultan.

The curriculum in the Great and the Small Halls was largely preparatory. The average age of admission to the Hall of the Commissariat or of the Treasury was twenty-two and the average length of the course was four years each. Here was trained the special entourage of the sultan.

In the hall of the expeditionary force pages were taught to wash and take care of the sultan's linen when he was on campaign or traveling, and they were also the members of the military band. The pages were thus taught to become proficient at sewing, embroidery, leatherwork, the making of bows, arrows and quivers, the repairing of guns, and, naturally, military music. Upon graduating from this hall and not being promoted to the last hall, these pages received commissions in the imperial guard.

The pages of privy commissariat kept in order and prepared the sultan's favorite sweets, molded and distributed the ordinary candles in the apartments of the palace, manufactured and dispensed to the public on behalf of the sultan the pastilles and amulets of amber and musk in great demand as aphrodisiacs. The chief of the commissary attended the sultan during the serving of meals and mixed his drinks.

An idea of what is meant by the privy commissariat can be gained from Tavernier's description: "Here was stored a full assortment of drugs, above all of potent antidotes for poison; the rare and costly spices, perfumes, and aromatics brought from Egypt, Arabia, and the Indies; the huge candles brought from Wallachia, for lighting the Selamlik, the Harem, and Palace Mosques; vast quantities of jams, marmalades, and other sweetmeats; a supply of drinking water from the two Chamlijas and from the stream of St. Simon in the old palace; the delectable syrups manufactured to order in "Grand Cairo" which were the foundation of many of the royal drinks; and the great pieces of ambergris sent by the Pasha of Yemen which was one of the ingredients of the favorite variety of sherbets."

The pages of the treasury were charged with duties in

connection with the imperial treasury and its contents. This treasury, quite separate from the state treasury, was the repository of booty of war and surplus wealth, the rich gifts accumulated by the sultans from the foundation of the monarchy. The only actual revenue received into it was from Egypt and its adjacent provinces but at the height of the Ottoman power this treasury was considered one of the seven wonders of the world.

Pages from the treasury were distinguished from the other pages by a rich bonnet which was estimated to have been worth twelve hundred ducats.

According to Sir Paul Rycaut, who was secretary to the Earl of Winchelsea, ambassador of Charles II to Mahomet Han IV, the more melancholy and less physicallly brilliant of the pages were likely to end up with secretarial jobs in the treasury from which they might eventually be promoted to the secretariat of state.

The pages of the royal bedchamber were the seniors of the school and it was from these that vacancies in the government were filled. Like seniors in any Western school they had many privileges, only these were grown men in their late twenties who had been through a decade and a half of rigorous discipline, such as not being punished like the others and occasionally even being able to maintain a family outside the seraglio which they could visit on certain occasions. They wore rich habits of brocade and cloth of gold, and top members of this hall, being truly *chamberlains,* though they ministered formally to the sultan's personal needs, were in fact being trained to govern vast and complicated establishments.

Their titles included chief swordbearer, master of the horse, master of the wardrobe, and master of the turban.

The master of the horse (like a Christian royal equerry) commanded "1000 equerries, 600 grooms, 6000 herdsmen, numerous rangers, saddlers, camel-drivers, mule-teers, 800 tent-pitchers, many of them also trained exe-cutioners always at his beck and call. . . ."

The master of the turban followed behind the sultan when he went out officially and with him carried a second turban "which was the one to receive the applause and adu-lation of the multitude who dared not raise their heads at the passing of the actual sultan."

Then there was the chief parer of nails, the chief barber who shaved the sultan's cranium, the keeper of the robes who perfumed the sultan's endless wardrobe with the deli-cate essence of aloes, the chief turban winder, the master of the napkin, chief ewer keeper, chief taster (with a suit-able number of subtasters) to see that no poison reached the regal palate.

Pages who had held such offices in the hall of the royal bedchamber upon graduation automatically received the rank of pasha and were appointed as viziers, lord admirals, heads of the Janissaries, or generals of the cav-alry. And those who had not held office passed straight into the imperial guard or were appointed as governors of important towns or outlying districts.

Ata Bey, the Turkish historian who made a thorough study of the Palace School, gives some impressive figures to demonstrate the effectiveness of the system in terms of what it was designed for: of sixty grand viziers whose careers he traced, forty-eight were educated in the Palace School as compared with twelve who rose to the post from outer service. Other official graduates included twenty-three lords of the admiralty.

Thus the Palace School produced the men who were to run the empire.

But it was the eunuchs who picked the candidates who were to enter the school, it was the eunuchs who were in charge of the administration and surveillance of the school; it was the eunuchs who recommended to the sultan which students were worthy of his special attention to be promoted and eventually achieve positions of authority.

The Chief White Eunuch, apart from his official position as grand master of ceremonies, head gatekeeper to the seraglio (in control of everyone who might enter or leave), chief of inner service, was thus not only confidential agent to the sultan but director-in-chief of the Palace School. In the early days he controlled all messages, petitions, and state documents addressed to the sultan, and alone was permitted to speak to the sultan in person. Immediately below the Chief White Eunuch two more were in charge of the treasury and the commissariat, heading up the corps of pages attached to these departments, the one responsible for the contents of the treasury and all inner-service payments, the other supervising not only the contents of the private commissariat but the entire kitchen staff and food for the palace.

For those who are interested in food, and the various ways it has been prepared on this planet, some extraordinary figures are available.

Bon, the Venetian diplomat, describes the amount of meat supplied each day for the Grand Seraglio at the beginning of the seventeenth century as "from one to two hundred head of mutton; one hundred of lamb, or kid in season; forty of veal—the favorite meat of the eunuchs—thirty to fifty brace of geese or goslings; one to two hundred of foul or chicken, and the same of pigeons." The yearly aggregate of that supply as given by Aubrey de la Montray a hundred years later was: "Thirty thousand head of beef, sixty thousand of mutton, twenty thousand of veal, ten thousand of kid, two hundred thousand fouls, one hundred thousand pigeons, three thousand turkeys, three hundred and twenty-four hare. . . ."

That the Turks were not really great meat eaters can be seen from the list of other commodities delivered to the Eunuch in Charge of the Commissariat in the year 1660-61 as set down in the manuscript of Eyyni Qanun Namesi: "Thirty-six thousand bushels of rice, three thousand pounds of vermicelli, twenty-five hundred bushels of chick-peas, the same amount of lentils, twenty-five bushels of eggplant, six hundredweight of onions, twelve barrels of starch, sixty thousand pounds of honey, forty thousand pounds of yellow wax, six thousand loaves of sugar, nine hundred and eighty pounds of saffron, twelve thousand pounds of salt, seven hundred and eighty camel loads of ice, five hundred jars of olive oil, seventy barrels of vinegar, twenty large barrels of lemon juice, thirty barrels of verjuice, six hundred and ninety three pounds of henna, twenty-four hundred and seventy-five pounds of sal volatile, and eighty-two pounds of amber. . . ."

To this Penzer adds: "Once a year two of the royal galleons took wood to Alexandria and brought back to the Grand Seraglio cargoes of rice, vermicelli, peas, beans, lentils, dates, plums, prunes, spices, tobacco, sugar, syrup, and other sweets of all kinds. The vast quantities of honey, the chief substitute at that time for sugar, came from the provinces of Wallachia, Moldavia and Transylvania as did the palace supply of apples. The pomegranates of which six thousand of the sweet variety and six thousand of the sour were annually consumed in the palace, were brought from Brusa. Other fresh fruits and vegetables, with the exception of eggplant, which was brought from Egypt as a rare delicacy, were produced in sufficient quantities in the gardens of the Grand Seraglio and the royal gardens in the vicinity of Constantinople. The general supply of olive oil came from Coronea and Modena, and the private supply of the sultan from Crete. The use of fresh butter was almost unknown then as it is now to the Turks.

"So-called 'cooked' butter (perhaps salted butter) shipped in ox-bladders from Moldavia and from Black Sea ports of Tnais and Kaffa was, however, employed to a considerable degree for cooking purposes. For the Privy Commissariat in the Third Court and for the larders of a few of the great pashas the Venetian Bailie was accustomed to supply a quantity of Milan cheese, which was much esteemed."

Ice, or frozen snow, which was employed chiefly for making sherbet, was brought by camel caravan from the slopes of Mount Olympus near Brusa—at an estimated annual cost of eighty thousand francs.

To give an idea of the business of cooking alone, on the four days a week when the divan met, an extra four or five thousand meals were served. Each of the ten kitchens was under the direction of a steward responsible to a eunuch. Below these officials the cooks were divided into ranks of chefs, apprentices and assistants, and attached to these were a special corps of butchers, grocers, chandlers, dairymen, icemen, water-carriers, collectors of fine herbs, and tinners, etc.

The number of confectioners alone employed in the Grand Seraglio is variously estimated to have been from four- to six hundred, and in their kitchens were manufactured the candies, crystallized fruits, preserves, syrups, sherbets, pastries and other desserts of which the Turks were and are still inordinately fond, the confectioners being a distinct branch of the kitchen service designated by a white cap—the toque of the modern chef.

Baron Wenceslas Wratislaw, who dined in the sultan's presence at the time of Shakespeare, gives a vivid description of the scene: "We saw how the Turkish Emperor is served. First come about two hundred cup-bearers, or servers, dressed almost uniformly in red silk dresses, and with caps on their heads like those of the Janissaries, except that about a span above the head they were embroidered with gold. These having placed themselves in a row from the kitchen to the Sultan's apartment, first did fitting reverence to all by an inclination of the head, and then stood close to each other, just as if they had been painted figures . . . When it was dinner time, the superintendent of the kitchen brought from the kitchen a porcelain dish, and another covered dish, handed it to the waiter nearest him, he to a third, and so on till it came to the one who stood nearest to the Emperor's apartment. There, again, stood another chamberlain, and one handed it to another, and the viands were carried very quickly, and without the slightest noise or clatter, to the Emperor's table. Several of them again placed themselves in a similar row to the place where the Pashas and my lords the ambassadors were ready to eat, and handed the dishes from one to another, till they placed them on the table."

To this picture Bon added the detail that as the trays were brought from the kitchen they were fitted over with covers of black felt, lined with white ones, whereas on their return the covers were reversed.

But to return to the eunuchs. Next in the hierarchy came the assistant head of the Palace School who controlled the great and small halls and the hall of the expeditionary force; he was generally in charge of school discipline and ran the whole seraglio in the absence of the sultan.

Each hall then had a eunuch who was held personally responsible for order and discipline in his hall, the pages of which were subdivided into groups of ten, each of which was presided over by a eunuch whose duty it was to keep order during the day, preside at meals, and, at night, prevent lewdness among the pages.

The young *eunuch* arrivals in the seraglio were set to learn Turkish and were then trained to occupy the various positions hierarchically all the way up to that of Chief White Eunuch who held the highest position under the sultan along with the grand vizier.

Those who showed promise were advanced along each step of the ladder, whereas the duller ones came to occupy low positions such as guards.

Another of the uses to which the sultan put the eunuchs was as members of the sultan's special secret service and as private executioners.

One of the chief eunuchs who was retired to Egypt was used by Suleiman the Magnificent to rout the Portuguese from their trading posts along the Indian Ocean. "Although the Pasha was eighty years old and so fat that four men were required to support him when he moved, he built a fleet carrying the galleys in sections over the Egyptian desert to the Red Sea. He launched seventy vessels, sacked the Arab ports near Aden and sailed by the Persian Gulf to the river Indus. While the Portuguese repulsed him from their port at Diu, their oriental trade suffered severely and their colonies were crippled."

Thus it can be seen that the organization of the white

eunuchs constituted a rigid and elaborate hierarchy numbering about a hundred and twenty at the end of the seventeenth century. The six leading officials were assigned special apartments whereas the rest were allotted to the various halls where they acted as surveillance officers. Selected for admission to the palace at about the same age as the pages or even a little younger, the white eunuchs received precisely the same education as the pages, usually completing the entire course including service in the Hall of the Royal Bedchamber.

As A. C. Muradgea, Baron d'Ohsson, in his picture of the Ottoman Empire which he dedicated to the king of Sweden, summed up the system: "For three centuries the chief of the white eunuchs was the first officer of the palace, a post which he relinquished only to become governor of a province, most often that of Egypt. Many were raised to the dignity of Grand Vizier . . . Most of them were distinguished for their talents and for their military accomplishments, but the most remarkable was Ghazanfer-Agha, Hungarian by birth, who was captured as a youth and raised among the pages of the seraglio, after embracing Mohammedanism. Giving in to the Sultan Selim II's wishes he underwent the operation in order to become an officer of the white eunuchs, the only ones who then personally attended the Sultan. He became Capou-Agha, a position which he maintained during the reigns of Selim II, Mourad III and Mohammed III, exerting a great influence on public affairs till he died in a revolt of the troops in 1603."

For many years the white eunuchs were thus largely in control of the Ottoman Empire, but gradually they were dispossessed of their prerogatives by—of all rivals—the corps of colored eunuchs.

4

BLACK GUARDIANS OF FELICITY

Now comes another whole side of the seraglio, the one, as both Penzer and Miller point out, most commonly associated with the word seraglio but which should properly be known as the *haremlik*, or harem for short. In Arabic "haram" is unlawful as opposed to "halal," lawful, and came to be used for that part of a Moslem's house occupied by the women in which it was unlawful for strangers to trespass. Softened by the Turks into harem and with the suffix "lik" meaning place, haremlik became the proper word in Turkish for that part of the house which was opposed to the *selamlik*, or area where the man of the house could greet his friends and transact business with strangers, the word "salam" meaning welcome.

Access to the harem of the seraglio was forbidden all men but the sultan, with very occasional exceptions, and in order to maintain this absolute seclusion the corps of Black Eunuchs was instituted.

In a central position between the divan and the harem quarters, the black eunuchs formed the last impassable barrier in the seraglio: but not satisfied with guarding and administering the harem, gradually over a period of years, they encroached upon the white eunuchs' territory till they succeeded in taking over most of their functions as well.

Obtained from Arab slave dealers who captured them in the heart of Africa, the black eunuchs were brought to the seraglio as boys, even younger at times than the pages, and were then subjected to training as rigorous as that of the pages, though slightly different.

Young Negro children would at times be sold into slavery by their impoverished African families to be made into eunuchs in the hope that they might thus attain position and riches in a seraglio, but most of them were captured by slave hunters.

Well-armed Arab raiders on horseback would gallop into a village in the tropical regions of Africa, often as far south as below the equator, and carry off boys between the ages of seven and ten whom they would place astride their saddles, disappearing into the "trackless" desert to their base of operations.

Sometimes battles would ensue between the raiders and the outraged parents, but the well-armed and swiftly mounted hunters usually got the better of the village natives, occasionally taking grown men and women, though these fetched far smaller prices, depending on their vigor and beauty. Tied by the necks in rows the victims would be dragged across the hot desert on long exhausting marches, many of them, especially the boys, dying on the way; but the price of a young eunuch was high enough for the Arab raiders to make a good profit if barely one out of ten survived.

Most of the young boys were dragged to the convents of Christian Coptic monks such as the ones at Gisa, Assiout and especially the monastery of Deir-El-Abiad near Sohag in Upper Egypt, and there castrated.

For those who survived the ordeal, the monks received in return, not only an excellent price, but the essential protection of the Lords of Islam for this valuable function which the Mohammedans were themselves not allowed to perform.

The only humanitarian note in this otherwise sad affair was the story of the chief eunuch of the mother of the Kadiv Ismail Pasha of Egypt who in 1868 established a eunuch factory at Massaua on the Red Sea. To run it he engaged an Italian doctor (possibly one of the earliest instances of that country's efforts in Eritrea!) who, for twenty years, castrated small boys who were then sold in Egypt and Constantinople, undermining the good monks' business (or the monks' good business) and incidentally making fortunes for both the eunuch Khalil Agha and for the Italian doctor who would answer those who reproached him the origin of his riches by saying that he had gained them as a benefactor of humanity, operating strictly according to the techniques of his profession which would lose but one out of ten of the victims compared with the eight or nine lost by the monks. His conscience, he maintained, was at peace for having snatched so many young boys from the jaws of death!

Up to the time of the Crimean War the commerce of

slave cargoes was free in the eastern Mediterranean, and black eunuchs could enter the Ottoman Empire directly from the Red Sea, from Djeddah, or from Tripoli, proceeding to markets in several cities, but principally in Cairo and Constantinople, where they could be bought along with slaves of either sex. Thereafter, up to the fall of the Ottoman Empire, though the slave market fell off, thanks to the dictates of the French and British allies, there was always a satisfactory clandestine market for eunuchs. The Anglo-Turkish convention of 1868 forbade the sale of black slaves (though it left it open for white Circassian women to populate the Ottoman harems), and British consulates kept what was known as a sharp eye on the landing of black slaves in Constantinople, taking those they discovered to special establishments (operated at the expense of the Ottoman Empire) where they were housed until such time as they could be placed as free servants in the houses of the rich.

It was the pretext of suppressing these slave traders that facilitated the carving out of large protectorates and colonies in Africa by the French and British—which in turn led to some rivalry between them, and eventually to the Anglo-French agreement of 1889 which divided up Africa, enabling French parliamentarians to boast that with the fall of Ghat "the trans-Saharan traffic of slaves had received a deadly blow" and for Lord Salisbury to quip that *"le coq Gaulois"* had now obtained a vast expanse of sand, nine times as large as France where "it could scratch at its ease."

In any case, British and French men-of-war cruised the Red Sea in search of the slavers' caiques and feluccas, confiscating their human merchandise and punishing the traffickers who thenceforward took to the more difficult land routes across Arabia Deserta and Morocco to exchange their eunuchs for arms, carpets, perfume and tea. And though the prices rose, governors of outlying territories continued to buy them and send them to the court as presents; the governor of Djeddah, on a trip to Constantinople shortly after the turn of the century, is reported to have taken twenty of them, between ten and fifteen years old, some of whom he offered to his protectors and some of whom he kept for his private use.

An Egyptian doctor, named Zambaco, who in the course of many years' practice and travel in the Ottoman Empire treated many eunuchs as his patients, gives a detailed description of the effects of the operation, as well as intimate glimpses into the life and nature of eunuchs in the Ottoman Empire.

Of the fully castrated eunuchs, says the doctor, he found many different types belonging to various races: some dark-skinned with thick protruding lips, underhung jaws, receding foreheads, flattened noses, and crinkly hair, some with scars on their faces done in their infancy to indicate their tribe, all from Central Africa. Those from Abyssinia he described as bronzed, of an almost golden color, well proportioned and with fine regular features—narrow lips, delicate noses, high foreheads and soft intelligent eyes, their hair not crinkly, their teeth white and even. These qualities, he remarked, made them specially sought after, their value being even higher than white Circassians, though still less than was offered for those with specially hideous and repellent features, crippled and misshapen bodies, who were valued by masters of a jealous nature.

These came mostly from the upper Sudan rather than from Abyssinia, their frightening expressions, according to the doctor, persisting despite decades in the midst of "a cultivated atmosphere," almost as if they became fiercer in the process of guarding "the fruit which they themselves might not savor."

Describing the physical effects of castration the doctor, who had occasion to study the problem intimately, pointed out that if the operation took place in infancy, before puberty, the body was modified in a way similar to castrated animals, there being a striking difference in the proportions of the skeleton, the arms and legs growing much faster than the trunk. Eunuchs on horseback, or especially ponies (for which they seemed to have a peculiar predilection), offered a very curious sight, their feet appearing to drag on the ground. Their arms, like those of monkeys, reached to their knees and sometimes even lower, with long thin fingers. Later in life they tended to become fat, with large breasts and flabby shanks.

Castrated before puberty, the eunuch maintained a cracked feminine voice throughout life, but, according to the doctor, and in contradiction to Carter Stent and his Chinese eunuchs, when castrated after full growth, a virile voice remained, which he attributed to the larynx not being subject to regression.

Among the minor complaints suffered by eunuchs, various sources have listed weak bladders, loss of memory, insomnia, bad eyesight, a distaste for alcohol, which quickly made them drunk, and the reputed incapacity for swallowing hard boiled eggs!

Normally obliged to squat like women in order to urinate, eunuchs developed the habit of carrying silver quills in their turbans, which, when inserted, enabled them to urinate at a distance. To prevent accidental wettings they carried a nail on a string with which to plug the urethra.

Observing many eunuchs from a psychological point of view, the doctor came to the conclusion that the operation causes striking psychic changes in the individual such as lack of vitality, gaiety, or action, as well as an inclination to sadness and laziness. Eunuchs, he wrote, are indolent, servile, without energy, often cowards, cruel and bitter; some remain perpetual children, bad-tempered and unhappy. Others, said he, have been known to be intelligent, amiable and capable of serious undertakings, even of being very cultivated. They are extremely jealous, proud, haughty and showoffs in front of their inferiors, though exceptions have been known to be sweet, affable, gay, and even affectionate, it being not unusual for female slaves in the harem to fall madly in love with eunuchs with whom they were closely associated.

Odd as it may sound, some eunuchs, especially when they reached a high enough position, were allowed to marry. Richard Burton, who managed to gain the confidence of a eunuch's wife, says she told him her husband practiced "the manifold *plaisirs de la petite oie* (masturbation, tribadism, irrumation, *têtebeche, feuille-de-rose,* etc.)" till they induced the venereal orgasm by means of the secretion of the prostate gland, and that at the critical moment she would be obliged to hold up a little pillow for her husband to bite, lest he tear her cheeks and breasts.

More commonly the eunuch's erogenous zones would shift, so that, as well as being an active sapphist, he became what was so prevalent in Rome—a passive pederast, capable, they say, of an almost vaginal orgasm.

Eunuchs of the palace, says Dr. Zambaco, were usually

well bred and exquisitely polite; loving luxury they often owned jewelry of considerable value, and some even amassed fortunes through the generosity of their master or mistresses with which they could afford to have mosques constructed or to invest in considerable philanthropic works, for the benefit, naturally, of their souls in a life to come—especially as everything they possessed in this one reverted to their owner at death.

Abyssinian eunuchs, according to the doctor, were usually the most gifted and often made fine diplomats. Former subjects of the Negus, they were originally Orthodox Christians till captured, castrated and confirmed to Mohammedanism.

Describing eunuchs in the sultan's palace at Constantinople, which he visited, the doctor remarked that they led a pleasant happy life, especially the favorites in the harem, loving horses, jewelry, wigs, perfume, children and cock fights, and giving themselves a great deal of importance. Having reached a certain age, however, they were inclined to become bigoted, passing their time reading religious books and saying prayers in order to prepare themselves an indemnity in future life for the privations received in this one, to the point, says he, of becoming religious fanatics. Nor is it surprising, adds the doctor, that "those who have been deprived of the gift of procreation should devote themselves to a cult which promises them all manner of satisfaction in the way of luscious semi-naked damsels in an Islamic paradise to come."

Many spent the better part of the day when not occupied with their duties, reading the Koran, and saying prayers with genuflections and prostrations in conformity with Islamic rites.

As a note of warning, the doctor pointed out that despite the refinements of their education the eunuchs were likely to be carried away by fits of temper which reached degrees of ferocity verging on mania, and that when riding out on their beautiful horses, finely arrayed and bejeweled, to accompany the sultan or his women, they carried hippopotamus hide whips with which they would lash out mercilessly against anyone hazarding an indiscreet peep at the veiled beauties under their guard.

A distinguished eyewitness and unhappy recipient of just such an outburst, Sir Henry Bulwer, younger brother of Lord Lytton, the novelist, was lashed by a eunuch on the outskirts of Constantinople in 1858 because he had dared return the smile of "a mischievous lady travelling in a richly equipped carriage," having made the mistake of going for a walk in the neighborhood of Pera without his normal escort of well-armed janissaries to indicate his title as accredited British ambassador to the Sublime Porte.

Apropos of which Reich points out that heretofore scientists seem to have been unaware of the contradiction which lay in the fact that individuals who were castrated *before* puberty showed a diminished sexuality, whereas those castrated *after* puberty did not lose their sexual excitability and were capable of copulation. "They did not," says Reich, "ask themselves why it was that eunuchs developed a strong sadism. It was only many years later—when I began to see the mechanisms of sexual energy—that I understood the phenomenon. After puberty, sexuality is fully developed, and castration takes little effect. The sexual energy is at work in the whole body and not just in the interstitial tissues of the gonads. The sadism observed in eunuchs is nothing but the sexual energy which, deprived of its normal function, now manifests itself in the body musculature."

In general, the Negro eunuchs treated by Dr. Zambaco as well as being inclined to sadism exuded a disagreeable odor which they masked with aromatics, musk, essence of roses and cloves; the Abyssinians, more happily, being "gifted by nature with slight odor of musk."

Once they reached the palace of the sultan, young Negro eunuchs were selected by senior black eunuchs, much as was done with the pages, on the basis of their physical qualities, talents and intelligence—in this case the values being reversed—the uglier and more deformed ones being chosen to be trained for positions of trust, close to the women of the harem, whereas the better-looking ones were likely to be relegated to minor positions, further from trouble, such as the outer doors, passages, and courtyards.

Yet the spirit of competition prevailed here as with the pages, and the canniest, if not the most intriguing, rose step by step up the rungs of a hierarchy similar to that of the white eunuchs.

Though their training was in no way as thorough as that of their white colleagues, in the long run they were to supplant the whites.

Like the pages they received new names, slept in dormitories, were tutored in Turkish etiquette and Islamic religion, and broken into the various jobs required of them, for which they received pay which was much higher than that of their white counterparts, and rose as they were singled out by their superior black eunuchs.

Bon, the Venetian source of most of the best data about the seraglio, thus describes the young black eunuchs: "They are watched and disciplined like the other boys of the Seraglio till at a certain age they are ready for service. They are then removed thence and sent to the women and placed under others (black eunuchs) in the service of the Sultana, being under the command of their chief, the Chief Black Eunuch, Kislar Aga, or Head of the Virgins. They have a considerable allowance of sixty to a hundred *aspri* a day, two robes of finest silk, clothes, and other things for their needs, throughout the year, besides what is plentifully bestowed on them from other quarters. They bear the names of flowers such as Hyacinth, Narcissus, Rose, and Carnation; since as they are in the service of women they have names suitable to virginity, whiteness and fragrance."

Immured for life, from the moment they entered the seraglio they were never allowed to leave until they had graduated to higher positions and then only to perform special missions for the harem members, the lower echelons, says Penzer, not even coming in contact with members of the white eunuchs, who never entered the precinct of the harem.

The Chief Black Eunuch held one of the highest and sometimes even *the* highest rank in the empire after the sultan, a pasha with three tails, and member of the privy council; he alone could approach the sultan at any time of night as well as by day, and was described as "the most illustrious of the officers who approach his August Person, and worthy of the confidence of monarchs and sovereigns."

Confidential messenger between the sultan and the sultan's mother (who, as will be seen, was the most important personage in the harem), he came also to be confidential messenger between the sultan and the grand vizier, gradually encroaching on the positions of the white eunuchs, making appointment to most of the leading positions not only in the seraglio but in the empire at large, becoming "the most feared and consequently the most bribed official in the Empire." As Barnette Miller put it: "With the rise to power of the royal harem, the highest dignitaries of the state were obliged to make large gifts to the black eunuchs, or even to pension them, in order to maintain themselves in power. . . ."

Even as early as the fifteenth century the power of the Chief Black Eunuch was considerable, and, as Angiolello, a Venetian who was in service in the Grand Seraglio, presumably as a page, from about 1453 to 1481, wrote in his memoirs, the women of the palace were guarded by "a Saracen eunuch who has the right to correct and chastise all persons in the palace and who receives a salary of one hundred aspres a day, besides living expenses and a retinue of slaves—to say nothing of the many gifts from the Great Turk, a house outside the palace, and a large villa about six miles distant from Constantinople which has been presented to him. He is free to do as he likes three or four hours during the day, but at night he must always remain in the palace. . . ."

Occupying a private suite which consisted of coffee room, bedroom, smoking room and lavatory, near the sultan's own quarters, the Chief Black Eunuch had access to his master at any time. Among his responsibilities was the education of the sultan's male children or princes, as well as of all the women of the harem, and to assist him in carrying out his duties outside the palace he was in command of a huge corps of former Christian slaves selected for their bodily strength from the discards from the palace school (or not taken into the janissaries) which were organized into what was known as the outer service.

Next after the Chief Black Eunuch was the grand treasurer, also with the rank of pasha with three tails who handled the financial affairs of the harem. There followed the chief liaison officer known as Mussahib, with eight or ten officers under him who were on duty in pairs throughout the day to carry orders from the sultan to the harem. Then came the master of the chamber, chief gatekeeper of the apartments, and all the various levels of the female hierarchy of the harem.

If I appear to have lingered disproportionately on the minutiae of life among the black and white eunuchs and the pages of the Grand Seraglio, it is not because of the intrinsic fascination of so extraordinary a system, but because they illustrate so aptly the theories of Freud and Reich, and because some may have lost sight of the fact that we, in the West, in moments of emergency, though supposedly free and democratic citizens, still tend to rely on human beings thus sinisterly educated, forgetting, apparently, that the emergencies may have been engendered by this very type, and by the system which perpetuates them.

At the foundation of authoritarian patriarchal culture and economic slavery, says Reich, lies sexual repression; it is, he insists, "of a social-economic and not biological origin."

From what he learned in his sex hygiene clinics in authoritarian Central Europe it became clear to Reich that the function of suppression of infantile and adolescent sexuality was to facilitate for parents the submissiveness of children.

To this Freud has added: "Fear of revolt among the oppressed then becomes a motive for stricter regulations. A highwater mark in this type of development has been reached in our Western European civilization. Psychologically, it is fully justified in beginning by censoring any manifestations of the sexual life of children, for there would be no prospect of curbing the sexual desires of adults if the ground had not been prepared for it in childhood. Nonetheless there is no sort of justification for the lengths beyond this to which civilized society goes in actually denying the existence of these manifestations."

The real unconscious goal of education, as Reich saw it, was the formation of what he called the "sex-negative" character structure. "But nobody," says he, "seems to have thought of the devastating results of this psychic castration on humanity."

But before looking deeper into psychic castration, just as it was necessary to describe the Palace School in order to understand the functions of the white eunuchs, in order to understand those of the black—who at one time numbered close to a thousand—a picture of harem life itself is essential: hence the following peep at a finishing school for nymphets.

5

THE SECRET WORLD OF THE ODALISQUE

Most of what is known about the seraglio—which for four hundred years remained a constant source of mystery and fascination to the West—was gleaned from the reports or memoirs of European diplomats accredited to the Porte, and, occasionally, from runaway slaves who somehow managed to escape with an inside story.

As one inspired historian put it: "Tales of the allurements of the harem of the Grand Seigneur fired the imagination of the world. Travelers eagerly sought and embroidered upon the gossip that filtered out from its jealously kept confines through the eunuchs, pages and from all who knew or professed to know its secrets. Its mystery, so nearly impenetrable, only enhanced its fascination. And yet, by the subtle sign language with which the Seraglio conversed across its barriers, hints reached the ears of foreign ambassadors, hints of fierce, unleashed jealousies, hints of love which is one of the most extraordinary that ever lived. . . ."

Male novelists—stymied by the heavily gated and massive outer walls, access through the single passage of which was denied by giant black eunuchs to all but the sultan and an occasional doctor—have conjured the very sunlight to take them where, in body, they could not venture.

This sunlight, rhapsodized one of these recreators of atmosphere, as it shines right over the walls "is reflected on the miniature, lead-roofed pleasure domes of a congeries of buildings under which as many as two thousand women live and wait upon the Sultan's pleasure; it is shaded by plane trees, cypress and umbrella pine; it steals through rose-colored blinds to paint its magic designs on the silken pallets where the slaves of the harem languorously recline with no sound but the buzzing of a bee and the far off cry of the sea gull. There, delicate limbs are encased in transparent trousers of rose-colored silk or other hues varying as vary the fancies of several hundred women conscious of the charms for which they were sought throughout Europe, Asia and Africa; the moon-pallor of the fragile Persians sets off the warm olive cheeks of the sun-ripened daughters of Arabia, Egypt or Algiers; soft bosoms palpitate beneath the white damask vests embroidered with gold which only half conceal them; deep dark eyes, set off by kohl-stained lashes, prepare to dart their most bewitching glances; red perfumed lips prepare to pout;

arms gleaming white, are twined and entwined, while henna stained fingertips toy with love charms sold by gypsies, and the air around the women is heavy with the aroma of seduction."

Or, as one English traveler summed it up: "In the harem an army of Virgins make it the only study of their life to obtain the single nod of invitation to the bed of their Great Master."

As late as 1926, Sir George Young who, in his own words, did "a good deal of digging in historic dustbins," remarked that "Up till now the seraglio Hareem and Hirkai Sherif Odassi (chamber of the Holy Mantle) remained two of the very few places on earth that no Anglo-Saxon or American has yet trod."

N. M. Penzer in his detailed study of what remains of the Sultan's Seraglio maintained that "During the whole period over which the Seraglio continued to be the Royal Residence the number of people who claim with good justification to have seen any part of it past the Gate of Felicity can be counted on the fingers of one hand. Even if we include men who were at one time actually employed in the Inside Service of the Seraglio itself the total still remains under a dozen."

And as for the actual harem: "So secret and jealously guarded was the harem and all that happened inside it that nothing of any consequence was ever known (let alone seen) until after the deposition of Abdul-Hamid II in 1909. And even since that date the number of people who have visited any of the closed rooms is a mere handful."

Nevertheless a handful of males *did* enter the harem, and from what they have described, along with the evidence brought out by the black eunuchs or by harem girls, who, as will later be explained, occasionally got married off to Turkish officials, or from the tales of the Jewish women who were allowed to enter and trade with the inmates, all of which have been accumulated through the years by various authors, a fairly convincing picture of the institution can be put together.

One of the first Europeans to catch an actual glimpse of the sultan's women in the harem, without paying for the audacity with his head or any other part of his anatomy, was a young English organ builder, Thomas Dallam. Sent to Constantinople in the summer of 1599 to install an organ he had built and which was being donated by Queen Elizabeth to the sultan in return for special trading privileges for the British Levant Company, he obtained an extraordinary and quite illicit bird's-eye view of part of the harem never before penetrated by Western men.

It took Dallam over a month to install the instrument in the sultan's palace (it having been badly soaked on the long sea voyage from England), but once this was accomplished the sultan was so pleased with its music he became infuriated when he discovered that no one but Dallam could play the machine.

To induce Dallam to spend the rest of his life in Turkey, the Sultan tried every available means of painless persuasion; but Dallam demurred, inventing an apocryphal wife and children pining for him in England, to which the Grand Turk replied with a solution, quoted from Dallam:

". . . they told me that yf I would staye the Grand Sinyor would give tow wifes, either tow of his concubines or els tow virgins of the beste I could chuse my selfe, in cittie or countrie."

Further to whet the Englishman's appetite the Sultan hit upon the idea of having Dallam summoned to the palace while he, the Sultan, was out of town, so that the Englishman might peep at what was in store for him if he elected to stay.

Because of this ingenious lure the world is now privy to the following description.

"When I came to the grait the wale was verrie thicke, and graited on bothe the sides with iron verrie strongly; but through the graite I did se thirtie of the Grand Sinyor's Concubines that weare playinge with a bale in another courte. At the firste sighte of me I thoughte they had bene younge men, but when I saw the hare of their heades hange doone on their backes, platted together with a tasle of smale pearle hanginge in the lower end of it, and by other plaine tokens, I did know them to be women, and verrie prettie ones in deede.

"Theie wore upon theier heades nothing bute a little capp of clothe of goulde, which did but cover the crowne of her heade, no bandes aboute their neckes, nor anythinge but faire cheans of pearle and a juell hanginge on their brests, and juels in their ears; their coats weare like a souldier's mandilyon, som of reed sattan and som of blew, and som of other collors, and girded like a lace of contraire collor; they wore britchis of samatie, a fine clothe made of coton wool, as whyte as snow and as fine as lane; for I could desarne the skin of their thies through it. These britchis cam doone to their mydlege; som of them did weare fine cordovan buskins, and some had their leges naked, with a goulde ringe on the smale of her legg; on her foute a velvett panttoble 4 or 5 inches hie. I stood so longe loukinge upon them that he which had showed me all this kindness began to be verrie angrie with me. He made a wrye mouthe, and stamped with his foute to make me give over looking; the which I was verrie lothe to dow, for that sighte did please me wondrous well. . . .

"Then I wente awaye with this Jemoglane [inner-service page] to the place wherare we lefte my drugaman or intarpreter, and I tould my intarpreter that I had sene 30 of the Grand Sinyores Concobines; but my interpreter advised me that by no meanes I should speake of it, whearby any Turke myghte hear of it; for if it weare knowne to som Turks, it would presente deathe to him that showed me them. He durste not louke upon them him selfe. Although I louked so longe upon them, theie saw not me, nether all that whyle louked towards that place. Yf they had sene me, they would have wondred as moche at me, or how I cam thether, as I did to se them."

Finally, afraid the sultan might try some more painful method of persuasion, Dallam managed to skip town in a British freighter and make his way safely to London, where, no doubt, his story caused some eyebrows to be raised in the local pubs.

Like the pages of the Palace School, the girls of the harem were almost entirely captured Christian slaves converted to Mohammedanism. As Miller says: "At the height of its power the harem of the Grand Seraglio was filled with the very flower of the slave markets of the East. The rigid process of selection begun in the slave markets was carried still further by the educational system of the harem and by the intense rivalry which prevailed among the women there."

During Suleiman's reign there were about three hundred women in the royal harem, but by the time of his grandson Murad III the number had risen to eleven or twelve hundred, all of them either captured in war, sold into slavery by their parents, or presented to the sultan by officials courting favor.

The early sultans had been in the habit of marrying, but since Bayazid I it became customary for the sultan not to be officially married to any of his women. Historians point out that this came about because the price of the sultana's dower was so great it overtaxed the exchequer. But Aaron Hill, a Restoration playwright who got his facts while working as a secretary to the British ambassador in Turkey, writing in the seventeenth century, maintains that the sultan was disabused from marriage partly for political reasons (so as not to be officially allied to any family), but mostly so that "the Greatest and most Unexpected turns of Fate, shall never wound the Princes Honour, in obliging him to see a Wife become the Victim of Licentious Insolence, and he himself an hapless witness to her shameful Usage."

The point in question was the unpleasant experience of that "ancient and unhappy Emperor Bayazid whose dearly beloved wife Dehespeena was by the victorious Tam-er-lane before the face of her distracted Husband, Ravish'd by the Conqueror."

Thereafter, the princes who succeeded Bayazid resolved "for the Future, to avoid so black and piercing Misfortune, and made a Law that none shou'd Marry ever after on the Throne of Turkey, which has been observ'd with such Religious constancy, that two late Emperours have been depos'd and little urg'd against their Governments, but that they took the Liberty of Marriage, and thereby Infring'd the solemn Prohibition of their Wiser Predecessors."

The women of the seraglio, like the pages of the Palace

School, and all the eunuchs, remained the personal private slaves of the sultan with whom he might do as he pleased.

Most of the girls were brought into the seraglio even younger than the pages, usually between eight and ten years old, but, on occasion, extremely beautiful older ones were admitted after the strictest physical examination.

Ottaviano Bon, the Venetian Bailo, gives an excellent description of the system, the flavor of which is retained in the translation of Robert Withers, published in London in 1650:

"Now those which are kept up for their beauties, are all young virgins, taken and stolen from forraign Nations; who after they have been instructed in good behaviour, and can play upon instruments, sing, dance, and sew curiously; they are given to the Grand Signor as presents of great value . . . These virgins immediately after their coming into the Seraglio are made Turks; which is done by using this ceremony only; to hold up their forefinger and say these words; law illawheh illaw Allawh, Muhammed resoul Allawh; That is, there is no God but God alone, and Mahomet is the messenger of God. And according as they are in age and disposition (being proved and examined by an old woman called Kahiyah Gadun, that is, as we say, the mother of the maides) so they are placed in a room with the others of same age, spirit, and inclination, to dwell and live together.

"Now in the women's lodgings, they live just as Nunnes do in great Nunneries: for these virgins, have very large rooms to live in: and their bedchambers will hold almost a hundred of them a piece. They sleep upon Sofaes, which are built longwise on both sides of the room, and a large space left in the midst to go to and fro about their business.

"Their beds are very coarse and hard (for the Turks neither use featherbeds nor corded bedsteads) made of flocks of wooll: and by every ten virgins there lies an old woman: and all the night long there are many lamps burning, so that one may see plainly throughout the whole room: which doth both keep the young wenches from wantonness, and serve upon any occasion which may happen in the night. Near unto the said bedchambers they have their *Bagnos* [baths] for their use at all times: with many fountains out of which they are served with water: and above their chambers there are divers rooms, where they sit and sew: and there they keep their boxes, and chests in which they lay up their apparrell.

"They feed by whole Camaradaes, and are served and waited upon by other women: nor do they want anything whatsoever that is necessary for them.

"There are other places likewise for them, where they go to school, to learn to speak and read (if they will) the Turkish tongue, to sew also, and to play on divers instruments: and so they spend the day with their mistresses, who are all ancient women: some hours notwithstanding, being allowed them for their recreation, to walk in their gardens, and use such sports as they familiarly exercise themselves withall."

What then, lay before these girls?

The very highest they could aspire to was the rank of dowager sultana—this by the composite but gradual process of bearing a male child to the sultan, being treated as the "first" among his women, outliving him, seeing their son enthroned, and, finally, becoming the dowager ruler of the whole harem.

In theory each of the girls, once trained, stood a fair

chance, allowing for physical and mental differences, of attaining this highest position, or, having failed, of being sent out of the seraglio at the age of twenty-five, with the chance, when lucky, of being married to some minor official of the Empire.

Like the pages and the eunuchs, the girls were obliged to sever all connection with their past; on entering the seraglio they received new names such as Nourisaba (Dawn), Gulbahar (Rose of Spring), Dilbeste (Heart-Binder), Hayati (Life-Giver), or, appropriately enough, Sfayi (Pleasure-Giver)!

On graduating from their studies, in which their individual talents for either singing, dancing, sewing or whatever, had been singled out and developed, the young virgins prepared themselves to rise up the ladder of hierarchic positions in the harem by the practice of "the one art to which all their other talents were but dressing": the Art of Making Love.

On their success in this highly competitive venture, rested each girl's chance of advancement. With one happy stroke, as in a children's game of ludo, they might be advanced a couple of dozen moves, or, by an unhappy move, be doomed to stagnate till the end of the game.

What then were the rules of this paragon of parlor games?

To be off to a good start a girl must contrive, by whatever means she could manage, to catch the eye of the sultan on those occasions when either he visited their quarters or they were called upon to entertain him in his own apartments or gardens (under the ever watchful eyes of the corps of black eunuchs).

Having succeeded not only in catching the sultan's eye

but in arresting it, a girl stood a chance of being advanced to the position of "Guzdeh," literally "in the sultan's eye." All that was necessary was for the sultan to glance at a girl approvingly or make some remark about her, for the girl to be separated from the rest in a private apartment where she would be taken care of by servants until such a time as she was given an actual chance at bat.

Bon's description of a sultan's method of making his choice is very similar to that employed by the emperors of China:

"When he is prepared for a fresh mate, he gives notice to the said Kahiya Cadun of his purpose, who immediately bestirs herself like a crafty baud, and chooseth out such as shee judgeth to be the most amiable, the fairest of all; and having placed them in a good order in a room, in two ranks, like so many pictures, half on the one side, and half on the other; she forthwith brings in the King, who walking four or five times in the midst of them, and having view'd them well, taketh good notice within himself of her that he best liketh, but says nothing; only as he goeth out again, he throweth a handkerchief into that virgin's hand; by which token she knoweth that she is to lie with him that night. . . ."

Michel Baudier de Languedoc, historian to Louis XIV, writing in 1621, aptly describes the sultan in this ceremony as walking up and down among his fluttering virgins *"comme feroit un papillon au milieu de plusieurs feux brillians."*

Other authors maintain the handkerchief was dropped at the girl's feet, and she, in great humility (and heaven knows what other emotions) would pick it up, kiss it, and place it on her head.

If all went well, and the sultan was still in the mood by nightfall, he then summoned the Chief Black Eunuch and commanded him that his handkerchief "mislaid in the harem" be brought to him by whoever might have "found it."

Meanwhile, in anticipation of just such an event, the lucky damsel was being bathed, depilated, shampooed, perfumed, mascaraed, hennaed, anointed, finely dressed, and, according to some authorities, plied with strong liquor (to dispel shyness) and with strong aphrodisiacs (to help in the performance of her delicate duties).

Of the Gran Seignor's bedchamber Baudier says: ". . . he complies with the custom of the country, or rather that of all the Eastern parts. There is no bedstead set up, but towards Evening his Pages spread three Quilts one upon the other, at one of the corners of the Chamber, and place over it a Canopy of Cloth of Gold, garnish'd with an embroidery of Pearls."

Added to this were half a dozen pillows heaped at the head, all in richly embroidered muslin cases. No second sheet was necessary as the coverlets were lined with fine white linen. In winter the sultan slept under two "ziberline furs, or certain black foxes whose fur is very soft, wearing a pair of ratine pants, whereas in summer he undressed completely and sleeps between sheets, a piece of maroquin being laid between the bottom sheet and the uppermost mattress or quilt to avoid causing sticky perspiration."

But to return to Bon's description of what happens to the chosen girl: ". . . at night she is brought to sleep with the Grand Signor in the women's lodgings, where there are chambers set apart for that business only. And being in bed together they have two great wax lights burning by them all night; one at the bed's feet, and the other by the door: besides there are appointed (by the Cadun) divers old Black moore women, to watch in turns that night in the chamber, by two at a time; one of them to sit by the light at the bed's feet, and the other by the door; and when they will they change, and another two supply their rooms, without making the least noise imaginable, so that the King is not any whit disturbed."

A poetic addition to this scene has been provided by the young English playwright Aaron Hill who was in Turkey at the beginning of the eighteenth century:

"The Sultan all this while expects her in the Bed to which she is directed, by two large white Tapers, burning in the Room; I should have told you, that she enters, only cover'd with a Wrapping Night-gown, and advancing to the Feet of the Grand Signior's Bed, falls down upon her Knees, and in an humble manner askes this Question.

" 'A slave to your Commands, Great Monarch, waits your beckon; may, or may she not be now admitted?'

"You may be sure the Sultan says Yes, and if impatient to possess her Beauties, takes her in as soon and kindly as your self young Reader would your Mistress: But alas poor Women! common Custom generally forces them to a more humble Entrance, for, in token of Submission, dropping their Night-gown, they must gently raise the Bed Cloaths at the Feet, and so creep gradually up to those Embraces, which an Englishman wou'd be so civil to believe deserving of a kinder Welcome; and an Englishwoman, if I know them rightly, think too worthy to bestow in such a mortifying and submisse manner."

To this Baudier adds a bit of information he claims to have obtained from a Jewish doctor who served for some years in the palace, to the effect that the governess who stands guard at the foot of the bed encourages the girl to keep up her good work, so that the night may make her fortune, it being the custom in Turkey, according to Baudier, for old women to assist young lovers on their wedding night by calling on their own experience to exhort the young virgin to perform in a manner best designed to please. Other women meanwhile wait at the door with bowls of scented water to wash the girl, it also being a Moslem custom that no man may know a woman twice without her having been washed between.

But back to Bon: "In the morning, when his highness riseth (for he riseth first) he changeth all his apparell from top to toe, leaving those which he wore to her that he lay withall, and all the money that was in his pockets, were it never so much; and so departeth to his own lodgings; from thence also he sendeth her immediately a present of jewels, money, and vests, of great value, agreeable to the satisfaction and content which he received from her that night."

So far, so good. If the damsel has made the grade, and is invited to a repeat performance, her fortune, too, may be made.

However, if, by misdeed or mischance, the wretch has failed to please the sultan with her natural gifts and acquired art, she has, quite literally, had it. The odds of her ever being summoned again to do better, in face of the competition of several hundred of the world's "fairest and lustiest maidens" is worse than numerical; she will find herself on a descending spiral, the end of which, quite literally, may be a cul-de-sac.

Taken by the Chief Black Eunuch to the chief gardener,

unwanted women from the harem would be placed in a sack, weighted with stones, taken to the fish gate, put in a light rowing boat, and, by night, towed towards the open water opposite Seraglio Point "there to be consigned to the murky waters of the Bosphorus."

According to N. M. Penzer, as many as three hundred women were drowned at one time, the most terrible instance being during the reign of Ibrahim, who, after one of his debauches, suddenly decided to drown his complete harem just for the fun of getting a new one, with the result that several hundred women were put in sacks and thrown into the Bosphorus, of whom only one is known to have escaped, being picked up by a passing vessel, and ultimately reaching Paris.

The tale is told of a diver sent down after a wreck off Seraglio Point, who immediately signaled to be drawn up, explaining in a quaking voice that at the bottom of the sea was a great number of bowing sacks, each containing the dead body of a woman standing upright, their heads protruding, their feet held down by the weighted bottom, swaying slowly to and fro with the current.

On the other hand, if a girl succeeded on her first night of love and was summoned again, her position was not only radically changed—she was assigned separate quarters, given one or more black eunuchs, several slaves to serve her, a special allowance and sufficient clothes for her new position (no sleeping partner of the sultan ever being allowed to be seen twice by her master wearing the same clothes)—but in her new position of "Ikbal"—"glorified"—she entered upon a whole new phase of the game in which the stakes began to be really worth the while.

If she could manage to be called to the sultan's bed

often enough for him to acquire the taste, and for her to become pregnant, her position became even more changed: to this end she was likely to resort not only to sorcerer's charms and knicknacks, but to all sorts of exotic and spicy helpmeets containing "the hottest substances known in the orient such as musk, amber, bezoar, aloes, ginger, pepper, cinnamon, cloves, etc. . . ." *ad limito phantasia,* which, though a sort of gilding of the lily, were reputed in the East to be of sizable aphrodisiacal potency.

Another system, used upon special occasions of palace rejoicing, was known as *Khalvet,* during which the harem as a whole was admitted to the sultan's privy gardens. The normal procedure was for all the windows in the adjacent buildings of the third court to be closed. The pages were then ordered to leave those buildings (on pain of death were they to be caught malingering) while the women were conducted to the gardens by the black eunuchs.

Information on what took place during these wanton escapades was not easily come by, but Jean-Claude Flachat, a French manufacturer accredited to the sultan, who became a good friend of the Chief Black Eunuch, was able to obtain the following detailed description by bribing him with some automaton toys he had invented:

" . . . when all is ready the Grand Seigneur causes *kalvet* (the state of complete privacy, either alone or with the harem) to be announced. The Bostanchis (head gardeners) stand on guard outside, and the black eunuchs inside. All the sultanas come from the Karem (harem) after the Sultan. The Keslar Aga, at the head of the other eunuchs, officiates. The women rush out on all sides, like a swarm of bees settling on the flowers and stopping continually at the honey they find. There are numbers of them of every kind and sort. The Keslar Aga has assured me several times that the gaiety of these occasions seems to bring out any skill they claim to possess, or arts which they display in anything they do to amuse. Those little games that poets invented for Cupid and the nymphs may give some slight idea. Each tries to distinguish herself; they are all a mass of charms; each has the same object to accomplish. One has never seen elsewhere to what lengths the resources of the intellect can go with young women who want to seduce a man they love through vanity, and especially by natural inclination. The grace of the dance, the melody of the voice, the harmony of the music, the elegance of the dresses, the wit of the conversation, the ecstasies, the effeminacy, and love—the most voluptuous, I may add, that the cleverest coquetry has invented—all unite in this delightful spot under the eyes of the Sultan.

"The Kiahia Caden (chief Cadin) finally presents to him the girl that most takes his fancy. No pains have been spared to ensure her success. She hastens to exhibit every pleasing talent she possesses. The handkerchief that he throws to her signifies his wish to be alone with her. The curtain which covers the sofa on which he is sitting is made to fall. The Keslar Aga remains to pull it aside again at the first signal, and the other women, who have scattered here and there, all occupied—some with dancing, others with singing, these with playing on instruments, and those with partaking of refreshments—all come to the kiosque in a moment to pay their respects to the Sultan and congratulate the new favourite. The fete continues some time longer, and terminates by the distribution which the Keslar Aga makes of jewels, stuffs, and trinkets, following the wishes of his master. The presents are proportional to the pleasure received."

To this the poetic Mr. Hill adds a variant in his smoothly scanning prose, helping one to visualize, if not to hear, smell, taste, and cutaneously enjoy this enchanted garden where "you walk as in a dream, thro' all the odoriferous ecstasies of Nature's Blessings. . . ." but it is so long it would require a chapter to itself.

To Mr. Hill's aesthetic appreciation of the sultan's lubricious pastimes the Rumanian nobleman Dimitriu Cantemir added some nuggets on the peculiar taste of Ibrahim:

"In the palace garden call'd Chas, he frequently assembled all the virgins, made them strip themselves, and himself naked, neighing like a stallion, ran among them, and as it were ravish'd one or other kicking and struggling by his order."

Ibrahim, says Cantemir, was as dedicated to lust as his predecessor Murad had been to wine, and reports that "he spent all his time in sensual pleasures, and when nature was exhausted with the frequent repetition of venereal delights, he endeavour'd to restore it with potions and art. Every Friday, which is the Turkish Sabbath, he dedicated to Venus, and commanded a beautiful Virgin richly habited to be brought to him by his Mother, Prime Vizier, or some other Great man. He cover'd the walls of his chamber with looking glass, that his love-battles might seem to be acted in several places at once. He order'd his pillows to be fluffed with rich furs, that the bed destin'd for the imperial pleasure might be the more precious. Nay he put whole sable skins under him, in a notion that his lust would be inflam'd, if his love-toil were render'd more difficult by the glowing of his knees."

Cantemir further reports that Ibrahim made a collection of "great and voluminous books of pictures, expressing the various ways of coition, whereby he ever invented some new and before unknown posture," adding that the public treasury, which had been diminished by Murad's drunkenness, was by Ibrahim's luxury and lust "quite exhausted, and the sinews of the Empire, which were applied by his ancestors to repulse their enemies and inlarge their dominion, were by him us'd to the destruction of his body."

Sir Raul Rycaut, the British diplomat and consular agent, in his delightful "History of the Ottoman Empire from 1623 to 1677" gives an even more salacious report on Sultan Ibrahim, of whose court he had firsthand knowledge: "Not withstanding the great number of women within the Seraglio, all of which were at the Devotion of the Sultan; yet Ibrahim not being contented therewith, passing one day to Scutari, had by chance cast his eye on an object which much pleased him; what it was, becomes not the modesty of my pen to relate; but being returned to his Seraglio, he sent Orders to the Vizier, to seek out for him the biggest, and best proportioned Woman which was to be found in all Constantinople, and the parts thereabout."

What it was that so attracted the sultan's fancy is, however, unblushingly described by Cantemir: "Happening to see by chance the privy parts of a wild heifer, he sent the shape of them in gold all over the Empire (presumably having had them first cast from plaster!), with the orders to make enquiry, whether a woman made just in that manner could be found for his lust. At last, they say, such a woman was found and received into the women's apartment."

For the remainder of the story we must revert to Sir

Paul. ". . . Emissaries were dispatched into all Quarters of the City; at length they happily procured a tall Armenian Woman, well proportioned according to her height, and a Giantess for her Stature; which being found, she was presently washed and perfumed in the Bath, and as richly Cloathed and Adorned as the shortness of time would permit: There was no great difficulty to persuade her to become Turk, having so high preferment in her prospect. So that being introduced to the Grand Signior's presence, he became immediately Enamoured, and was so pleased with her Society, that he preferred her before all the Women of his Court; an Evidence whereof he gave, in that he could not deny her in any request she could make, and particularly about that time the Pashaluck of Damascus being void, this Woman begged it for herself, substituting another in Office, who was accountable to her for all the Profits and Emoluments thereof: By these particulars of favour the Queen-Mother becoming jealous, one day inviting her to dinner, caused her to be strangled, and persuaded Ibrahim that she died suddenly of a violent Sickness, at which the poor Man was greatly afflicted."

Sic transit Armena.

But whereas the sultan's immediate object was to satisfy his pleasure, that of the maidens was to become with child.

The race consisted in being first to bear a boy, or, failing that, to place in number two, three, or four positions, which might pay off as well as the winner—there being always the chance that those ahead might somehow manage to get themselves disqualified.

To bear a male child meant for the kadin in question getting herself in position for the grand prize.

As the redoubtable Bon puts it: "If it so fall out that

any one of them doth conceive by him, and bring forth his first begotten childe; then she is called by the name of Sultana Queen: and if it be a son, she is confirmed and established by great feasts, and solemnities; and forthwith hath a dwelling assigned unto her apart, and many stately rooms well furnished: and many servants to attend upon her. . . .

"The other women (however they bring forth issue) are not called Queens; yet they are called Sultanas, because they had had carnal commerce with the king. . . ."

These, however, were limited to seven, most sultans being content with four. The reason commonly adduced being that Mohammedan law contained an exotic clause requiring a man to sleep with his wife (rather than with some younger or more appetizing slave) at least once a week, the night of holy Friday being normally reserved to the number one wife.

Though technically the kadins weren't wives, the law still seemed to apply, and four appears to have been the favorite number—allowing a balance between four days for connubial satisfaction and three for amorous experiment.

Normally each kadin would share her master's bed on one appointed night of the week, and, if invited before dinner, would have it served in the sultan's quarters, though at a separate table.

Seldom would the sultan visit the kadins in their private apartments where they lived with their young children (and retinue of eunuchs and female servants), unless the kadin or one of her children were ill, whereupon, says the Baron d'Ohsson, in his *Tableau general de L'Empire Othomen*: "Whenever the Sultan would thus happen to enter the harem on a non-ceremonious visit he wore slippers heeled with silver that he might make sufficient clatter for all the female inhabitants to scatter before his presence," it being considered bad form and most disrespectful to be caught, so to speak, underfoot.

The second, and even more important leg of the "double" consisted in lasting the full course of hurdles, outliving the sultan, keeping a son alive against all rivals—no easy venture in a palace teeming with professional executioners where fratricide and genicide were legalized and primogeniture no guarantee of succession, and where the weapons of murder included such subtleties as the poisoned vest which, when donned, caused a rapid, agonizing, and apparently inexplicable death.

But whoever succeeded became queen mother of the *new* sultan and the real sovereign in the harem.

As Penzer points out: "The ruler of the harem is not the Sultan, nor the head wife or First Kadin (recognized concubine) but the Sultan's mother, the *sultan validé*. Turks recognize that a man can have many wives, that he can get rid of unwanted ones and take others at will, but that he can have only one mother, and it is she, therefore, who occupies the unique place of honour that nothing can alter save death. To her are entrusted the most personal and private belongings of her son, his women. The power of the *Sultan Validé* is enormous, not only in the harem, but throughout the Empire."

Here we return to the role of the Black Eunuchs. Though the *sultan validé* was the official ruler of the harem, the Chief Black Eunuch, acting as a sort of prime minister, and by virtue of his official position as liaison officer between the *sultan validé* and the rest of the harem, and between the harem and the outside world, was in a better position to wield actual power, much as the Prime Minister of England can wield more power than the actual sovereign.

"As for the rest of the women which are not so fortunate as to be beloved of the King," says Bon, they "must still live together, and diet with the rest of the young virgins: wasting their youthfull dayes amongst themselves in evil thoughts: (for they are too strictly lookt unto to offend in act)." A subject on which he expands a little further by adding the comic note that "it is not lawful for anyone to bring ought in unto them, with which they may commit the deads of beastly, and unnaturall uncleanness; so that if they have a will to eat radishes, cucumbers, gourds, or such like meats; they are sent in unto them sliced, to deprive them of the means of playing the wantons: for they being all young, lusty, and lascivious wenches, and wanting the society of men (which would better instruct them, and questionlesse far better employ them) are doubtless of themselves inclined to that which is naught, and will often be possest with unchast thoughts."

In support of this last contention the Greek-born historians Habesci—who spent many years in service with the seraglio of Mustapha III and claimed to possess details "no other man ever had it in his power to lay before the public, or, if he had, did not dare to communicate"—affirms that "the most infamous lasciviousness is likewise common in the chambers of the girls. Nor is it at all astonishing that handsome girls, well fed, undergoing neither fatigue nor vexation; girls that have nothing to do but to prepare themselves for sensual pleasures, and who think of nothing but Venus and her son, should give way to unnatural lasciviousness for want of the proper means of gratifying their amorous inclinations. Notwithstanding the consciousness of the fatal doom that awaits them, if they are discovered, the violence of their passions makes them rush precipitately upon their ruin. Alas! How many of these unhappy girls are thrown, tied together in guilty couples, into the sea, from that part of the Seraglio which faces Kadi-Roa (Calcedonia). In the reign of Sultan Mustapha III, some hundreds were the victims of their incontinence, and not a year passes, at present, though the governesses use the utmost vigilance to keep them in order without some such sacrifices, so shocking to humanity, that if we did not draw a veil over the subject, the minuter descriptions we are able to give would offend the eyes of chastity, and too deeply affect the sympathizing hearts of well disposed readers."

A few minute details were, however, added by Penzer, who says that "a eunuch in touch with the outside world could easily smuggle artificial phalli and similar erotic succedania into the harem and to a certain extent play the part of Lesbian, which by its very novelty and perversion might help to satisfy the cravings of a bored and neglected woman."

Of the maidens who failed to reach the sultan's bed, or, having reached it, failed to hold him with her charms, they were, at twenty-five—if no worse fate had befallen them—carted off to the old seraglio, described by Hill as: "a prison to receive . . . whole shoals of barren, sick, or antiquated Ladies."

A "Palace of Tears," as it came to be called, it served as a place of banishment for the entire harem of a deceased sultan.

Aubrey de la Montraye, a French writer of the seventeenth century who had once managed to insinuate himself into the "new" seraglio—while the sultan was in Adrianople—by impersonating the assistant of a Swiss clockmaker from Pera who had been summoned to mend some pendulums, describes the scene in the old seraglio in pathetic terms: "Thither at the death of each sultan, were sent his wives and favorites, and here also were brought the grandmothers, the unmarried sisters, and aunts, the milk-relatives, and the contumacious, sickly, and barren concubines of the reigning sultan. . . . The women imprisoned within its walls were without exception sent there by reason of the deaths of their husbands, the execution of their sons, or loss of royal favour."

From this living tomb, guarded by second rate eunuchs, there were, apart from death, only two methods of escaping a celibate life of imprisonment: by becoming *sultan validé,* or, if lucky enough to have saved up enough money while at the seraglio, to be given in marriage to a government or army official who might seek one's hand for the influence he might thus obtain at court.

When Murad IV succeeded to the throne by the simple process of exterminating his seventeen brothers, his mother alone escaped the fate of his father's innumerable bedfellows. As Montraye describes the scene: "Directly after these poor princes, who people say possess'd great beauty, had been buried, the populace waited at the gate to witness the departure from the seraglio of their mothers and all the other wives of the king, with their children and their goods. All the carriages, coaches, mules, and horses of the court were employed for the purpose. Besides the wives of the king and the twenty-seven daughters, there were two hundred others, consisting of nurses and slaves, and they were taken to the Eschi Seraglio [the old seraglio], where the wives and the daughters of the king reside, with their aghas, that is eunuchs, who guard and serve them in a royal fashion. There they can weep, as much as they like, for their dead sons, a thing that was forbidden at the other grand seraglio, under penalty of capital punishment, and there by degrees they will marry according to the custom of the Kingdom. Inside the grand seraglio there remain only the wives with child, and there they stay until their children are born."

Of all the inmates of the seraglio, the luckiest were probably the sultan's daughters—of which there were sometimes several score! If they were not strangled at birth, or their umbilical cord was not left untied, they were not only well taken care of for the rest of their lives, but were afforded all kinds of privileges. "Brought up with tender care by their mothers in the seraglio, they were (sometimes while still in swaddling clothes) engaged to rich pashas, who had no choice but to accede to the sultan's wishes, an honor which was likely to cost them a fortune."

But among all their privileges, of which Castellan, in his six-volume opus on the mores of the Turks, lists a great number—making them unique among women in the Ottoman Empire—there was one proviso which reduced the sister of a sultan to a lot inferior to the commonest fishwife. All their children, whether boys or girls, had to be killed at birth.

The rivalry of feudal houses for the succession, which so plagued Europe, were, in the Ottoman Empire, a physical impossibility.

The whole purpose of the system, as Miller underlines it, was to guarantee the absolute supremacy of the sultan ruling a vast congeries of vassal states through a hierarchy of officials trained to serve him faithfully for the tenure of their life *only*.

To make sure that no faction could contest the throne by claim of royal blood, no daughter of a sultan could bear a child that lived, while the fate of the sultan's sons was one of the most dangerous and unpleasant in history. Those of the sultan's sons who were allowed to survive birth were kept alive purely as material to guarantee the succession, but every precaution was taken to insure that only *one* could safely do so.

Mohammed the Conqueror legislated fratricide into law, making it legal if not mandatory for a future sultan to kill off all his brothers and half-brothers. A prison called the "qafes," or cages, existed within the seraglio to which all the young princes were consigned after reaching puberty. There they were kept like steers to insure the succession, but forbidden during their captivity to procreate.

The women with whom—as a palliative to such a dull existence—they too were provided, were subject to having their ovaries removed, or, if by some slip an heir was born, it was instantly disposed of.

As an example of fratricidal exuberance, King Hassa of Tunis managed to reign in security by the process of murdering forty-four brothers with whom his father had "inconsiderately" encumbered him, devoting himself thereafter, as one historian added, "to a life of unspeakable vice in his harem of four hundred boys."

Only the *designated* heir to the sultan—and this might be either a son or a brother of the sultan, as primogeniture was not the rule—was given a certain freedom. After his apprenticeship at government learned in the Palace School, along with the other pages (who would eventually be his lieutenants and administrators) he was sent out to learn the art of government in practice by being assigned as governor, at a very early age, to some outlying province.

Ibrahim, some of whose characteristics have been noted, has been, on the other hand, excused by some historians for his excesses in the harem because of the fact that he came to the throne at a late age after spending most of his life imprisoned in the qafes, an imprisonment which had made him almost blind.

This, in sum, was harem life in the grand seraglio of the grand signor. But the harem was not limited to sultans. Pashas, beys, beylebeys, anyone in fact who could afford it, was entitled to a harem of four official wives and as many concubines as he could happily support. The expensive proviso, however, of having to maintain each *legal* wife on an equal footing was inclined to keep the great majority of Ottomans monogamous.

Still, there are some fascinating tales about what went on behind the shutters of the seraglios of the rich.

Their eventual decline and almost disappearance has been attributed, at least by one opulent pasha, to the arrival of the twentieth century with its status symbols. Obliged by Moslem law to produce, instead of the usual beads and bolts of cloth for each and every spouse, a grand piano and a French governess, even the most stalwart of pashas was induced to modify his household, except, of course, for Abdul Hamid, the last of the Ottoman sultans to inhabit the grand seraglio.

6
SIC SEMPER TYRANNIS

Of medium height, rickety, hooknosed, and with hollow cheeks on which a fast-growing beard was "clumsily dyed with a mixture of coffee and gall-nut," Abdul Hamid II has been described as a neurotic monomaniac who "kept alive on his nerves."

Despite the recent and humane attempts of historians to portray him as a well-meaning, but unfortunately born, anachronism, who, beneath a despotic veneer, had the interest of his country at heart, it would be hard to find a better—or worse—example of what he both symbolized and was: "the Sick Man of Europe."

Having come to the throne in an atmosphere of sortilege and insanity, complete with the pinpricked dolls of his incumbent brother, his regime provides an even more devastating picture of the decadence and hopelessness of an authoritarian state than was provided by the holocaust of the Third Reich—though, by a strange quirk of fate, Abdul Hamid did not end his days in the bunker he had prepared for such an eventuality.

So terrified was he that the beautiful seraglio palace of his forefathers might not afford him sufficient protection against "his own people," he built himself, at their expense, a new palace on the heights of Yildiz overlooking the Bosphorus.

There he entrenched himself, as if to sustain a seige, in a fortress the outer walls of which were of concrete and steel, the inner ones, all of twelve feet thick, being provided with special vaultlike doors which could only open outward.

In private apartments, for which the Turkish ambassador to Paris got an estimated £80,000 to do the interior decorating—with results described as "more suitable in a house of ill-repute"—Abdul Hamid immured himself in the hope of being able to withstand any popular uprising or military mutiny.

As an extra precaution he added to these fortifications a kiosk "of artificial rock" somewhat like Hitler's dugout, inlaid with mother-of-pearl and ivory, guaranteed by its constructor to be impervious to fire, earthquake, or any then known projectile, supplied with specially reinforced doors with complicated locks, alarms and hidden springs.

Frightened of dusk, and terrified of darkness, he would go to bed late, and sleep very little, insisting that the whole palace, down to the smallest room and out-of-the-way lobby be brilliantly illuminated from twilight to dawn; hating silence almost as much as the dark, he ordered the palace orchestra to play till the wee hours of the morning, and guards to march ceaselessly up and down outside his doors but just within earshot, so as to calm his nerves with the rhythmic sound of their footsteps.

To help him drop into an uneasy sleep on the reclining chair which served him as bed, a chamberlain was required—from behind an arras—to read him detailed descriptions of assassinations and executions, which "though stories of crime excite him and prevent him sleeping, as soon as his reader reaches a passage where blood flows, the Sultan immediately becomes calm and falls asleep."

Not unlike the modern newspaper subscriber, his favorite reading matter dealt with rape, assassination, the abduction of children, substitution of wills, incendiarism, and any act of violence; to keep him well supplied with such copy, his court librarian—filling the function of the modern tabloid editor—was charged with cutting out and translating the more lurid pulps from foreign countries as well as the regular contents of the *Gazette de Police de Paris,* presumably because of the piquancy and higher Hooper rating of the dragnet reports of the French *Police des Moeurs.*

As a result, notes one chronicler, "it was not surprising that the Sultan would frequently complain of nightmares and immediately summon a sorcerer [Freud was just then discovering Breuer] to analyze the meaning of his dreams!"

By day, though his fears were less nightmarish, he behaved as if in constant dread of plots against his life, carrying revolvers secreted in specially built pockets which he would whip out and shoot at the slightest provocation.

In an even more secret refuge, actually carved out of rock, and reached by a labyrinth of secret stairways "known only to the sultan and a faithful servant," he would spend his very bad nights. There he is reported to have kept his most secret and valued possessions, such as informers' reports on members of his privy council.

All the knickknacks of the imperiled authoritarian are here almost grotesquely caricatured.

The surveillance of his enemies, real or imaginary, appears to have engrossed most of Abdul Hamid's attention. To be informed, he created "a vast system of espionage," not only in the empire, but as far as he could throughout the world.

All his reports and documents he first required to be disinfected in a special stove. And so terrified was he of the bacteriological world, he had special *lavabos* placed throughout his apartments in which he could constantly wash his hands. He also spent many hours studying bacteriology and antiseptics so as to be able personally to analyze any kind of food to see if it were poisoned.

An early riser, he is said by members of his council to have devoted almost all his working hours to the study of reports "sent by spies from every quarter of the globe, and which are laid out for him on his desk by his confidential eunuch, Djafar-Agha."

An unflattering glimpse of the sultan's life at Yildiz is given by a young Greek, Georges Dorys, whose father, a prince of Samos, was one of the sultan's ministers. Though the picture of degradation, fear, and corruption he paints may be colored by partisan politics, as he was a member of the "Young Turks," his facts have the professional qualifications of a journalist trained as a subcorrespondent for *The Times*.

Some of the more lurid details of the private life of the sultan he may have obtained from his father, but the extraordinary social and political atmosphere which fermented around the palace he obtained firsthand, having been brought up there, at least till his own political opinions brought him to the attention of police spies and forced him to take refuge in Paris, where, at the turn of the century, he revealed what he knew in a sizzling little booklet, *The Private Life of the Sultan of Turkey.*

According to Dorys, the sultan's statesmanship consisted entirely of organizing espionage, and an attempt to obtain his ends both at home and abroad through a vast system of corruption.

Plus ça change, plus c'est la même chose!

Dorys estimates, though he does not reveal the source of his data, that in the six months after the Armenian Massacres, 235,000 pounds Turkish were spent and approximately 640 decorations handed out in the form of hush money to various European newspapers, the sultan going so far as to try to bribe the *London Times,* and being quoted to the effect that "with a million pounds Turkish we could silence Bismarck."

What figure may have been allotted to try to hush *The Times* does not appear in his record; but to be convinced that such methods, far from being abandoned, have been improved on, one need but look at the modern lobbying of some Central American and Caribbean countries.

As for his ministers and councilors, Dorys quotes the Sultan as saying "let them rob, so long as they serve me."

As his chief weapons, says Dorys, the sultan used secret condemnation, banishments, and mass executions, employing secret courts which he would enjoy witnessing (like his forefathers) from behind a curtain, being able thus to savor not only the trials but the third-degree methods of "mediaeval torture some of the refinements of which were suggested by his court 'buffon' Kiathan Imamy," such as the application of scalding hardboiled eggs under the armpits, a form of torture reputed so to upset the victim's nervous system as to drive him mad.

To this torture one of the eunuchs, Mousaffer Agha, is said to have been subjected and then exiled to Mecca, for having, so the story goes, divulged Yildiz secrets to the British Embassy.

To hide the fact that executions had taken place, says the young Greek author, the sultan would have them carried out in outlying parts of the empire by a special clandestine organization for summary executions, but his fondness for blood, adds Dorys, was such that it would induce him to have the severed heads of victims sent to the Porte that he might view them; and if the place of execution had been far away, the heads were embalmed, no longer as by his forefathers wrapped in herbs and tucked into a saddlebag, but with the more modernly Victorian formaldehyde.

As Dorys describes the end of the long history of the grand seraglio: "Under Abdul Hamid the tyranny and absolutism remained, but none of the glamor that had once made it a fascinating system."

By the turn of the century, around beautiful Seraglio Point, a foul, belching railway cut a swathe of Manchestrian drabness.

The eunuchs—of which there still were over a hundred —now dressed, as did the sultan, in *stambouline* frock coats of Victorian black. The fantastic heron-plumed headdress of the Chief Black Eunuch was replaced by a plain red fez. In Dorys' words: "An enormous Negro, more hideous than the others, crossed the courtyard with a slouching gait. It is His Highness the Grand Eunuch of the Imperial Harem, who bears the official title of Dar-us-seadet-us-cherife-aghassy, or Guardian of the Gates of Felicity."

As his forefathers had done before him, Abdul Hamid made special use of the eunuchs as informers and executioners, but, says Dorys, "now recruited almost entirely from the more primitive recess of Africa, owing to the vigilant anti-slavery efforts of the European powers, the palace and therefore to a large extent the empire, was literally in the grip of ignorant, superstitious maniacs."

Of the once powerful Janissaries nothing had existed for almost a century. The Palace School had become an "academic anachronism," whereas the guards, trained by Prussian experts, now drilled in khaki.

In the harem, with its close to four hundred inmates, the women dressed in cheap imitations of the Paris fashions, their quarters decorated with neo-Gothic Victorian furniture, complete with aspidistras and antimacassars.

"Far from evoking the fugitive vision of a fairy-like and unknown world," says Dorys, "it was of a cruel and revolting sequestration of young, beautiful and ardent women, whose charm and freshness and even their lives belonged absolutely to one master—a melancholy and deformed monomaniac."

Dorys' further description of the women in the harem, here slightly paraphrased, takes on the overtones of the inspired novelist.

"An incessant and exasperating surveillance shackles

them even in their prison, and the enervating, unhealthy atmosphere which they breathe constantly renders them different from other women. In the absence of a master whose very name makes them tremble, they are nervous, irritable, capricious and perverse.

"When not dancing they spend their time in real childishness, playing with dolls, or imitating the cries of animals, the crow of a cock, the buzzing of a fly, the barking of a dog, or else they smear the faces of their Negress attendants with flour, put them up to tricks, quarrel among each other . . . in short, try anything to pass away the time.

"Lying on divans or silk-covered sofas, squatting on Boukara rugs, in careless attitudes that set off the symmetrical lines of their bodies and express eloquently enough the sadness of their empty existence, most of them follow with their eyes the blue spirals formed by the perfumed smoke of their cigarette or *narghileh,* and with a ring-covered hand toy with the amber beads of their tesbih, a kind of chaplet made of amber to amuse the fingers of Orientals with an innocent occupation.

"Others sip syrups, partake of sherbets, munch ice, chew gum, or suck a thousand kinds of sweetmeats, which they all love as well as tobacco, flowers, perfume, especially musk and violet, of which the Sultan is particularly fond.

"They adore cats, parrots, doves, coffee, cards and suggestive stories; and they crave two things, because they are prohibited (and because they are women), wine and raki—which the kindness of a eunuch sometimes procures them.

"The time they cannot 'kill' they abandon to sadness, and they think unceasingly of their far-distant country, their forsaken home, their long-lost parents, the gloomy future, their impossible lover, an old master, depressingly ugly."

In 1909 with the fall of Abdul Hamid's regime, some 370 women and 127 eunuchs were discovered immured in Yildiz. Of these a few of the sultan's favorites stuck with him to the end, living out with him the balance of his exile, mostly in Salonika.

Of the rest a grim and pathetic description has been given by Francis McCullagh in his *Fall of Abdul-el-Hamid,* written in 1910.

"One of the most mournful processions of the many mournful processions of fallen grandeur that passed through the streets during these days was one composed of the ladies from the ex-Sultan's Harem on their way from Yildiz to the Top-Kapu Palace [the seraglio]. These unfortunate ladies were of all ages between fifteen and fifty and so numerous that it took thirty-one carriages to convey them and their attendants. Some of them were sent to the Old Seraglio in Stamboul, but this old palace of the early Sultans had fallen into such a state of disrepair that it was found to be unsuitable for them and they were sent back again to Yildiz. Finally they were all collected in the Top-Kapu Palace in connection with one of the strangest ceremonies that ever took place even there. It is well known that most of the ladies in the harems of the Turkish Sultans were Circassians, the Circassian girls being very much esteemed on account of their beauty and being consequently very expensive.

"As Abdul-Hamid's Seraglio was no exception to this general rule, the Turkish Government telegraphed to the different Circassian villages in Anatolia, notifying them that every family which happened to have any of its female members in the ex-Sultan's Harem was at liberty to take them home, no matter whether the girls had been originally sold by their parents or had (as was the case in some instances) been torn from their homes by force.

"In consequence of this, a large number of Circassian mountaineers came in their picturesque garb into Constantinople, and on a certain fixed day they were conducted in a body to the Old Palace of Top-Kapu, where, in the presence of a Turkish Commission, they were ushered into a long hall filled with the ex-Sultan's concubines, cadines and odalisques, all of whom then were allowed to unveil themselves for the occasion. The scene that followed was very touching. Daughters fell into the arms of their fathers whom they had not seen for years. Sisters embraced brothers or cousins, and in some instances relatives met who had never met before, and were only able to establish their relationship by means of long and mutual explanations.

"The contrast between the delicate complexions and costly attire of the women and the rough, weather-beaten appearance of the ill-clad mountaineers who had come to fetch them was not the least striking feature of the extraordinary scene; and in some instances the poor relatives were quite dazzled by the beautiful faces, the graceful manners, and the rich apparel of their kinswomen. The latter seemed all very glad, however, to get away; and as a rule they lost no time in packing their trunks and departing, sometimes after a very affectionate leave-taking of their other odalisques. The number of female slaves thus liberated was two hundred and thirteen.

"Clad in Circassian peasant dress, they are now in all probability milking cows and doing farm work in Anatolia. . . . This joyful reunion in the Top-Kapu Palace had its sad side, however, as more than one of the men did not find the face he sought. Some of the girls had died, some had been put to death by Abdul-Hamid, and others of them after Abdul-Hamid's fall, and been brought with him to Salonika by the ex-Sultan or quietly drafted into the harems of imperial princes who had taken a fancy to them. Moreover a good many of the women, especially those who had already passed their first youth, were disheartened to learn that nobody came to fetch them. Apparently their relatives had died or migrated, or did not relish the prospect of bringing back into their miserable mountain huts women no longer young, who had contracted expensive tastes and forgotten the language of their childhood. . . . These unfortunate ladies will probably pine away the rest of their lives in company with the other ladies—remnants of the Harems of the past Sultans—who fill the Top-Kapu Palace and who, in the best manner of the *Arabian Nights,* sigh audibly at the barred and latticed windows and have on one or two occasions dropped roses and perfumed handkerchiefs before good-looking youths passing in the street below."

With their passing, the grand seraglio ceased entirely to be a royal abode. In April, 1924, it ceased also to be royal domain, when it was attached administratively to the museums of Stamboul, and thereby formally declared the property of the Turkish Republic.

Of the eunuchs, most of them were dispersed, though some came to a rough end, such as Djalar-Agha, "a huge swollen, balloon-like creature of extraordinary stature," who was hanged at Galata bridge for having "plotted against the Constitution and distributed large sums of money."

Of his colleagues, some fared better, such as Nadir

Agha, "a slim, intelligent, girlish creature who had been bought from an Egyptian slave merchant at the age of ten for 150 francs" who is said by McCullagh to have trimmed his sails to the new wind and managed to play quite a role, even after the fall of his master Abdul Hamid, mostly because of his intimate knowledge of the seraglio in which he had been brought up and of "whose secret caches of treasure buried in inaccessible and unguessable spots he alone was aware."

In the 1950's, planning a trip to Istamboul, I obtained from a professor of Turkish at Columbia University an address which might have enabled me to talk to one of the last of the surviving eunuchs of the Grand Seraglio. Unfortunately the advent of the Eisenhower Administration forced me even deeper into the stacks, and I missed an opportunity which now may be quite irretrievable.

From a family friend, however, the wife of an American official less squeamish about the Eisenhower regime and quite free to travel abroad—I did obtain an eyewitness description of the inside of one of the last great harems of an Oriental potentate still flourishing today.

One of the few American women at that time—the mid-1950's—to have been admitted to an audience with his Majesty Abdul Azziz ibn al Saud, King of Arabia, she was introduced into his seraglio where she caught a glimpse of a large number of women enjoying a private screening of some Hollywood production, had lunch with the number one wife, and was then introduced into the presence of the king by a tall black Negro of about fifty, who, as he was the only male she saw in the entire harem with the exception of the king and his young children (of whom the king admitted fathering fifty) she presumed to be a eunuch.

Whether eunuch or trusty, she was too southernly prim to inquire, and, as he was unlikely to offer her visual evidence of his state, the question must remain unanswered; however, it is doubtful that such a patriarch as King Saud would be likely to allow in his harem (through which several hundred women are reputed to have passed), a tall dark and manly-looking Negro, merely on trust—and in such a climate!

Furthermore Saudi Arabian friends of mine have made no bones about the fact that eunuchs still guard the harems of their compatriots in Arabia.

7
ANGELIC CHOIRS

While Abdul Hamid sat gazing out at the Aegean, twiddling his *tesbih* and plotting how, with the enormous sums he had looted and hoarded in Swiss and London banks, he could regain the Eastern throne of his forefathers, a Turkish-born eunuch named Mustapha, then a resident in the capital city of Abdul Hamid's less exotic colleague (but one who attempted with many of the same means to keep alive an authoritarian *regime* beyond the endurance of his people, the not yet emperor, but sometime kingling, Victor Emmanuel III) was acting, that is, the eunuch was acting as *Kappellmeister* to the Vatican Chapel.

Indeed, this Mustapha was the last of a long line of some of the most extraordinary creatures in history, who, through several preceding centuries, reached heights of popularity and received emoluments for their art, as great or even greater than any modern serf of the celluloid.

In the Christian world, if Matthew was the tested cause for religious eunuchs, to St. Paul can be assigned their use as singers.

Within the sanctified area of the temple, Paul wanted women to be silent; yet someone had to sing the praises of the Lord in the required "high angelic voice of innocents."

For a while a chorus of virginal maidens and pre-pubescent boys was employed. Then something better was discovered: a creature, presumably innocent of sex, with an ethereal, otherworldly, almost angelic voice: the eunuch.

And true it is that they have an extraordinary psychic effect upon the listener.

One of the first reports of their use in the West—according to the late drama critic C. J. Bulliet—was at the wedding of Emperor Caracalla for whom a chorus of soprano singers was especially manufactured by Plautinianus, the father of the bride, an African by birth, who seized several young boys from well-to-do Roman families, had them castrated and trained as choristers.

Sozomen, the first historian to deal with castrati as singers, tells how in Byzantium the Empress Eudoxia, whose minister Eutropius was a eunuch, charged another eunuch, Brison, with organizing a choir of orthodox castrates for singing the Christian hymns which St. John of Chrysostom (who was against the practice of castration) rejoiced in opposing to the then current and popular pagan choir reunions. When the quarrel ensued between the rival groups, Brison got hit on the head with a stone. To avenge the insult the empress forbade choirs of noncastrates; only orthodox castrates were allowed to continue.

Thus the custom got established.

From the Eastern Church it passed to the Catholic, and by the twelfth century the number of eunuch singers had grown and spread throughout Europe. By 1137 even Smolensk could boast of a eunuch professor of song called Manuel.

The elaborate *a capella* style, which began to flourish about the middle of the fifteenth century, necessitated, say musical historians, a much wider range and higher degree of virtuosity than anything that had gone before; the existing choirboys became inadequate.

Even the *falsetti*, a type of singer, most of whom were trained in a special school in Spain to sing the parts of soprani in a high falsetto tenor, could not fit the bill: their voices—as described by those who heard them—had a peculiar and somewhat unpleasant quality and they could not reach as high as true soprani.

That there is a close relation between the larynx and the testes is a fact obvious to any family with a teen-age boy. A doctor who dissected the throat of a eunuch who had been castrated young found the larynx to be a third less developed than in normal males and the circumference of the glottis much smaller. This difference results in a change of timbre from contralto to high soprano—often with voices as beautiful and with more power and control than those of women.

Here was an opening for the rapid propagation of eunuchs.

By the sixteenth century they were filling the churches and private chapels of Europe. In 1569 there were six in the chapel of the Duke of Bavaria under the direction of Orlando di Lasso, who was to revolutionize plain-chant and the musical education of castrates.

Finally castrati made an appearance even in the pontifical chapel from which they had so far been excluded because the church officially frowned on the practice of mutilating men.

Girolamo Rossini, the first castrato to sing in the papal choir was, nonetheless, promptly chased out by his ungelded rivals presumably because of the serious professional threat he posed, especially to the Spanish-trained *falsetti.* Discouraged, Rossini decided to quit competing altogether and don the habit of a Franciscan—an order in which singing was forbidden—but Pope Clement VIII was so taken with the effect he produced in the choir he ordered him back.

This was the beginning of the end for the Spanish falsetti: by the time the last one died in 1625 castrati were well in control in the Vatican as well as other chapels.

It was also the beginning of a new trend in song. Noting that the Church, which had openly deplored castration, was now closing an eye, and that, though it did not encourage the practice, it seemed happy to accept into its choir, without much questioning as to how and why, this new and special type of singer, the poor, especially of Naples, began to have their children castrated in numbers. Outside Neapolitan barbershops signs began to appear: *"Qui si castrano maravigliosamente i putti."*

By the end of the eighteenth century as many as two thousand children were being castrated in a single year in

Italy. To excuse the practice, apologists coined a sophistical syllogism: Man was distinguished from animals by his voice; voice must be a faculty more precious than virility; if to embellish the voice required suppression of virility it could be done without fear of impiety.

In 1588 Sixtus V, in whose pontificate the dome of St. Peter's was finished, and who wished to clean up the "lawlessness and licentiousness" left by his predecessor Gregory XIII, forbade women to appear in public on the stage. The ban fell into disuse but was reinstated in 1676 by Innocent XI (known as Papa Minga, because he was forever saying No) and throughout the eighteenth century in Rome women remained barred from the stage.

Here was another natural opening for the castrato; also an extra source of income to be tapped. If a castrato was to fail to secure a place in some chapel, he could now be counted on to find employment in the theatres as a "sopranista."

Among the poorer classes it was the practice to select and sell outright to some teacher or musical institution—there were as many as four conservatories in Naples alone—any child who showed musical promise.

Where a family could manage to scrape together the necessary money for several years of hard training, they could invest in a singer of their own, who might produce lavishly for them in their old age.

It is said of one famous castrato that when approached for money by a poor old man who turned out to be his father, he answered: "Willingly! But in the same coin." Whereupon he threw an empty purse at the old man's feet.

Schools of song spread throughout Italy and castrati began to receive intense musical training, many of them acquiring "an impeccable style and an astonishing facility for improvising on a given theme."

Unlike boys, who could barely be taught to read music before their voices would break, the eunuch could be trained and trained till he had mastered the science, whereupon the brilliance, lightness, and strength of his voice would last a very long time. One castrato kept his voice beyond eighty, as flexible, they say, as any young man's.

Castrati could sing a whole octave above the normal voice of women, had a clear timbre and were, obviously, a great deal more powerful than choirboys.

As a result of this training the art of singing and *il bel canto* reached a perfection, as one critic put it, "that in all probability will never more be attained."

By the 1780's practically every church in Italy had its castrati in the choir and in Rome alone there were more than two hundred.

Favored by princes both lay and clerical, castrati began to be treated like collection pieces by cardinals for their choirs.

Even Richelieu had his Bertod, and at the court of Versailles, not to be outdone, Louis XIII had a certain number of *incommodés,* as they were euphemistically called, for his chapel.

The Duke of Württemburg, to be assured of a proper supply, imported from Poland two surgeons to furnish him, at their discretion, with soprani.

Some statistician computed that in the eighteenth century 70 per cent of all male singers were castrati.

Meanwhile opera had developed. For two centuries it was to afford castrati their greatest fame, making them conversation pieces from Lisbon to Vladivostock.

As the vogue for opera spread through Europe, the

castrato, with his effeminate airs, his high voice, and his extraordinary mastery of the art of singing, was the natural substitute for women. But it did not stop there: they encroached even on the men.

As no natural man's voice could have encompassed the fantastic bravura passages that were so much admired and came to be considered indispensable, tenors were relegated to the roles of old men, basses reserved for such special effects as Neptune's oracle in *Idomeneo*.

In the Venetian period *all* the male characters were assigned to sopranos and contraltos.

Lured by the higher pay offered by enterprising impresarios, castrati (who were not allowed to sing in both chapel *and* theater) began to abandon the choirbox: soon the churches were obliged to make do with the leftovers from the opera.

In an attempt to reverse the trend, Clement XIV ordered theater managers to employ women. Too late: castrati had caught the popular fancy, and by the time Niccolini tried to stage his opera *Selvaggio* with female soprani it was "howled off the stage in the middle of the second act."

When edicts were issued to limit singing to *hommes complets*, eunuchs got around the ban, as the priests had done earlier, by carrying their "superfluities" on their person, a performance facilitated by glassmakers in Venice who developed the specialty of blowing them into colored glass—often in the form of a cherry branch with two red pendant fruits!

In the theater the castrato could earn as much as 1,000 scudi a month. One, Caffarelli, was paid 72,000 gold francs for a three-month season in Lisbon in 1775.

What a chance to indulge in their congenital—or ex-genital—compulsion for gambling! De Brosse tells of one castrato, Benetto, who lost £10,000 in a single night.

Many rose to unheard of pinnacles of fame, amassing fortunes like those of Hollywood stars and receiving more adulation than any Presley or Sinatra. What's more, they could even outdo Bing Crosby, keeping to the stage as long as half a century before retiring to luxury.

Throughout Europe they traveled from court to court: whole cities would turn out to greet them; they were treated like idols and had their portraits painted by the most renowned of artists.

Of royalty they became the favorites and intimates. Farinello, who was almost adopted by the king of Spain, was obliged to sing nightly to his patron for ten straight years, repeating the same favorite tunes an estimated 3,600 times.

The queen of Sweden sent a ship especially to bring Burney to Stockholm.

Caffarelli bought himself a dukedom, built a palace (which he left to his nephew) and on the door had put *Amphio Thebas, Ego domum*, to which some wag added *Ille cum, sine tu*—a play on the words of the Greek legend according to which the walls of Thebes were supposed to have been built with stones put together by the music of Amphion's lyre. Stones, of course, being the biblical euphemism for what was most lacking in eunuchs.

Indeed, the castrato seemed to get the best out of life—money, adulation of the public, even love affairs without worry: the one evident drawback was oblivion in posterity: they could have no children, and, as neither the tape recorder nor the record player had been invented, leave no mark behind—with the fascinating exception of Moreschi, of whom half a dozen rare renditions are extant in a private collection of recordings in New Haven.

The rest, perforce, had to be satisfied with the pleasures of the moment.

Being *spadones* with the verge intact, many of them were able to indulge in a considerable love life, without the risk of compromising alliances or the begetting of bastards; as popular superstition believed them to be impotent, it was easier for them to dally with a wife without arousing the husband.

Casolino, by adopting the ruse of calling on his paramour dressed in his stage costumes as a female, is said to have been able to carry on an affair with a lady of society right under her husband's nose.

It was not uncommon for castrati to go about town in women's clothes. Once, to make the turnabout complete, one of Casanova's lady friends appeared on stage pretending to be a castrato, having had to pass the examination—women then being forbidden on stage—of an elderly and gullible priest, which she managed to do by taping "an instrument" to her body, as Casanova puts it, "in the appropriate position."

But not all were as clever or as successful as Casolino. Several, as reported in the local chronicles of the times, were murdered by jealous husbands, whereas poor Caffarelli, after spending the night in the garden of his mistress hidden in an empty cistern where he had been driven by her irate husband, nearly died of the resulting cold.

In the main, being androgynous in aspect it was not unnatural that they should incline to an ambisexual love life—especially in the Holy City, which, as Casanova remarked, "tended to make a pederast of every male."

In the Rome of 1729 Montesquieu described seeing two little creatures at the "Capranica" dressed as women: "the two most lovely creatures I have seen in my life and who would inspire the taste of Gomorrah even in a person most refractory to its depravity."

To which Casanova adds a detailed description of a favorite of Cardinal Borghese: "His body encased in a beautifully made *busto* he had the figure of a nymph and what seems extraordinary, his neck and shoulders were in no way inferior to those of a woman, and it was mostly with these that the master made such ravages among his admirers. Though you knew the negative nature of this *disgraziato,* if curiosity drew your eyes to his breasts a strange enchantment would agitate your senses to the point of falling madly in love before realizing what was happening. To resist and not be caught one had to be as frigid as a German. When he walked about the stage waiting for his aria his step was both majestic and voluptuous and when he threw glances towards the boxes the tender and modest rolling of his black eyes smote right to the heart. Clearly he wished to inflame those who loved him as a man, and who most likely would not have loved him as a woman."

Goethe, though a German, turned out to be not at all frigid to their charms. When first he heard a castrato singing he says he felt a delight unknown to him before.

"I reflected on the reasons why these singers pleased me so greatly, and I think I have found it. In these representations the concept of imitation and of art was invariably more strongly felt, and through their able performance a sort of conscious illusion was produced. Thus a double pleasure is given, in that these persons are not women, but only represent women. The young men have studied the properties of the female sex in its being and behavior; they know them thoroughly and reproduce them like an artist; they represent, not themselves, but a nature absolutely foreign to them."

However, it was more than their mere appearance which caused the fascination. Something in their voices, and in the art with which they sang, must have been enormously, universally, appealing.

Bontempi, in his *Historica Musica,* describes his compatriot Ferri as the most extraordinary singer who ever existed: "It is impossible to give an idea of the clarity of his voice, of its agility and of the ease with which he managed the most difficult passages, perfect tone, brilliant vivacity of trills, and perfect breathing. He would often go into rapid and difficult passages with all the chiaroscuro of crescendos and diminuendos and just as he would seem worn out, without breath, start an endless trill going up and down the chromatic scale for two good octaves always absolutely sure of himself. It looked like a game, and the muscles of his face showed not the slightest contraction."

Such virtuosity made them the darlings of the stage and in the limelight they could do pretty much as they pleased.

The opera, as the institution developed, with anteroom for refreshments and gambling, boxes which served as regular drawing rooms and places of assignation for masked encounters, was an ideal setting for the antics of castrati.

They could, and did, choose their own costumes—which resulted in some incongruous scenes such as a Caesar in olive breeches, flowered knee socks, red-heeled shoes with sparkling buckles, powdered cheeks and a head of golden tresses.

They could, and did, interpolate their own favorite arias into quite a different opera, make special bold entrances to the accompaniment of trumpets.

So much did they love the mad scenes which gave them full scope for coloratura and so much did the audience like to be dazzled by them that one critic complained, "Coloratura continued to proliferate like frog spawn in a pond."

To accomplish such bravura required a great deal of practice, and it is said that good castrati would spend several hours a day in front of a mirror teaching themselves the art of singing extraordinarily complex pieces without contortions of expression.

It was an art which required exertion; the story is told of one castrato who died on the stage of the San Carlo opera house in Naples in the effort to reach a very high note.

Another, a "natural born" eunuchoid, one day was said to have exerted himself to such an extent in singing an aria that "of a sudden those parts which had so long been concealed by nature, dropped into place"—causing him, in turn, to be dropped *from* his place.

In the end it was this very exertion at complexity and virtuosity which became their undoing. So far did they stray from the original music and design of an opera that finally the composers rebelled.

Already Gluck and Mozart, by their addition of dramatic qualities to opera, rendered it unsuitable for eunuchs. But it was Rossini with his music dramas such as *Moses in Egyp*t who gained the reputation of having "sung the burial service" over castrati in opera. Complaining that they "startled" rather than "moved," that they made of music what the Jesuits did with poetry and eloquence, "placing Lucian before Virgil, and Seneca before Cicero," he decided to remedy the situation by writing directly into the score such *fioriture* as castrati could handle "without doing outrage to the melody."

The final blow came in Milan where Rossini was preparing to stage his *Aureliano in Palmira.*

At the third rehearsal the eunuch Velluti, whom Rossini had never heard, but by whom he was much impressed, suddenly added such a *"sfoggio di gorghezzi, volate strilli, salti di ottava, abusi di semitoni, aggruppamenti di note, scale cromatiche,* etc.," that the original design of the aria was quite lost. Enraged at the virtuoso's lavish embroidery of music which Rossini considered quite florid enough, the maestro vowed never again to let his singers depart from the written notes. Velluti, in turn, vowed never to sing Rossini's music again.

The end was nigh. Allegri after a magnificent rendition of the "Miserere" remarked: "When we are gone the *bel canto* can intone its own miserere."

The critics raged against them, especially after the extraordinarily acute and timely monograph of the Marquis Algarotti, a Venetian nobleman in London who, among his several accomplishments, became the lover of Lady Mary Montagu, famed for her descriptions of the Grand Seraglio while the wife of the British envoy to the Porte:

"When one neglects the essential rules and does not have a real taste for music, one runs the risk of denaturizing the most lovely music, of taking from it its strength and majesty, of rendering it effeminate and licentious, of weakening its expressiveness by a mass of rolls, cadences, hammerings, rocking, pealings, and conclusions."

Not only rulers of taste but of state turned against

castrati. Napoleon, who, when he heard Crescentini sing in Zingarelli's *Romeo and Juliet,* in 1809, had granted him the order of the Iron Crown, now changed his mind and put a stop to their singing in the empire; when Francis I regained possession of Milan he ostracized castrati from the stage.

With the public too, they were falling from favor. Already Wagner and Verdi were coming into vogue; the last castrato to be heard in London was Pergetti in the season of 1844.

With the French occupation of Rome in 1851, Pope Pius IX promulgated a bull abolishing once and for all castration of singers.

Pius X confirmed the edict and put a stop to the recruitment of castrati for the Sistine Chapel.

Yet they lingered in the Vatican chapel well into the twentieth century. The last *Kappellmeister*, Mustapha, director of papal music till 1895, lived till 1912. And the very last to sing publicly was Allessandro Moreschi, who died in 1922—the year Victor Emmanuel summoned Mussolini to Rome—having sung at the funerals of both King Humbert I and Victor Emmanuel II.

8
KEYS TO THE KINGDOM

Christian involvement with castration goes deeper than the larynx and further than meets the eye.

Indeed, in one sense, Christians might be called the greatest castrators of them all, having removed 100,000 phalli from an entire pantheon of pagan statues and left hardly a verge intact. The sudden swing from pagan eroticism to Christian asceticism—as is so often the case with popular movements—was as drastic as the swing from being persecuted to being persecutors, though both reactions appear to have been rooted in the faith that the soul's salvation was all that mattered.

The emphasis on celibacy in the gospels is plentiful

enough; there is more in the so-called apocryphal writings of the period, and in the writings of the early fathers celibacy and virginity are lauded to the sky.

Celibacy does not necessarily mean castration, but, as one historian remarked, in the hot-blooded Mediterranean where continence for a man was considered superhuman, once it was established by prophecy that the end of the Judeo-Christian world was at hand, and that reproduction was therefore pointless, "it appears to have been but a step to self-castration."

That Mediterraneans are particularly subject to the temptations of St. Anthony is graphically admitted by that early Father of the Church, St. Jerome, who, to avoid the bevies of girls conjured up by his overheated mind, took refuge in the desert among wild beasts and scorpions, but still complained: "My face was pale and my frame chilled from fasting, yet my mind was burning with the cravings of desire, and the fires of lust flamed up from my flesh that was as that of a corpse."

To Origen, the editorially prolific father of the Church, these cravings of the flesh became so importunate that, to preach the gospel to women unimpeded, he resorted to self-castration. Others followed his lead.

In the early Christian world two schools of thought thus developed, which, strangely enough, have remained in vogue to the present day.

On one side stood those who took Jesus, via Matthew, to mean literally that to attain the necessary state of sinlessness to enter the kingdom of heaven, the offending organ should be cut off; on the other—and this was the school officially adopted by the Church—stood those who maintained that only "spiritual" eunuchism was required for the avoidance of sin, and even this proviso was later watered down in favor of the sacrament of "matrimony"—except for priests and members of religious orders and those striving to attain perfection.

As Gibbon reports the development: "The use of marriage was permitted only to his [Adam's] fallen posterity, as a necessary expedient to continue the human species, and as a restraint, however imperfect, on the natural licentiousness of desire." To which he adds editorially: "The hesitation of the orthodox casuists on this interesting subject betrays the perplexity of men unwilling to approve an institution which they were compelled to tolerate."

What Gibbon calls "the chaste severity of the fathers" and their "abhorrence of every enjoyment which might gratify the sensual, and degrade the spiritual nature of man" led Frazer to remark that "in their anxiety to save their own souls and the souls of others, they were content to leave the material world, which they identified with the principle of evil, to perish around them."

Robert Briffault was even more scathing: "The uncompromising attitude of the Christian Fathers, which caused many Christian converts to castrate themselves, condemned marriage as inconsistent with religion, pronounced woman to be the gate of hell, and declared the extinction of the human race preferable to its propagation through sexual intercourse, has offered the foundation of those standards of sexual morality which have ever since been current in the tradition of Western civilization."

Actually, such fathers of the early Church as St. Basil, St. John Chrysostom, St. Cyril and St. Augustine, were on the side of a "spiritual" eunuchism, also because they maintained that the vital element in the fight against "sexual pollution" was the exercise of that free will which God had granted to all men, and that to allow for victory temptation must be present, or, at least, possible—relying, as an extra safety valve, in case free will went astray, on the sacrament of penitence "ever at hand to whiten a filthied conscience."

In the orthodox world it was this school, offering to the divinity not the organ but its function, which prevailed. Those in the other camp who stood for physical castration were branded heretics, and if little trace is left of them, it is partly, no doubt, because their writings were either destroyed or declared apocryphal.

The traces that are left are indeed pretty meager.

The earliest and most renowned sect of Christian emasculators, the so-called Valesians, were said to be followers of a third-century Arab, Valesius, who, having imitated Origen's example of self-emasculation, is supposed to have developed a sect in Arabia Deserta which not only considered castration essential to the priesthood but to the world at large.

According to Epiphanius, fourth-century bishop of Salamis on Cyprus, these Valesians not only castrated themselves but believed it their duty to effect the operation on their guests or anyone who fell into their hands, pretending as they did so, to be following the biblical injunction in Matthew. The main result, as far as can be deduced from the evidence, is that travelers avoided the area "lest they fall prey to such fanaticism."

Elaborating on St. Epiphanius—who maintained the heresy flourished among the inhabitants of Bachatis, near Philadelphia beyond the Jordan—later writers claimed that it was Valesius himself who would tie to a bench any unfortunate victim who fell into his hands, then cut off his member on the pretext that by "wiping out the race in this world he would be saving it for the next."

But as St. Epiphanius' lifelong pursuit was an attempt to refute Origen and his followers as heretics, going so far, in his role of bishop, even to refuse Origen what seemed to be a well deserved aureola for martyrdom, and as the *Britannica* says of Epiphanius, "his prejudice and his credulity outweigh his erudition," there may be ground for wondering how much of this Valesian story is even historical. In the end the Valesians are said to have been bloodily exterminated to a man.

True or false, Valesius' theory about this world and the next remained at the heart of a very persistent creed. Whether Valesius and his castrators existed or not, the practice subsisted *sub rosa*: it has survived to this day; and there exists in the twentieth century a fundamentalist sect whose members assert that they alone of all the Christian denominations follow the reiterated teachings of Jesus that castration is the only hope for the avoidance of carnal sin and for affecting His Second Coming.

Of their importance, more later.

Officially the Church considered all such sects as heretical and the 325 A.D. Council of Nicea banned castration as a means of maintaining celibacy for a priest, a ban reconfirmed by the second Council of Arles: "Eunuchs may be received into the number of the clergy but those who castrate themselves shall not be received."

When Leontius of Antioch, to whom this wording was apparently not clear-cut, decided to conquer a passion he had developed for a woman of his household by cutting off what bothered him, Pope Leo I forbade castration altogether, and priests were thereafter forbidden to say mass unless in possession of their manhood.

The word possession, however, seems to have been freely interpreted, at least to judge by the priest in Boccaccio's tale who carried the desiccated relic of his former manhood in a snuffbox till it was discovered and mistakenly swallowed by a small boy because of its resemblance to dried figs.

Actually the Nicene fathers had made no new enactment but merely confirmed existing Apostolic canons dating as far back as the first ecumenical council: "If anyone in sickness has been subjected by physicians to a surgical operation, or if he has been castrated by barbarians, let him remain among the clergy; but if anyone in sound health has castrated himself it behoves that such an one, if already enrolled among the clergy, should cease from his ministry, and that from henceforth no such person should be promoted. But, as it is evident that this is said of those who wilfully do the thing and presume to castrate themselves, so if any have been made eunuchs by barbarians, or their masters, or should otherwise be found worthy, such men the canon admits to the clergy."

What the canons condemned, as has been seen, the Emperor Constantine forbade by law: "If anyone shall anywhere in the Roman Empire after this decree make eunuchs, he shall be punished with death. If the owner of the place where the deed is perpetuated was aware of it, his goods shall be confiscated."

But the practice continued clandestinely. Those who, either because they considered it the true gospel, or felt they could not be celibate otherwise, continued to resort to the knife, or the red-hot poker.

In the East the custom persisted uninterruptedly, especially in Byzantium, and in Russia was resorted to by several metropolitans, including Jean and Ephen.

As Gnosticism gave way to Manichaeism, says Kenneth Rexroth, there followed on Paulicianism and Bogomolism "a whole covey of Russian Heresies and the famous Cathari and the Albigensian Crusade."

In Russia the "heresy" was to take hold on the grand scale, developing into one of the most extraordinary and little known of Christian sects, a sect which, according to one modern writer, is now "politically the most important in the world" because—so goes his thesis—not only do its followers abide by the supposed teachings of Jesus on castration, but follow literally his teachings on the subject of communism.

In the opinion of this authority—a New York medical doctor and author of several books—the whole of Medievalism and the Middle Ages is but the story of the effects and consequences on the Western world of the Nazarene communism in the gospels. Only when the Roman Church discovered that communism was both impractical, says he, and dangerous as a rule of life among the rank and file, did the Church abandon the doctrine and consider poverty along with chastity as suitable only for those in holy orders.

As effective as the substitution of the sacrament of marriage for true asceticism and celibacy, says he, was the abandonment of the Nazarene canon on usury. The result, in his words, was that "the Renaissance and the rise of modern civilization became possible."

In this, of course, he is echoing Frazer, who says the obsession lasted a thousand years till "the revival of Roman Law, of the Aristotelian philosophy, of ancient art and literature at the close of the Middle Ages, marked the return of Europe to native ideals of life and conduct, to saner, manlier views of the world," adding that "the tide of Oriental invasion was turned at last."

Nevertheless, some fundamentalist Christian sects clung to theistic communism as an obligatory pattern of life, and some still clung to castration.

When the Reformation hit Russia, various protestant "Raskolniki" sects who rejected the ministrations of the Church and its priests reverted to early Christian and even pagan rituals.

One of these sects, the Khlistis, reverted to one of the earliest pagan beliefs which had been merged in Christianity: the belief that Jesus Christ was continually being reincarnated in the persons of members of their sect.

They also reverted to one of the earliest rituals of the Christian Church, the Agapes, or "love feasts," their theory being that normal procreation was a sin, that men should not marry, or, if married, should live with their wives as if they were sisters, intercourse being permitted only as a sort of religious rite to prolong the species.

According to renegades who have described them, these rites ended up, after the usual vertiginous dancing, flagellation and incoherent cries, in free-for-all promiscuous sexual orgies, the theory being that "the carnal love which we feel for our sisters is sanctified by the presence of the Holy Ghost. The child conceived in this promiscuity is the Child of God. The woman who carries it in her belly is the Mother of God."

From this protestant group developed a sect which reverted even more drastically to what it considered the original Nazarene gospel, maintaining that mankind, to redeem itself from original sin, must, as in their opinion Christ and his apostles had done, mutilate its genitals.

According to the theology of the Skoptsi, as the members of this sect were known, Adam and Eve had originally been created sexless, but after the Fall, the halves of the forbidden fruit were grafted upon them as testicles and breasts: it was thus the duty of all good Christians to restore the disfigured image of God to its original state of purity.

Though at first glance a wild conceit it appears less so the more it is scrutinized, and is certainly no more obscure or far-fetched than the tale of the talking snake and the mysterious tree of temptation.

Simulating the religious dances of the priests of Cybele, who, as will be seen, were their historic predecessors, and working themselves up into frenzies, they would cut off their testicles and then the phallus, using sharp knives, red-hot pokers, or both, while the women were excised of their nipples, breasts, clitoris, labia majora and minora, and, in some cases, subjected to complete hysterectomies.

Renegades from the "heresy" told of private ceremonies in which the priest, brandishing a knife or razor before the neophyte, would proclaim, "Here is the weapon with which to destroy sin!" and, as he excised the testicles: "Behold the crushed serpent. Behold the head of Adam!"

At public ceremonies at midnight, the victim would be undressed, held by the arms by two adepts while the operator, kneeling before him, spread his legs, put a ligature around the testicles, excised them with a neat stroke of the razor, to a chorus from the onlookers of "Christ is resurrected."

Thereafter the victim would be starved for several days and the wound bathed with alum or cowdung.

One of the basic ceremonies for women—also as reported by a renegade—was to get a young virgin of fifteen or sixteen, put her naked into a warm bath where several old women made an incision on the left breast, removed it, cut it up into small pieces and distributed it to the onlooking adepts, who would ceremoniously swallow a morsel.

Maturer women would then be bound with a long white cloth into which two holes the size of a half dollar had been cut, through which the nipples and part of the breasts were forced. With the formula "Christ is resurrected," operators on either side of the victim, each armed with a razor, would slice off the part of the breast forced through the hole.

Mad as such methods may appear, they are no more far-fetched, and, in a way, more expeditious, than those used by some cloistered and saintly Catholics such as the nuns, who, having taken the vow of chastity, were required to apply cataplasms of hot grease to their breasts, tying them more tightly each day until, in two or three weeks, they were quite emptied of their substance, the mammary glands destroyed, and nothing was left but a pair of empty sacks; or St. Martin, who, according to Sulpice, subjected his body to such incredible austerities that after his death his member was so atrophied that "one could not notice it if one had not known where to look for it where it should have been"; or the devout Francisca of France in whose canonization bull it avers that to quench the flames of desire she resorted to the device of pouring boiling bacon fat onto her pudenda!

The first score or so of Skoptsi to be discovered by the authorities in Russia belonged to a group headed by an Andrei Ivanov. Arrested in 1771, they were sent to Siberia.

Three years later sixty more were discovered in the province of Tambov and also sent to Siberia with their new leader, Selivanov, presumed by historians to be the same Ivanov, who, having escaped, reappeared under a variant name.

Tortured, whipped and having had boiling wax poured on his head, Selivanov was sent to hard labor. As a result of this treatment he became a martyr in the eyes of his followers. His creed, instead of being hurt, began to spread.

According to his followers, Selivanov was a new incarnation of Christ; in their psalms he was venerated as such.

To the Skoptsi there was no unbreakable barrier between heaven and earth. When men finished their lives on earth they went to live in a seventh heaven among the gods. In their opinion God the father, the Son, and the Holy Ghost, the mother of God, and the saints and apostles, were all able to descend from heaven and become incarnate among the virtuous faithful, to help men conquer the flesh and liberate their souls.

It was to redeem the world from the original sin of Adam and Eve, so they maintained, that Christ had first incarnated himself among men, castrating himself and preaching the doctrine to his followers.

This process was to continue until the Apocalyptic figure of 144,000 saints (Revelation 14:4) totally undefiled by women, had gained the kingdom of heaven, whereupon all would be summoned to a final judgment after which Christ would proceed to universal castration and the world would be turned into a veritable and eternal paradise.

To account for the lack of explicit details in the gospel they maintained that under the Emperor Constantine corrupt Christians had emasculated the biblical texts.

According to the Skoptsi, the patriarchs of the Old Testament were eunuchs, as were the Jewish prophets, circumcision being but a euphemism for castration.

The struggle between body and soul, they maintained, was otherwise irreducible: to combat sexual desire, chastity was not sufficient. Only castration could safeguard against sin.

Whether to simplify the creed for those to whom it was preached or because there was sufficient rumor to justify the story, the Skoptsi claimed that Selivanov was not only a reincarnation of Christ but of Czar Peter III, which they explained by saying that when his wife Catherine Alekseevna had realized he was a Skopet and had tried to dispose of him, the plot had failed thanks to the complicity of a palace guard, also a Skopet, who had changed clothes with Peter III and been killed in his place.

Peter's death has indeed been a historical mystery, there being no eyewitness report of his actual death or murder. That he was impotent and that Catherine—who has been labeled *"la piu famosa futatrice nel mondo"* used a lover to beget her progeny, is generally admitted—even by Catherine in her own memoirs.

In any case, so current was the rumor about Peter being alive in the person of Selivanov that Czar Paul I, hearing of it, had his presumed father summoned to St. Petersburg to offer him the throne, an act which might have changed the course of history had not Selivanov asked him to submit to castration, at which point the incumbent Czar had his postulant relative placed in a madhouse.

Paul's successor, Alexander I, renowned for his mystical leanings, had Selivanov moved to a monastery in Smolensk, and soon thereafter, partly thanks to the intervention of the royal court chamberlain of Poland, Alexis Jelanski, himself reputed a Skopet, and partly to the intercession of the czar's intimate, the Baroness de Kruedner, Selivanov was freed and allowed to return to St. Petersburg.

Thus began what was known as the "golden age" of the Skoptsi, and Selivanov's house in Moscow became known as the "new Jerusalem."

Thanks to Jelanski's influence at court the sect flourished and its ideas spread throughout Russia, percolating as high as the aristocratic entourage of the czar, infiltrating the high clergy, and subverting such respectable members of society as the directors of state banks.

Soon the Skoptsi leader became so wealthy, so famous, and so powerful that Jelanski proposed to the czar a "theocratic constitution" which would place the entire empire in the hands of the Skoptsi through the device of a "divine chancellery" at the head of which Selivanov was to guide the actions of the czar by revealing to him the "Divine Will."

To protect the members of this conspiracy from any action by the police a rich member of the sect, Solodovnikov, had a special building erected for Selivanov, a safe retreat with no windows onto the streets, which could not be entered without a password and for which Solodovnikov was able to obtain "from a very highly placed person" a letter forbidding the police access.

But when an ominous number of the officers in the capital were discovered to be castrates, the police, fearing the security of Mother Russia might be endangered, took steps to suppress the sect.

Alexander himself abdicated, to lead—so the story went—a hermit's life under the name of Feodor Kousmich in a log cabin in the Siberian wilderness near Tomsk, his disappearance being accounted for by his supposed death in 1825 at Taganrog, where a soldier was said to have been buried in his stead.

Meanwhile Selivanov, the savior, ordered "into retreat" at the monastery of Souzdal, is said to have gone right on receiving a chain of pilgrims who came to be blessed by him and to seize as holy relics "locks of his hair, scraps of his food, bits of his wearing apparel, and even his dejecta."

In 1832, Selivanov died, they say a centenarian; but to keep alive the myth of his resurrection his body is supposed to have been placed in an unmarked grave.

For the Skoptsi it was once more Siberia and the mines. But persecution, as so often happens, seemed to augment their numbers; those condemned even managed to make proselytes among their prison guards whom they relieved of their manhood.

From an estimated 20,000 at mid-century, the number of Skoptsi kept growing, taking in members from (or disposing of the members of) all classes—nobles, officers, bourgeois, but mostly peasants.

And the sect also flourished financially. In 1869, in the house of a man called Plotzine, the police are said to have found 48 million rubles belonging to the Skoptsi. Whatever the figure, bankers, cashiers, moneychangers abounded among the adherents of the sect, and their financial dealings spread as far as Odessa and Bucharest.

Plotzine, sent to Siberia, is reported to have set up a steamship yard on the Pacific coast so that, when his first steamer was launched in 1879, he could jump aboard and sail for San Francisco along with some coreligionists, there to form the first Skoptsi chapter in the United States.

One of the subtler methods the Skoptsi developed for gaining recruits was to offer loans to small businessmen, obliging them, in case of default, to be initiated into the sect at the cost of their manhood.

Another method was to buy the children of impoverished peasants—paying as much as $500 a child—to be brought up as castrated "virgin" members of the sect.

Interpreting the New Testament, and especially the Apocalyptic words of John, to mean that adult male initiates who had even once been "defiled" by women could not count towards the 144,000 virgin males required for Christ's return, they endeavored to swell the number of "virgins" both through the acquisition of children and by castrating their own sons.

Though it is nigh impossible to obtain reliable figures for such a clandestine sect, at the height of their popularity, toward the end of the last century, there were said to have been as many as 100,000 Skoptsi in Russia.

When persecution was resumed many sought refuge in Rumania. There they were allowed to continue their ceremonies of castration in their own temples which survive to this day.

It was from Rumania just over half a century ago, that a Muscovite, Lissine, proclaiming himself to be the "second redeemer" and another incarnation of Peter III, set off to visit Russia in the hope of presenting himself to the czar as the new messiah. Receiving much homage in the south he was emboldened to proceed as far as Moscow but was arrested at the height of a Skoptsi ceremony and dispatched to Siberia.

Events in 1905 caused the authorities to be more tolerant of the sect; but not for long. By 1910 they were once more being deported to Siberia or fleeing to Rumania.

To keep the sect alive in the twentieth century members were allowed to procreate one or two children before mutilation; as recruiting became more difficult, they began to lure impoverished young men into the sect with the offer of two horses and a carriage (in return for their manhood), with the result that most of the adepts became cabbies by profession—a familiar sight to tourists of Bucharest up to the First World War and even after, when they reappeared as taxi drivers. Their special quarters in the city remained as before, "opulent buildings with huge carriage doors painted green which cut off their high-walled houses from poorer quarters around them." Those who have talked with these Skoptsi describe them as extremely well-behaved, sober, puritanical, vegetarian teetotalers who never smoked or played cards, who never got into trouble with the police, were renowned for their politeness, and who steadfastly maintained that salvation could only be obtained by a rigorous denial of the flesh.

The last important public notice of Skoptsi in the Soviet Union was in 1929 when the police discovered a clan of them in both Leningrad and Moscow. In their secret reunions, they were apparently predicting another coming of Peter III. At a public trial in Leningrad, among the several defendants, figured three "ex-millionaires."

Here the story would end, were it not for an extraordinary epilogue produced by the American physician, Dr. Emanuel Josephson, who maintains that by virtue of their dominance of the Soviet Politburo, the Skoptsi are now the most important if little known Christian sect in the world. To support this theory there is the evidence of several American newspapermen and columnists who, at one time or other, have run across the story.

The trials, says Josephson, were merely a front, directed against "capitalist Skoptsi defectors" who had wielded the wealth of the sect in their own interest; true Skoptsi had been given preferment in the Soviet Union.

Fundamentalists, says Josephson, by virtue of their implicit following of what they consider biblical injunctions about castration, the Skoptsi also followed the "fundamental, vital, and constantly reiterated teaching of Jesus on the subject of communism"—a communism which provided for all communicants as well as for financing the gaining and support of converts, based directly on such statements in the gospels as Acts 4:32-35:

> . . . neither said any of them that the things which he possessed was his own; but they had all things in common. Neither was there any among them that lacked; for as many as were possessors of lands and houses sold them, and brought the prices of the things that were sold and laid them down at the apostles' feet; and distribution was made unto every man according as he had need.

To the Skoptsi, the principal sin in the gospels—and one for which the sinners were punished by the Lord with death—was *not being a Communist,* as a striking example of which they cite the deaths of Ananias and his wife Sapphira as related in Acts 5:1-11.

Being theistic Communists from the beginning of the sect, it was inevitable, says Josephson, that when the Bolsheviks came to take over Russia the Skoptsi would be sought out by the Bolsheviks "with whom they found themselves in a natural position of allies in all matters but religion."

The Skoptsi, having operated a near watertight clandestine party for over a century, with a knowledge of the most closely guarded secrets of Russia's court, its bankers, industrialists and politicians, would indeed be ideally qualified to serve as Communist spies. This, says Josephson, is what they did, rising quickly in the behind the scenes struggle for power till, in 1921, "as many as four members of the Russian Soviet Council were Skoptsi."

Gradually, says Josephson, they infiltrated so high as to gain control of the Politburo, and, with Malenkov, the premiership!

All of this could easily sound like crackpot propaganda and until absolute proof is forthcoming must obviously be taken with caution: yet so far the historical facts are easily verifiable, and the data adduced is from writers and newspapermen who should be responsible. What is more, after the experiments of Pavlov and the purges of Stalin nothing out of Russia bears passing up without scrutiny.

George Malenkov, says Josephson, "is notoriously and obviously a Skopet, a eunuch castrated in his youth. His face is smooth-skinned and has never required shaving. His voice is so girlishly high-pitched that he avoids public speaking and generally has had his public speeches read by others."

When I tracked Dr. Josephson to his booklined Manhattan studio, he informed me that the main source of his information was the son of a former U.S. ambassador to St. Petersburg who, brought up in Czarist Russia, had become a professor in geochemistry at the University of St.

Petersburg and who, before he fled the revolution, had lived for some time as the neighbor of a Skoptsi community and been allowed to attend their ceremonies.

On August 13, 1953, columnist Lee Mortimer jolted readers of the New York *Daily News* with an exclusive story to the effect that Malenkov was most probably a castrate.

"When Malenkov was a young man," wrote Mortimer, "he joined a queer Oriental religious cult in which all had to be eunuchs. It was thought the millennium would be ushered in when the membership reached 144,000. This early experience accounts for his pudgy appearance and his often extremely feminine thought-processes."

On August 20, Mortimer elaborated with a second piece in the *Daily News* identifying the cult as the Skoptsi and adding that Malenkov had first come to Stalin's attention because of the fact that the Skoptsi eunuchs had for many years held "a virtual monopoly on public offices in the Urals and Russian Asia."

In December of the same year, the story was corroborated in a magazine piece by T. L. Cummings, Jr., for twenty years, says Josephson, a correspondent in Russia and Central Europe:

"With a great show of indignation, the Communists made a pretense of outlawing the Skoptsi following the Revolution of 1918. Actually the cult had been outlawed for years, while the Communists had received valuable help from influential Skoptsi in staging the Revolution. To this day, few if any Skoptsi have featured in Red purges as victims, while the Soviet government is still studded with them."

Cummings then went on to describe the then newly appointed premier of the U.S.S.R.

"Physically, Malenkov is unprepossessing. Fifty-two years old, standing only five feet seven inches tall, he is abnormally obese, weighing better than 250 pounds. His piglike black eyes—alert and watchful—are the only signs of life in his moon-shaped face.

"He has many feminine traits—a high-pitched voice which rises to a scream when he is enraged, a mincing gait, and layers of lard on his breast and thighs.

"His first mate was a young and pretty stenographer whom he married when he was in his early thirties. During most of this marriage, Malenkov was scarcely ever at home. Once, for a two-month period, he slept on a cot in the office of the Central Committee of the Communist Party.

"Malenkov's third wife—to whom he is still married—is Elena Krushchev, sister of the present secretary-general of the Communist Party. A transvestite, she likes to wear male attire whenever possible."

Martin Ebon in his biography of Stalin's successor confirms the story that Malenkov was married to "former actress and singer Elena Khrushchev, now director of Moscow University," and in a book by Stalin's nephew, Budu Svanidze, there is a photograph of Elena taken at a bathing beach in the Crimea, sporting in the water with Malenkov and Beria, and, like the men, wearing no top to her bathing trunks.

Budu Svanidze, who defected to the West and wrote a book on Malenkov published in London in 1953, says that as a young man Malenkov was sent by his parents to a seminary to become a priest, that his cheeks were puffy and smooth "the cheeks of a *Skopetz,*" and that when he shook his hand it was "small, warm and smooth as velvet, a real *Skopetz* hand."

He then noted that it was curious that "even after several generations the children of *Skopetz* are born with a characteristic eunuch appearance."

In a chapter on "Malenkov and Sex" Robert Frazier says that under Stalin's successor "the aim of the party is to produce a race of eunuchs of a type the world has never seen."

That Malenkov's recorded birthplace, Orenburg in the Urals, was a region to which numerous Skoptsi had been exiled and where they had formed large colonies, is a matter of historical fact.

Dr. Josephson points out that the circumstance under which Malenkov's father, a wealthy merchant, was not executed by the Reds, are indicative that he was a leader of one of the Skoptsi colonies which had joined forces with the Bolsheviks.

As for Malenkov's rise to power, it was sketched in by Cummings as follows:

"Malenkov arrived in the Russian capital in 1923 and studied at Moscow University and Moscow Technological Institute, becoming an engineer. At the former he was a spy for the Cheka or secret police. At the latter he was Communist Party secretary. From then on his jobs were consistently those of spy, informer, organizer, secretary, and—if necessary—the man who ordered but did not personally carry out executions.

"Not until it was certain that Trotsky was doomed as a Communist leader did Malenkov side openly with Stalin. Then, through Besso Lominadze, whom many believe to have been a Skoptsi, he met Stalin's personal secretary (also a Skoptsi) and was given a clerk's job in Stalin's office!

"He was only twenty-three years old."

From then on Malenkov rose rapidly to become "Stalin's secret inquisitor," handling—as Cummings put it—the details of interrogations too delicate to be entrusted to the secret police, making on-the-spot decisions after which either nothing was done, or the victim was conveniently made to disappear.

"In six years," says Cummings, "during the 'Big Purge' of the '30s, he was directly responsible for the execution, banishment, or imprisonment in concentration camps of 1,500,000 Communist Party members! The blood-letting was so great that even the Politburo became nauseated. Malenkov then made a scapegoat of Nikolai Yezhov, head of the NKVD, who was executed."

Some months later, in another story for the same magazine, Cummings added: "What Stalin didn't know was that Malenkov, cunning in the manner that only a eunuch can be, gradually began using his influence to move many other Skoptsi members into important posts."

"Malenkov's plan," says Cummings, "was obvious to everyone but Stalin, who realized it too late. Malenkov's bold objective was to have the Skoptsi take over Russia by quietly putting Stalin into the grave with a secret poison.

"The plan worked—and when Malenkov stepped into the premiership he gave his fellow-Skoptsi most of the important Kremlin jobs."

At this point Beria is supposed to have threatened to expose Malenkov and the rest of the Kremlin official staff for what they were, but was brought to a secret trial at which parts of the testimony were suppressed; he was accused of treason, convicted, and executed.

From then on, says Dr. Josephson, the Skoptsi had a clear road, "going so far as to replace with their own converts even those leaders of the satellite states who were not already members of the sect."

On June 4, 1957, the New York *World Telegram* carried a story by United Press staff writer Bruce W. Munn which led off boldly: "Hungarian Premier Janos Kadar was emasculated on Russian orders to make him subservient to the Kremlin."

The evidence for this statement, said he, had been collected by the United Nations special committee investigating the anti-Communist revolt in Hungary—though it was not included in any detail.

Earlier the same year *Time* Magazine reported that it was Hungarian party boss Matyas Rakosi, in whose villa basement torture cells had been discovered, who pulled out Kadar's fingernails and castrated him.

François Fejto, in his book *Behind the Rape of Hungary*, quotes to the effect that Kadar was emasculated by his fellow communist Vladimir Farkas, known as "the torturer," one of the chiefs of the dreaded AVO secret police.

This evidence was corroborated by Sandor Kiss, Secretary General of the Executive Committee of the Hungarian Revolutionary Committee, who testified before the House Committee on Un-American Activities, March 20, 1957, saying that Kadar had himself admitted in a meeting at Hungarian Communist Party Headquarters that he had been tortured by Farkas and his son, "that his teeth had been knocked out and that he had been castrated."

To explain Kadar's sudden *volte face* and submission to the Russians at the crucial point in the revolt, Fejto says that many Hungarians believe Kadar "was abducted by the Russians on November 1, and that he consented to turn against Nagy, to dissociate himself from the insurrection, and to condone the intervention, only after being 'worked over' for several days." Not till November 9, says Fejto, did Kadar return to Budapest, and then he stayed out of the limelight for several days. "Later, when he appeared publicly, his eyes were those of a man tormented by uncertainty."

Shortly thereafter, to climax the drama, a New York magazine published an article by Dr. Ferenc Tatar, a self-styled Hungarian refugee in the United States, which it called "one of the most horrible stories of the century." In it Dr. Tatar admitted that on a dark and rainy night he had castrated Janos Kadar, then premier of Hungary, in the old city of Pest.

"Flanked by two guards," says Tatar, "my old friend Kadar was taken down and down into the cellar where there were the old familiar torture chambers.

"Kadar was in a kind of coma. I ordered him strapped down to an operating table. His clothing was removed. He sank back, his eyes saddened, but he did not lose consciousness for the eyes looked up at me with horror. He could not speak but the brain understood.

"I took up a scalpel and did what I was told to do. After it was over, I looked at his face and it was the face of a child. Never will I forget it, for big tears rolled down his cheeks. There was no sound. I had castrated my friend Kadar.

"May God forgive me."

Dr. Tatar excuses his action by saying that in a Communist regime you have to do what you are told—or else! He maintains the Russians ordered the operation in order to make of Kadar a puppet.

Dr. Josephson, however, claims that Kadar, far from having had the operation imposed on him, was a willing initiate into the Skoptsi fraternity, but one who lacked the courage to emasculate himself, or to have it done by the sect's castraters; a qualified physician—an old friend of his—was therefore summoned to perform the operation, but kept in ignorance of its real purport and meaning.

In any case, says Josephson, after the Skoptsi had disposed of Stalin and assumed Soviet power, Malenkov visited Budapest and greeted his fellow "white goose" Janos Kadar "with the characteristic hand-to-arm grip of the international dictatorship conspiracy."

All of which is hard to prove, one way or the other, at least without such a test as the one described by historians as having been used by a conclave of cardinals to determine tactilely and with the aid of a *chaise percée* whether a new pope was in fact in possession of the manly parts required to pontificate. Furthermore, it must be remembered that it is just such a canard—hard to put a finger on—which gets circulated about almost any controversial political figure. Remember what they said about Hitler, Goering, Himmler and Goebbels, as whistled in the ditty in the film *Bridge on the River Quai?*

But to return to the broader scene, if what Dr. Josephson says about the Skoptsi is true, the great battle for dominion of men's minds and for control of their lives would be back where it started at the beginning of Christianity—a dispute between spiritual and physical eunuchism!

That the Catholic Church is run by members of the first sort, is plain enough.

Strange would it be indeed if the main force opposing the Church turned out to be one run by the second, or "heretical" sort of eunuchs, similar to the ones which the Church inveighed against at the beginning!

9
THE COCKS OF CYBELE

Yet the subject of castration has barely been scratched.

Before the Skoptsi, there were earlier sects of Christians who ablated their organs for religious purposes.

Before them, pagans did likewise.

One of the most extraordinary accounts, and the one most quoted because of its detail, is that of Lucian.

On a certain day in spring, to celebrate the vernal equinox—so the Samasotan satiricist informs us—eunuch priests who were attached to the temple of the Syrian goddess Astarte would work themselves into a religious frenzy, whirl to the sound of pipes and drumbeat, flagellate each other, slash their arms with knives, asperge the area with blood.

The effect of this on the bystanding worshipers, roused as they were by orgies of promiscuous intercourse, by an atmosphere heavy with aphrodisiacal perfumes, by music the strains of which appear to have been entrancing, was to rip off their clothes, leap naked among the eunuch priests, snatch up short swords and castrate themselves. The severed parts they would then brandish through the streets to fling at whatever house struck their fancy, placing the inhabitants under the obligation of outfitting them as neophyte eunuchs with a complete set of women's apparel and "all the ornaments becoming a lady."

Lucian suggests they emasculated themselves to imitate the mythological Attis, who, when Rhea deprived him of his virility, "put off his manly garb and assumed the appearance of a woman and her dress, roaming over the whole world to perform her mysterious rites. . . ." The question, obviously, is who or what is meant by Attis and by Rhea!

As the Abbé Banier put it, "Fables are to be not otherwise accounted for than so many beautiful veils, under which the Truths of ancient history are concealed."

But what truths? The closer one looks into mythology the more one finds that all the gods and heroes of antiquity appear to have been castrated—Uranus, Cronus, Saturn, Attis, Osiris, Bacchus, Dionysus; the list could be extended indefinitely. Yet the veil which hides the reason appears as impenetrable as the Veil of Isis.

Whether Attis was a man, a god, a superior spirit, an anthropomorphized symbol of some celestial power or body, or all of these, the conceit and the ritual appear invaried whether his name be Attis, Adonis, Tammuz or any of a dozen other appellatives. As a castrated, dying and resuscitating god he was worshiped by Sumerians, Babylonians, Assyrians, Phoenicians, Canaanites, Hebrews, Egyptians, Greeks, and Romans; is worshiped, in fact, today.

Likewise, the same great goddess, whether called Astarte or Rhea, Aphrodite or Cybele, or any of *several* dozen names, was the deity to whom the manhood of the dying young god was sacrificed.

Whether to Artemis, Atargatis, Ishtar, Hecate or Bellona, ceremonies of castration took place in Phrygia, Lydia, Cappadocia, Pontus and Galatia—always to a similar goddess, and always one tended by eunuchs.

In Greece, the priests of Cybele, called Corybantes, celebrated the death and resurrection of her lover Attis by dancing around to the sound of cymbals, tambourines, flutes, and "savage" shouts. Whipping each other till the blood flowed, they would tear off their clothes, and at the height of their paroxysms seize their genitals and sever them with cries of joy. The excised parts, carefully collected, were then embalmed, wrapped in the neophytes' old clothes, and deposited in the nuptial chamber of the goddess.

Dancing—which for thousands of years has been a form of religious ceremony—and which at times can be taken as an imitation of the movement of heavenly bodies, was an essential prerequisite to the ritual. On this subject Annie Besant has an odd bit of data in which she describes the choric dances of the priests of Babylon as representing the movement of the planets round the sun, then goes on with the clairvoyant reconstruction of an ancient ceremony in which "above the altar the huge golden Sun gleamed faintly, and the planet Venus hung in the air, high in the vault above," and suddenly was present "the Supreme Lord of the Hierarchy . . . the Eternal Virgin in all the beauty of his unchanging youth. . . ."

Could the wild, snakelike, hair-waving, whirling, feathered dances—so similar in all the corners of the globe—depict some heavenly rondo? the wild movements of a passing comet? the chaos of a satellite captured out of space? the struggling intercourse of bodies in the sky?

And what of the intoxicating sound of the Phrygian pipes! Could they have been in imitation of the weird celestial harmonies of Pan, or the wild gyrations of some heavenly body, perhaps loosed from its accustomed bonds?

The beating of drums, the clashing of cymbals, the rattle of castanets conjure up all sorts of rites—from a whirling of witches to a conclave of dervishes.

Aristotle said the strains of the Phrygian musician could "make souls enthusiastic." Frazer, who agrees that musical notes "cannot be mere empty sounds" but must have "escaped from some higher sphere," attributes to music an essential role in inducing an ecstatic state and as a stimulus to prophecy.

To this John Sebastian Marlow Ward, a senior Mason and one-time head of the Intelligence Department of the "Federation of British Industries," by-lined in his book on the psychic manifestations of Christ as the Reverend Father Superior of the Abbey of Christ the King, a member of the orthodox Catholic Church, adds the curio that the ancients had a secret for producing music which intoxicated the brain of the worshiper and could work him into a frenzy. The secret, says Ward, rested in the use of eighths and quarter tones—adding that remnants of such music still exist in a remote part of Central America.

By the use of a strange mode musicians in the past were

supposed to be able to arouse in the hearts of humans any one of several sensations at will, an art not overlooked but not yet thoroughly exploited in our modern temples—the movies.

According to Diodorus the Sicilian, Osiris was the patron of dancers and musicians—as indeed, were the other representatives of the castrated deity; and Julius Firmicus Maternus is categoric in saying that the worshipers of Osiris shaved their heads, beat their breasts, gashed their shoulders, and inflicted wounds on their bodies in imitation of the cuts and gashes which Typhon made in the body of Osiris—an analogy which becomes all too clear in due course.

Throughout the Middle East the rituals were performed by eunuch priests.

The Ephesian Artemis or Diana was served by virgins and eunuch priests called Bagabuxsa—"having salvation through the deity"—and her statue was often represented with a necklace of testicles, the bleeding organs of emasculated priests.

Her high priest, called Megagysas, was a eunuch, vested in the same manner as the eunuch priests on Hittite bas-reliefs.

The ceremonies in honor of Mylitta included wild orgies, during which votaries castrated themselves in dedication to her service.

The priests of the God of Emesus were castrates and on his feast day would throw a human phallus onto the altar as an offering.

Atargatis the Palmyrene goddess who was venerated in Syria had eunuch priests who dressed themselves as women and were self-mutilated.

In Cyprus, at Amathonte and Paphos, and other main

cities on the island, service in the temples of Adonis and Astarte was reserved to eunuchs.

Cappadocia was known for the particularly bloody festivals of Cybele and Attis.

At Stratonice in Caria a eunuch held sacred office in connection with the worship of Zeus and Hecate.

In Egypt, where for centuries priests had sacrificed their virility as a first fruit to the gods, the priests of Isis shaved their heads and mutilated themselves in sorrow over the death of their god, Osiris.

Farther west, in Carthage, priests still castrated themselves as late as the time of Augustine, who took a poor view of them as they paraded through the streets and squares—"their hair perfumed, their faces powdered and made up, publicly begging so as to support their infamous existence."

In India, since Vedic times, men born eunuchs had been dedicated to a goddess Huligamma, and wore female attire. Other eunuchs were obtained by squatting men over a furrow where the earth could receive their blood as they were knifed.

Yet the ritual of castration appears to be but a diminution of what was once an even deadlier and more bloody rite, in which the victim, hung to a tree, was castrated so as to bleed to death, that his blood might fertilize the soil.

Gradually the severity of the ritual was mitigated further. The original method of cutting off the male member and letting the victim bleed to death was made less severe. Either the bleeding was stopped, and the victim allowed to live after forfeiting his member, or, in other cases, he was killed in a less painful way, usually by a stab in the flank, or a blow on the head.

At one point the testicles and penis of a bull seem to have been substituted for those of the man, and even this symbol was eventually replaced by cakes of wheat made by women to represent the male organs of their husbands.

Another part of the ritual appears to have been a sacramental meal in which the victim's body was eaten and his blood drunk.

At last the whole ritual of death and resurrection was turned into a drama—a mystery drama, which taught of immortal life beyond the grave.

But so long as the man representing the god was actually killed, his spirit was believed to pass to a younger and fresher body, ejecting or overshadowing the ordinary soul already resident therein.

During three days the divine soul was supposed to visit the underworld, the revelation of its adventures there being reserved for an inner circle of initiates. After three days the dead god was supposed to rise: the exact moment being marked by the appearance in the eastern sky of the planet Venus, the morning star.

This process formed the heart of an annual ceremony and between its exit from one body and before it entered another, the spirit was also supposed to reside in the bough of a tree, usually that of the acacia.

The priest-king—as representative on earth of the divinity—was the chosen victim, to be killed ritually. As Tammuz was slain in heaven, his human embodiment on earth also had to be slain, and the man who represented the incarnate God lost his personal name, taking in its place the title of the God. Thus the high priest of Cybele was called Attis, the priests of Bacchus were Bacchoi, of Sabazus the Saboi, and so on.

Ward, following closely on Frazer, says that the method of depositing the "external soul" in a safe and secret place outside the body was closely linked with totemism. Pillars of wood were not only symbols of the phallus but also the residing place of the Spirit of Vegetation; the belief was widespread that the souls of those waiting to become incarnate dwelt in trees.

Essentially this was the ritual described by Lucian in the second century of our era as taking place in Syria—a ritual which is at the heart of a continuity of ceremonies from the remote past to the present day, out of which there is evidence aplenty among many different peoples in many lands.

Among the Jews the ritual survived for centuries: from the time Jeremiah complained about the obscene phallic cakes which Jews used in connection with the worship of the goddess, to the time of Jerome who says that when Christ was born there was still a grove in Bethlehem sacred to Adonis where women wept for the dying god.

To a very late date Jewish women, like other worshipers of the great goddess, offered as substitutes for the male organs of their husbands models made out of the "flesh" of the slain corn god, and poured out wine to symbolize the blood which naturally flowed when the human male organ was cut off—as in the case of the priests of Cybele.

These worshipers believed that unless the goddess was offered these phallic cakes they would receive from her no harvest; and in order to "make themselves one with God," they ate the bread and drank some of the wine.

Though the ritual by now was mostly play-acting, Ward says that at a time of dread and danger, "blood and only human blood, could satisfy the Goddess."

The Song of Solomon, according to Ward, was but a ritual hymn of the fertility rite to Astarte: "It is the liturgy of the wooing and marriage of Astarte and Tammuz performed every year in Palestine in the Spring, which inevitably led up to the death, or loss, of the male God in order that the land might become fertile."

According to Ward, Josephus indicates that the Essenes, an ascetic sect of Jews who flourished at (and well before) the historic time of Christ, were really a reformed version of the old Tammuz cult who had spiritualized the ritual.

"The more closely we investigate the Essenes," says Ward, "the more clear it becomes that on the one hand they were derived from the old Tammuz cult, and on the other pass on some of their ceremonies to kindred secret societies, such as the Dervish rites," which have survived in Palestine into the twentieth century.

The celibacy adopted by the majority of the Essenes, says Ward, was almost certainly a mild substitute for the emasculation at one time demanded by the Great Mother, which was still exacted from the priests of the more primitive forms of the cult described by Lucian.

As an odd historic note Ward adds that the high priest of the order devoted to Diana of Ephesus was known by the title of Essen.

St. John, says Ward, seems to have been an Essene; Christ most probably was; and some of his disciples most certainly were.

G. R. S. Mead, who managed with a lifetime of research to rescue some of the early Christian sects from the hecatomb to which their more vociferous survivors had consigned them, says the Essenes refused to have anything to do with the actual blood-sacrifices of the temple-worship, *not* believing in the resurrection of the *physical* body, a tenet which the rest of the Pharisees held as cardinal.

When the Jewish sect which became the Catholic Church set up headquarters in Rome, the ancient cult of the goddess and the young dying god was re-established in a new synthesis. Though castration was apparently regarded as an "alien extravagance" in Rome, the goddess had already been brought there, together with her eunuch priests, in 204 B.C., as a result of the long-drawn second Punic War.

On the recommendation of the prophetess of the Sybilline books that a foreign foe could not otherwise be driven from the peninsula, a statue of the great goddess (faced it seems with a small black jagged meteorite) was brought to Rome and installed on the Palatine.

A bumper crop resulted; Hannibal cleared out for good.

Drawn through the streets of Rome by lions, the Phrygian Mother was attended by her eunuch priests, the Galli, who leapt and danced, "gashing themselves amid strains of outlandish music," attired in female garb with long hair fragrant with ointment.

With the establishment of the empire the cult was officially incorporated into the spring festival of Cybele and Attis, observed in March, very much as it has been in the East. On the twenty-second of that month a pine tree was felled and brought into the shrine of Cybele, its stem wrapped with woollen bands as if it were a corpse, decorated with wreaths of violets—sacred to Attis—and his image was placed in the center.

On March 23, the Day of Blood, the High Priest eunuch drew blood from his arms, worshipers worked themselves into a frenzy stirred by music and dancing, gashed themselves with knives till the blood flowed, poured it out on the sacred tree.

Those about to enter the priesthood would then castrate themselves in the usual manner and hurl the bleeding fragments at the image of the goddess.

As in Greece, sterile women appealed to the goddess and were lashed over the loins by the eunuch Galli, whose High Priest or Archigallus was called Attis.

Later the *Dies Sanguis* became the Hilaria, Festival of Joy, celebrated in Rome as carnival, with merriment, masquerades and licence.

Minor officials of the cult, the "metragyrtes" went from town to town attending the sick and selling images of the goddess, amulets supposed to cure all ills, and talismans of the phallus, carved, says Bruzon, from pomegranate roots.

By law they were authorized to beg, and maintained themselves through the "stips" as the donations were called.

Plutarch says old women in their retinue passed as sorceresses, and that they delivered their oracles extemporaneously or drew them by lot from certain books they carried with them, selling their "wretched predictions" to silly women who were charmed by the cadence of their verses.

Apuleius, in his *Golden Ass*, tells of his involvement with these eunuchs, as well as of being initiated into the mysteries of Isis, and of how he was brought back from the guise of an ass by eating the roses of Isis—a psychological conceit, of which more later.

As described by Apuleius, the eunuch priests of the Syrian goddess were by this time considered little more than sodomites and thieves, parading about with statues of the goddess on the back of an ass, telling fortunes and earning much money.

By the time of Voltaire there remained of these votaries of the mysteries, so he says, "nothing but some bands of tramps under the name of Egyptians, wandering about Europe with their castanets; dancing the dances of the priests of Isis; selling balm, curing the mange, and being covered by it, telling fortunes and stealing chickens. Such was the end of what had once been most sacred in half the known world."

When Christianity officially overcame the worship of the Great Mother (along with Mithraism) and various early Christian sects were classed as heretical, the ritual of Adonis either seems to have gone underground or to have been incorporated in the Church.

The similarities between the careers of the historic Jesus and the Lord Adonis are startling enough.

Within five days of being proclaimed a king, Jesus was ritually murdered. Before being crucified, or "hung on a tree," Christ was ritually scourged, robed in the purple robes of Adonis, crowned with the familiar acacia thorn, and in his hand was placed as scepter a reed—symbol of the god of vegetation.

At his death he was mocked as king of the Jews and stabbed in the side. The date—the traditional Good Friday—was the twenty-third of March, the Dies Sanguis.

Frazer was almost too specific in drawing a comparison: "When we reflect how often the Church has skillfully contrived to plant the seeds of the new faith on the old stock of paganism, we may surmise that the Easter celebration of the dead and risen Christ was grafted upon a similar celebration of the dead and risen Adonis, which, as we have seen reason to believe, was celebrated in Syria at the same season."

Good Catholics may be shocked to read him further: "The type, created by Greek artists, of the sorrowful goddess with her dying lover in her arms, resembles and may have been the model for the Pieta of Christian art, the Virgin with the dead body of her divine Son in her lap, of which the most celebrated example is the one by Michelangelo in St. Peter's."

Furthermore, Mithras too, who rivaled Jesus for religious domination in Rome, was a castrate, virgin-born, a mediator between God and man, celebrated a sacred bouquet of bread and wine, washed away the sins of the world in blood, and—most extraordinary of all, as will be seen in a later chapter—was equated by Herodotus with Venus.

What an amalgam of conceits!

Professor E. O. James summed up the results: "Within the context of one single and supreme transcendent Deity, the creator and ground of all existence, the Incarnate Lord was represented at once as the Son of God and Son of Mary the Madonna, while the Church and his Bride and mystical Body was the Mater Ecclesia. In this spiritualized and impressive theological setting the age-long widely diffused quest of life in a continual process of renewal, bound up with the resurrection of vegetation and the mystery of birth and generation, acquired a new significance which gave the ancient theme and its ritual, shorn of the deadlier fertility motifs, a permanent place and function in Christendom."

But the original Adonis cult was not extinguished by the triumph of Christianity. What the church did not stamp out of the old heathen rites, is transferred to various saints, especially the two St. Johns.

Elsewhere part of the ritual survived among the Druses, the Manichaeans, the Assassins, and other such sects. Through them it eventually was spread to Europe as a result of the crusades, when much of the ritual seems to have passed to the Knights Templar and through them to the Masonic orders.

Among the various Gnostic sects—of whom so little has been known till recently, except through their detractors—part of the theology, if not the ritual, appears to have survived: in a degraded form, say their detractors; in a highly spiritualized form, say their supporters.

Among the Druses of Lebanon, the old Syrian center of the Adonis cult, traces of phallic and fertility worship are still evident, and their veneration of certain angelic intermediaries is reminiscent not only of the Essenes who were under obligation not to betray the names of the angels, but of the Skoptsi sects.

Those Druses, says Ward, who have come into close contact with Europeans, often maintained they were connected with the Rosicrucians and Freemasonry.

Among the Mohammedans the old Tammuz cult survived to date in a reformed guise in the secret rites of the Dervishes. Through them, says Ward, it passed to the Masons, so that "out of crude beginnings, evolved the great mystery rites, and Freemasonry itself, wherein men were taught the doctrine of the resurrection of the soul and of life beyond the grave."

As an indication of the survival of part of the ritual, Ward—who as a Mason should know—points out that in some of the lodges up to a few years ago, after being stripped and bathed, candidates had a running noose fastened round their genitals as a reminder of the earlier rite.

Jessie L. Weston has concluded that the Holy Grail legends contain the remnants of the old Syrian cult, and that these legends owe their origin and dissemination to the Templars.

The significance of the phallus in the ritual of the Templars was recognized by the Inquisitors, says Ward, for with "fiendish cruelty" they attached heavy weights to that organ when torturing the knights, as if to say "Your rites centre round that member and so shall the tortures we inflict on you. .. ."

To Miss Weston it is clear that the wound suffered by the King-guardian is castration, and that the original Quest was to restore the vitality and also the virility of the Guardian of the Grail, known as the Fisher King, or Maimed King, so that fertility might revert to the wasteland.

"The dead body on the bier," says Miss Weston, "the Maimed King on the litter, correspond with the god, dead, or wounded in such a manner that he is deprived of his reproductive powers."

It is an analogy, says she, which has hitherto been too much ignored, "though certain scholars have evidently been aware of its existence." Among others she quotes Vellay to point out that the term "thigh" used in connection with the wounding of Adonis is merely a well-recognized euphemism for the genitals. "While the majority of the Grail texts," says she, "employ this term for the wound of the Fisher King (Parmi les cuisses), Wolfram von

Eschenbach (in his Parzifal) uses words which leave no doubt that here, as elsewhere, the term is to be understood in an euphemistic sense."

Other examples of the old rite have survived in England where the Lord of Misrule, who presided over the Christmas revels for twelve days, represented King Saturn, who, in the Saturnalia of the Roman legionaries, was "made king in mockery and then killed in earnest."

Saturn, in fact, turns out to be the kingpin of the story. Frazer says of the festivals in his honor that "if I am right, a man who personated a god or hero of the type of Tammuz or Adonis, enjoyed the favours of a woman who represented the great Semitic goddess Ishtar or Astarte; and after he had thus done his part towards securing, by means of sympathetic magic, the revival of plant life in spring, he was put to death. We may suppose that the death of this divine man was mourned over by his worshippers and especially by women, in much the same fashion as the women of Jerusalem wept for Tammuz at the gate of the temple and as Syrian damsels mourned the death of Adonis, while the river ran red with his blood."

In England Cybele reappeared as the May Queen and Attis as the Green Man—the Maypole, or sacred pine tree, representing both the Great Mother and the castrated god.

The custom was widespread throughout Europe: after midnight youths would go to the woods, cut down a tree, lop off its branches, leaving a few at the top, wrap around it purple bands and even attach to it a doll before taking it to the village at sunrise of May Day accompanied by the blowing of flutes and horns.

One of the most extraordinary indications of the universality of the Adonis rites, and of their survival into the present century, is the report of an American anthropologist in the Philippines.

In Mindanao, preliminary to sowing, a man was tied to a tree, arms above head, the whole male member was cut off and the man allowed to bleed to death, so that his fertilizing blood could drain into the soil. Later, to mitigate the pain, the victim was knocked on the head, a spear thrust into his side, and the whole body severed at the waistline.

In India, through the ages, after each harvest, the exhausted soil was thought to be renewed by the performance of fertility dances, during which human blood was used, or flesh of the victim buried in the field, or the ashes of his bones plowed into the land to insure a good harvest.

The rite was still practiced until suppressed by the British, at which point a goat or buffalo was substituted for the human victim.

In Korea, at the beginning of the twentieth century—on a certain night in the twelfth moon—so writes another American anthropologist, "the palace eunuchs, of whom there are some three hundred, perform a ceremony supposed to ensure a bountiful crop in the ensuing year."

In the East Indies an English traveler witnessed a dance in honor of the gods of the earth in which hermaphrodites danced till they fell to the ground foaming at the mouth and "pretended to foretell."

In Africa, among the Ekoi of southern Nigeria both men and women excised their genital organs to celebrate an annual festival in order to produce a plentiful harvest and immunity from thunderbolts, the victims apparently usually dying from loss of blood.

In the Congo, up till recently, youths were castrated "in order more fittingly to offer themselves to the phallic worship."

Another anthropologist, H. H. Johnson, describes curious eunuch dances in Africa to celebrate the new moon in which white cocks were thrown alive into the air, with clipped wings, then caught and plucked by eunuchs. Originally, so Johnson reports, humans were sacrificed, a young boy or girl being thrown into the air and then torn to pieces by the eunuchs: a custom, he adds, which fell off in the 1880's when "slaves got scarce and manners milder."

Among headhunting cannibals, according to Paul Wirz, a Swiss ethnologist, to celebrate the "beginning of the world," after several nights of promiscuous orgy a fine young virgin was made to cohabit publicly with a series of youths under a canopy of heavy logs which was allowed to drop on the final couple. The bodies of the boy and girl were then dragged out, cut up, roasted and devoured.

According to Leo Frobenius, among various tribes in Africa, between the death of one king and the installation of another, a holy fire was kindled by "twirling the male stick in the female base." In this ritual a pubescent boy and a virgin appeared completely naked to perform a ritual first copulation before the whole court, after which they were tossed into a prepared trench and buried alive.

Shilluk kings were also strangled and buried with a live virgin after a term of seven years, or earlier if the crops or herds were to fail.

In the Indian province of Malabar, though his term of office was longer, lasting a cycle of twelve years, the god-king's ordeal was more dreadful: he was required to mount a scaffold, castrate himself and cut off pieces of his body, until, feeling faint from the loss of blood, he was permitted to cut his throat.

In the New World, which may have a history considerably longer than most people have been prepared to believe, the Aztecs sacrificed to the corn goddess Chicomecohuatl a young girl of twelve or thirteen: thrown on her back on a heap of corn, her head was cut off, the blood caught in a tub, and a priest, having carefully flayed the headless trunk, would squeeze himself into her skin!

Prescott in his *Conquest of Mexico* tells how every year a man was chosen to represent a divine king, was married to four beautiful wives, who represented the goddess, and allowed to live in the greatest pomp and splendor. At the end of a year he was taken from the palace and sacrificed in full view of the people who but a few days before had treated him as master. This is reminiscent of Strabo's tale of "Albanians" in the Caucasus where a great sanctuary was dedicated to the "Moon," ruled by a High Priest, to which were attached a number of "Sacred Men." Sooner or later the Divine Spirit was supposed to descend into one of them as he wandered about through the forests prophesying. He was then seized and brought back to the temple, where he was kept in semiroyal state for a year, like the God-King in Mexico. At the end of that period he was sacrificed to the "Moon" by having a spear thrust in his side.

But far and away the most extraordinary of these human sacrifices, involving eunuchs, was the immolation of what is known as the "mujerado"—or man turned into woman.

An ancient Central American custom—which consisted of selecting the most virile and handsome man in a village and turning him into a woman—it survived in Mexican pueblos into this century.

The method for accomplishing the metamorphosis was as extraordinary as the result.

To begin with, manual onanism was practiced on the victim as many times a day as possible and in between times he was made to ride bareback on a horse. The effect of this was to produce extreme erethism, or abnormal excitability, to the point where eventually the movement of the horse alone caused ejaculation, then orgasm without ejaculation, till finally no orgasm at all was possible; the testes and penis would begin to shrink, erections ceased, and the organ gradually atrophied.

An American doctor who examined several of these individuals in the latter half of the nineteenth century found them to be beardless and devoid of pubic hair, the penis reduced to "the size of a thimble," with the overdeveloped breasts of a nursing woman, some of them having admitted nursing the children of mothers who had died.

The purpose of this strange ordeal to which they were subjected quite willingly, so it seems, was, as described by the doctor, to provide creatures essential for the "Saturnalia or orgies of these Indians" in which the "mujerado" played "the passive agent in pederastic ceremonies—reminiscent of Sodom and Gomorrah."

In the original ceremony, from which women were barred, the priests and elders of the village deposited within this sacrificial human goat in a manner which hardly needs describing, their seed, whereupon the whole was impaled and roasted alive so that the flames might carry heavenward to the propritiated deity the offering of the worshipers below.

Though the human sacrifice was no longer practiced at the time of the American doctor's report, the rest of the ceremony had apparently survived, and the "mujerado" was regularly put to his ancient use not only during the annual orgies, but whenever the chiefs felt the urge.

Examining these once handsome and virile young men, the doctor noted they had undergone a severe psychological as well as physical change, no longer frequented women, had lost their former courage, as well as their wives and children, but not, strangely enough, their standing in the village, which was one of esteem as participants in an ancient religious ceremony.

Altogether too extraordinary to go without some word of explanation.

10
VENUS AND ADONIS

What on earth—or in heaven—could motivate human beings to act in such a fantastic manner?

Is there an explanation somewhere available? Some physical, metaphysical, or natural explanation, some hint to lead to the solution of such a puzzle?

Who was this dying god to whom victims were sacrificed, who had himself been a sacrifice, and whose spirit seemed to lurk as well in a seed as in the solar orb, or for that matter in any of the celestial orbs with whom this planet has had intercourse?

Who is this ever-virgin, all-producing, mother goddess?

Some may consider the solutive phenomena as fantastic as the phenomena they are supposed to solve.

To Jessie L. Weston, who does not usually sound so academic, the first of the two divinities was the "somewhat elusive and impersonal entity who represents in anthropomorphic form the principle of animate nature, upon whose preservation, and unimpaired energies, the life of man, directly and indirectly depends."

Elan vital? The Life Force? Some universal cosmic energy?

Frazer is more *terre à terre*. To him, under the names of Osiris, Tammuz, Adonis, and Attis, the people of Egypt and of western Asia represented the yearly decay and revival of life, especially of vegetable life, "which they personified as a god who annually died and rose again from the dead." And year by year, says he, the corn-spirit was represented by human victims slain on the harvest field.

Frazer lists all kinds of examples of the ritual putting to death of king-priest heroes, including not only Osiris and his just mentioned namesakes, but Orpheus, Bacchus, Dionysus, Lycurgus, the kings of Tyre, Odin, Halfadan the Black, and even Romulus, saying that all together these legends point to a widespread practice of dismembering the body of a king or magician and burying the pieces in order to ensure the fertility of the ground "and probably also the fecundity of man and beast."

To Ward, the god was the same in heaven as on earth: Tammuz on earth, as representative of the sun-god enlivening matter, Moloch in heaven. Incarnate on earth, Tammuz was doomed to die in order that men might live. Ascending to heaven amid a roar of thunder, he became Moloch, who sent down the rain.

Apparently the earthly representative of the divinity was also the rainmaker, and "if the harvests failed," says

Frazer, "he would be given the blame, even paying with his life."

Certainly Tammuz—or Attis, or Adonis—was everywhere associated with sunlight, plant life and seed grain; and as the vegetation withered in its yearly cycle *something* appeared to die, or pass into the subterranean world, only to be resurrected at Easter.

The Sumerians quite plainly recognized in their withered autumn leaves the dead body of Tammuz. The eunuch priests of Attis, once ordained, donned long yellow robes "the color of autumn leaves."

The analogy of Attis with an ear of grain is clear enough. Every year the grain must be cut with a sickle, planted in the earth, there to die; but from this "dark place" comes forth new grain in the spring which grows to maturity and in turn is repealed and placed in the earth.

Father Lagrange was of the opinion that Adonis represented, not vegetation dying a natural death from summer heat or winter cold, but the grain falling beneath the reaper's sickle, then being crushed on threshing floor and millstone.

Ward suggests that on a material plane the whole civilization of the West is dependent on the development of food grain, and that to it can be attributed the doctrine of Resurrection. Certainly the God of Christianity is one who is killed, buried, resurrected and then eaten by the faithful! But so were his predecessors, Bacchus, Dionysus, etc.

Frazer is even more blunt: "It was no vague poetical sentiment," says he, "which prompted them to hail with joy the rebirth of vegetation and to mourn its decline. Hunger, felt or feared, was the mainspring of the worship of Adonis."

Yet he does admit there was more to it than that when he discusses the mystery of the resurrection of Osiris—a ritual performed for the benefit of every dead Egyptian: "As Osiris died and rose again from dead, so all men hoped to rise like him from death to eternal life."

Man too is a seed which must be planted in mother soil to develop. Furthermore, to be reborn into this life, or another, man must die, and, whether or not he is buried in the ground, to dust his body must return, and the dust too reverts to the elements, and so on in a cycle.

In analogy the lover of the Great Mother dies, from the fruit of their union comes forth the son; he in turn becomes the lover, dies, and is the parent of another son—who goes through a similar cycle.

The moral seems to be that form is evanescent, that life and its creator subsist despite the dying form.

In a pneumatic sense Isis, to the Egyptians, was Mother Nature surrounded by and robed in seven etherial mantles, "the spheres of ever-changing generations which metamorphose the ineffable, unimaginable, incomprehensible mother substance," whereas Osiris was the Mind, the Will, the Self, which makes all things but remains unchanged.

A second key is the conceit that in this universe, everything is somehow linked, that what is above affects what is below, and vice versa. The sea is as much in the fish as the fish in the sea.

In theosophist parlance: "From Gods to men, from Worlds to atoms, from Star to rush-light, from the Sun to the vital heat of the meanest organic being—the world of Form and Existence is an immense chain, whose links are all connected."

Tammuz can be, and is, the power of generation in the sun *and* in the leaves of a plant. What's more, he, or it, can be symbolized alike by a shining orb, the leaf of a tree, a virile young man (who gets castrated), the phallus itself, and, most obviously, in seed—running in a gamut of harmonics from the seed of grain to the seed of man, to the seed of all things germinating in the will of God.

As one Gnostic seer expressed the idea: "When I use the term 'will' I do so merely to suggest the idea of an operation transcending all volition, thought, or sensible action. And this universality also was not our dimensional and differentiable universe, which subsequently came into existence and was separated from other universes, but the Seed of all universes.

"This universal Seed contained everything in itself, potentially, in some fashion as the grain in the minutest point—roots, stems, branches, leaves, and the innumerable germs that come from the seeds of the plant, and which in their turn produce still other and other plants in manifold series."

With the process of generation still a mystery to biologists today, is it any wonder that the male has been for so long, and by so many people, considered but the vehicle through which some supernatural power could operate—that during coitus man is possessed by a god?

So thoroughly established is the idea that sperm constitutes the actual substance of the deity who uses the human male as his medium during the condition of sexual excitement, says Robert Briffault, that it has survived in mystic theological thought to the present day.

The ancient Egyptians, says he, represented the supreme self-created deity "as introducing his generative organs into his mouth, from which the seed presently issued forth as the Creative Word, or Logos." The assimilation of sperm with the word or Logos, he adds, "is indeed a current commonplace in Catholic casuistical theology."

This would explain the oft reported administration by Gnostic sects and Tibetan monks of sperm to communicants, as well as the original use of sperm in the "precious creme" of confirmation.

To Vellay, the myth of Adonis was all composed of a chain of analogous ideas, a drama which had its source in heaven: "the birth of the god, his death, his resurrection, the vicissitudes of his fate, are but the poetic expression of one symbol: the revolutions of the sun and the alternating seasons and terrestrial production and reproduction."

All the cults of Adonis, says Vellay, centered round this one conceit, as all the religious ceremonies centered round the phallus.

Dupuis, in his *Origine de Tous les Cultes,* says without reservation that Attis despoiled of his genitals is the sun in autumn, just as in spring he is worshiped in the erect phallus as the sun in its most generative power.

The ritual on earth was to duplicate in human form what appeared to be happening in the spheres above. Its purpose, apparently, to avert the permanent suspension of the reproductive energies of nature, dependent, first, on the sun, but also, as will be seen, on a second, and very powerful divinity: the killing and castrating mother and mistress, she who was the matrix, the ovoid void, the moist and earthy womb, the mother, mistress, nurse and killer.

Just as Tammuz was a heavenly as well as an earthly divinity, so was Ishtar: Goddess of Heaven *and* Goddess of Earth. Strangely enough, she was even known by the same name as Tammuz "The Green One." She is Maia, Mater, Matter; and Urania the Azure Queen, the blue of the vault of heaven, the blue in the depths of the ocean. Star-girt and resting on a crescent, an immaculate virgin mother, holding in her arms a virgin child, she is the prostitute goddess of sex, giver, preserver and destroyer of all, the undecaying eternal mother of the gods and universes.

A confusingly composite nature, it is somewhat simplified if viewed first as a physical heavenly body which in turn represents her pneumatic, metaphysical essence.

Yet even as a heavenly body there remains a confusion, both physical and symbolic, between the planet Venus and the satellite Luna.

The most widespread and constant symbol under which the great mother was known—never mind whether rightly or wrongly—was that of a triune deity of heaven, earth, and the underworld: the moon.

Whether it was as the moon itself that she was being worshiped—as some might be thought to be worshiping a plaster cast of a Madonna—or whether she was worshiped because of the obvious powers exerted over generation on this planet, or whether it was as a symbol of some deeper mystery of generation, all the great goddesses have at one time or another been assimilated with the moon in one of its innumerable phases relative to the sun and earth.

Yet almost as often the same deity has been assimilated with the planet Venus.

How to account for the confusion?

No one can have looked at the mythology of the world without being amazed at the constant confusion of epithets applied equally to the moon and to the planet Venus. Both—along with Isis and others—have been called the goddess of a thousand names; one French writer, Pierre Henri Larcher, in a booklet brought out in Paris in the year of the American Declaration of Independence, listed 248 principal names, surnames and epithets for the Goddess Venus—whether lunar or planetary—running through every letter of the alphabet from Acidalia to Zerynthia.

Classical sources not only confirm the Frenchman but add to the confusion.

Some have tried to explain away the mess by pointing out that Venus, the planet, is closely linked with the moon, and was, since antiquity, considered the moon's planet.

But behind this confusion must lie some simpler truth.

Why Venus should not be Venus, and the moon the moon seems hard to understand, unless at some time in the past the movement of heavenly bodies was so shaken up that the attributes of one got shifted to another.

Then there is the theory that the shifting heavenly bodies brought about several earthly cataclysms which came close to wiping out humanity, warping its memory in a fog of mass amnesia. Add to this the fact that the names of the divinities are in different languages in different localities, and the excuse for confusion is obvious—though nonetheless deplorable.

At one point the only explanation for Adonis seemed to be to equate it with the planet Venus itself; then a simpler way out was found by postulating an original planet or comet or disintegrating satellite no longer visible in the sky.

Certainly the symbol of a radiant orb, or of a swastika, is applicable to any celestial body. Nor does it simplify matters to refer to a horned or crescented body as the moon *alone*. Venus too has its phases, well described in antiquity before they were discovered to the modern world through the telescope of Galileo.

One means of simplifying the confusion is to follow the lead of the mythologists who consider the variously named divinities as representing various phases of the moon in daily, weekly, monthly, yearly, or other, phases.

At an early stage the Greeks called the moon Selene. Later they split her into two characters, Aphrodite the bright, and Hecate the dark; later still they made of her a three-headed triune goddess to represent three main phases of the moon: Artemis for the waxing, Selene for the waning, and Hecate for the dark.

In Islam this nomenclature persisted, and the three daughters of Allah are said to have been called Al-Ilat, Al-Uzza, and Manat. Though the *Encyclopedia of Islam* calls Al-Uzza the planet Venus!

On the Isle of Man the three phases of the Celtic moon goddess apparently were symbolized by a three-legged swastika, a very old symbol for satellite divinities but also for the mating of male and females bodies.

Later the moon phases were split into four, giving rise to our week of seven days.

The names of the goddess also varied from month to month throughout the year, though basically Aphrodite during the spring and summer, and Persephone—destruction and death—during the dark months of the year.

There are grounds enough for the moon to be considered a powerful deity, and data enough in prehistory to show that the world was well aware of the power exerted by the moon on our planet.

That it controls the seas, holding the waters at the present level and causing their tides, is a fact known to the schoolboy, though it wasn't till 1953 that it was established that the solar tides in the earth's atmosphere are sixteen times more powerful than the lunar tides in the atmosphere. On the seas it is the moon's oscillations which affect winds and currents. No wonder the moon is that patron of sailors. But then so is Venus!

As controller of the seasons—in a way far more direct than has yet been widely admitted—the moon was believed, since what is known as the dawn of history, to affect all agriculture, cause seeds to germinate, animals to bear young, women to become pregnant.

A nineteenth-century royal commission of scientists established that the genitals of certain shellfish wax and wane with the moon, though any Mediterranean fisherman could have told them so.

Is there any scientific basis for the cliché that the moon affects the cycle of women? At the turn of the century a Swedish scientist carried out experiments on several thousand women in Stockholm hospitals in which he established that there is a definite relation between the frequency of births—and thus of generation—which is coincident with the lunar month. Equally interesting is the fact that males are swayed in similar cycles.

In women, periodicity, though affected by various physiological and psychological causes, was proved by Svante Arrhenius, the Swedish physicist and chemist, to be strongly influenced by the rhythm of the moon.

Most interesting, he discovered that though it takes the moon twenty-nine and a half days to pass through all its phases from one full moon to the next, the period in which births were most numerous and at which most of the women underwent their cyclic functions recurred not every twenty-nine and a half days but every twenty-seven and one-third days.

Curiously, this is the exact time it takes the moon to turn once round the earth and arrive back at the spot over the earth whence it started—the time differential being accounted for by the fact that the earth has also moved.

In a previous and independent piece of research the same Swedish scientist established that the amount of "electricity" in the atmosphere varies in a rhythmic cycle, the maximum occuring every twenty-seven and one-third days!

That people as well as plants are affected nervously by thunderstorms and the amount of "electricity" in the air is common knowledge, but it wasn't till recently that it was discovered in Germany that this "electricity" was the cause, rather than sunlight and darkness, of the apparent waking and sleeping of flowers.

The changes of the moon's cycle are a calendar too obvious for anyone to miss. In Aryan mythology the moon is the oldest known measurer of time, and in the Babylonian story of creation—or, as appears more likely, re-creation—it is the moon who is the measurer.

To the ancient Arabs, the heavenly constellations were the houses of the moon, dividing the solar year into months, and the zodiacal belt was called the "girdle of Ishtar." Though who is Ishtar?

In Islam, Ramadan begins at the first glimpse of the new moon. In China, the new moon was proclaimed by heralds sent out by the royal astronomer.

In many lands, the duration of time was reckoned by nights and not by days. Caesar records that the Celts calculated by moons and nights. In England the fortnight is still current though sennight has almost vanished. Honeymoon is still going strong, and no one on either side of the Atlantic needs be reminded of the difference between Saturnday night and Moonday morning.

In the days when the three main phases of the moon were symbolized by three different deities, each phase and each goddess were given different attributes.

The waxing moon, patroness of seedlings, was the one to make things germinate and grow. During the first quarter of the moon the ground was prepared and seed sown so it would not rot. Throughout the ages the crescent moon has been so constant a charm for the increase of grain, flocks and family, that today, with our more modern ideas of value, at the new moon we turn over in our pockets, in the hope that it may increase—money!

Under the waning moon hay fields and grain fields were to be cut so they would not ferment or sprout. Trees were felled so the lumber could mature. Whereas sheep were shorn under the waxing moon that their fleece might grow back quickly—the horns of cattle are still cut today in the United States in the waning moon, so the animal will not bleed from the wound.

In the dark of the moon the destructive powers of nature were considered at their worst, bringing floods, storms and destructive pestilence. All things were then thought to be "minished and brought low." This was the time when it was said that the powers of sorcery and black magic could be evoked to work their mischief unchecked. The rites of this dark goddess were performed at night, and were especially concerned with placation in order to turn aside evil. The dark queen of ghosts swept through the night followed by baying hounds, and her "dreadful train of questing spirits." A picture with strong overtones of Venus! But whoever she was, this heavenly body, instead of being the giver of visions, was the cause of nightmares and "lunacy."

It was in her bright phase that the moon was most important and most efficacious, bringing fruitfulness to the earth, promoting fertility in man, animals, and vegetation.

It needs no 'enry 'iggins to note the similarity between the Babylonian Ishtar and the modern Easter.

Easter, according to innumerable authorities, was and still is a lunar festival. Yet it also marks the resurrection of the sun at the vernal equinox and is announced by the appearance in the east of the morning star—the planet Venus! Strangely enough, a historic date for the birth of Venus into our universe has been assigned by a modern scientist to the very moment of the biblical "passover"! And now comes an extraordinary compounding of rituals, as evident in the biblical descriptions of the worship of the golden calf as in Lucian's Syrian ceremonies.

Throughout antiquity the spring ceremonies were uniformly accompanied by a widespread indulgence in sexual intercourse. How did this sex fit into the picture?

From Vedic times in India the ritual was universal: the central glorious act of the ceremony—still symbolized by the fertile rabbit and the all-producing egg—following so closely on the Friday mourning for the dying God, was identical from Egypt to Asia Minor, from Babylon to Knossos: a ritual sacred sexual congress, the *hieros gamos*.

The birth of Aphrodite, goddess of sexual love, from the severed genitals of Uranus mixed with sea-foam, is a celestial phenomenon which will become clearer later.

In any case, as the deity of fertility, she represented the generative power in everything female, a power to be kept alive and fanned upon this planet by ritual coitus.

In the words of one woman writer: when women gave up the personal use of their own sexuality in these rites "the divine power enhanced, shined forth anew."

The symbolism was not, says this writer, "in the erect phallus or in the all-embracing woman" but in the moment of union, "in the act through which tension is released and energy put forth." Words that may go to the very heart of the creative process and give some meaning to the symbolism of the boy and the girl making fire in the African ritual.

They also explain the presence of thousands of temple harlots, and the orgies of promiscuity in which, as Hannay describes them, "men, women and children took part in open-air, public, stark-naked, priapic, adulterous orgies, when all bonds of relationship were untied, and sexual intercourse enjoyed in full sunshine in the presence of the whole population"—a custom which, in Imperial Rome, developed, or degenerated, depending on the point of view, into regular monthly festivals during which women were required to display the greatest possible abandon and gross sensuality the better to stimulate the fertilizing powers of the god.

As Briffault points out, it was a universal belief that such rituals promoted the growth of crops, that the seed planted in the ground would be ineffective unless accompanied by the planting of seed in woman—a custom, says Briffault, which is still current in Holland and Germany where peasants have intercourse in the fields as soon as the latter have been sown.

Frazer says that by performing certain magical rites they thought they could aid the god who was the principle of life, in his struggle with the opposing principle of death. "The ceremonies which they observed for this purpose were in substance a dramatic representation of the natural process which they wished to facilitate; for it is a familiar tenet of magic that you can produce any desired effect merely by imitating it. And as they now explained the fluctuations of growth and decay, of reproduction and dissolution, by the marriage, the death, and the birth or revival of the gods, their religious or rather magical dramas turned in great measure on these themes."

Far from being "degenerate" the indiscriminate sexuality of these ancient orgies might well have been less prurient than some of our modern discriminate promiscuity. In the orgy, by which was meant a religious ritual, the personal element may well have been subordinate, or at least incorporate, in a general accumulation and discharge of tension for a mass religious purpose.

In some early Christian sects—on which the Khlisti seem to have based their rituals—these was a conscious attempt to limit the indiscriminate urgings of the flesh, to channel them for a ritual form of godly procreation.

In any case, in antiquity, the function was severely organized; most everywhere the goddess was attended by priestesses and guardians known as "virgins," some of whom appear to have been required to abstain from sex, but most of whom were sacred prostitutes who received the "fertilizing energy of the deity" into their own person, a function they performed for the benefit of all.

In the temples of Ishtar these Hierodules, or sacred prostitutes, were called joy-maidens, or Ishtarity. Pledged to the service of the goddess they were not supposed to use "their sex, their attraction or their love" for their own satisfaction—a fact which makes the tale of Hero and Leander all the more poignant.

In some cases these prostitutes were reserved for the use of the king-priest, with whom he had temporary or lasting relations, but as sacred harlots they were also obliged to give themselves not only to the king, and the high priests, but to strangers (in whom the young god was supposed to be represented) or, at times, to any of the male worshipers of the goddess.

In Cyprus the religious orgies of prostitution in and about the temples of Paphos were such that "Paphia" became the generic word for prostitute.

According to Hannay, the worship of Paphos lay in a strongly organized college of priests and priestesses living in thousands round the temple, and the "sexual excesses of the devotees constituted the Cyprian cultus of the deification of lust."

Such wording and such a tone, were, no doubt, in Victorian times considered essential for the communication of such subjects, if not for the writer, at least for the general reader into whose closeted mind the seed was to be laid.

Some biblical readers may no doubt be shocked to hear that according to Dr. Inman there were close to a hundred cells at the Temple of Jerusalem for the Kadeshoth, or sacred prostitutes, Kadosh in Syrian meaning "sacred" and the title of both the sacred men and women dedicated to Astarte and Tammuz, the males—euphemistically called "dogs" in the Old Testament—being generally accused of not only ritual coitus but of sodomy.

In most of the sanctuaries the "priestesses" appear to have been dedicated to the service of the goddess for life—

or the better part of a lifetime—staying in them not only to perform the sexual rites but certain water rites reminiscent of "the Deluge," and to attend the sacred flame.

In many temples a sacred flame was kept perpetually burning, the fire being supposed to embody or represent the perpetual fertility of the goddess. The deity in fact was believed to *be* in the flame as it was in the light of heavenly bodies and even to be able to lie latent in a piece of wood—a conceit, as will be seen, far from the madness it may have seemed in the days of Queen Victoria.

The Latin for torch is vesta: hence the Vestal Virgins, whose principal celebration was the Festival of Candles. Nowadays, as anyone in Rome at the Feast of the Ascension will not easily forget, the whole of the torchlit city with its great and gloriously flaming central Mamma, faced by an equally flamboyant obelisk, is devoted to the Virgin Mary.

True, certain vestals, not only in Rome, but the world over, and as far back as history can trace, were reputed to be quite untouched, and any infringement of their vows was severely punished, usually by being buried alive.

But why, despite the fact she has many lovers and is the mother of many sons, is the great goddess always represented as virgin?

If this is taken as symbolic of the moon the conceit is comprehensible in that the body of the satellite appears continually to renew itself, going from slender and virginal to fully mature, in an endless cycle. In a deeper or more pneumatic symbolism, the idea is the more appropriate. In Lucian's philosophy Matter or Mater is alone eternal and imperishable, subject only to an eternity of metamorphosis whereas mind continually comes into being and dies!

Also the epithet virgin has the connotation of single, belonging to herself, not permanently wedded. On this point Frazer elaborated by saying that the Greek word *parthenos* "applied to Artemis, which we commonly translate Virgin, means no more than an unmarried woman, and in the early days the two things were by no means the same . . . there was no public worship of Artemis the Chaste; so far as her sacred titles bear on the relation of the sexes, they show that on the contrary, she was, like Diana in Italy, especially concerned with the loss of virginity and with child-bearing. . . ."

Needless to say, Artemis and Diana have both been used as epithets for the moon in one or other of her phases.

In a footnote, Frazer comments on the line of Isaiah, "and a virgin shall be with child," saying that the Hebrew word rendered there as "virgin" means no more than "young woman." To which he adds a remark consonant with his nineteenth-century point of view: "A correct translation would have obviated the necessity of a miracle."

Briffault provides another clue to the enigma. "The word virgin," says he, "is, of course, used in those titles in its primitive sense denoting 'unwed,' and connoting the very reverse of what the term has come to imply." The virgin Ishtar is also frequently addressed as 'The Prostitute'; and as she herself says, 'A prostitute compassionate am I.' She wears, says Briffault, the "posin," or veil, which, "as among the Jews, was the mark of both 'virgins' and prostitutes."

The correct Latin word for virgin, he adds, is not *virgo* but *virgo intacta,* adding that children born out of wedlock were called *parthenoi,* or *virgin-born.*

From the union of these temple "virgins," regarded as the human representatives of the Great Mother, with the representatives of the Young God, despite the use of "magic contraceptives made of honey and crocodile feces used by the priestesses of Isis in ritual prostitution," a fairly numerous supply of children could be expected, from whom more "Divine" young men could be selected for the blood sacrifices of the "Dying God."

E. M. Harding says that the priestesses of the goddess, in addition to performing the offices which represented her fertilizing and life-giving activities, also impersonated her in her dark and destructive aspect. Each year the Vestal Virgins at Rome would throw twenty-four manikins into the Tiber, and infant sacrifices are believed to have been regularly performed in honor of the goddess. Around a sacred stone representing the goddess Astarte, were reportedly discovered hundreds of skeletons of human infants.

In any case there is evidence aplenty of human sacrifices to the great goddess as well as to the dying god throughout the world.

The chief priestess of the Celtic goddess was required to act as executioner whenever a human sacrifice was made. She had to kill the victim with her own hands. The silver vessel into which the blood was poured was called the Cauldron of Regeneration. Blood was considered a regenerative potion or bath, and boiled it yielded "grace of inspiration." Thus, says McCullagh, in his *Religion of the Ancient Celts,* "in the Grail there was a fusion of the magic cauldron of Celtic paganism and the sacred chalice of Christianity, with the products made mystic and glorious in the most wonderful manner."

But it was not the priestesses alone who were required to prostitute themselves for money. In Phoenician temples women prostituted themselves for hire in the service of religion, believing, says Frazer, that by this conduct they propitiated the goddess and won her favor. "It was a law of the Amorites, that she who was about to marry should sit in fornication seven days by the gate." In Armenia, he adds, the noblest families dedicated their daughters to the service of the goddess Anaitis in her temple of Acilisena, where the damsels acted as prostitutes for a long time before they were given in marriage. And again, the Goddess Ma was served by a multitude of sacred harlots at Comana in Pontus, and "crowds of men and women flocked to her sanctuary." In Babylon, where even the daughters of the noblest families were required to dedicate their hymens to the goddess by lying with some stranger in the temple, all women were required to do so once in a lifetime, which goes to explain the passage in Herodotus:

"The worst Babylonian custom is that which compels every woman of the land once in her life to sit in the temple of love and have intercourse with some stranger . . . the men pass and make their choice. It matters not what the sum of money; the women will never refuse, for that were a sin, the money being by this act made sacred. After their intercourse she has made herself holy in the sight of the goddess and goes away to her home; and thereafter there is no bribe however great that will get her. So then the women that are tall and fair are soon free to depart, but the uncomely have long to wait because they cannot fulfill the law; for some of them remain for three years or four. There is a custom like to this in some parts of Cyprus."

Once a year women were also supposed to sacrifice their hair to the goddess, a bit of symbolism very clearly associated with the planet Venus, and it is related that those who hesitated were required to offer themselves, either in the temple or in the market place, to strangers, the gold they received as the price of their favors being offered to the goddess.

In the mysterious initiation during which women were required to sacrifice their virginity the act, when not performed by king, priest, or stranger, was accomplished with the aid of a non-human image of the phallus.

In India girls were regularly deflowered before their marriage by means of a linga, or stone phallus, unless it was one of ivory or metal. Roman brides likewise were required to sit on a priapic stone, though sometimes an accommodating priest would act as substitute.

Just as the heavenly marriage between the goddess of fertility and the young fertilizing god was considered absolutely vital to the fertility of women, crops and herbs, so the sacrifice of the maidenhead to the god was considered essential for a fruitful marriage. In this way developed the custom of the king, headman or priest impersonating the divinity with every local bride on the first night of marriage, a custom which survived in Europe into the Middle Ages with the *droit de seigneur,* and which, according to the report of a recent American ambassador to one of the Andean republics, is still current in certain remote villages of the Andes where the function is ritually performed on the young bride by the local parish priest, a custom which has given, so it appears, some cause for worry to the hierarchy, but which the local peasants insist on as part of the old form of worship.

The similarity between some of the ancient religious rites and the witchcraft of the Middle Ages is obvious enough. The sexual rites of the witches carried the significance of a union with the divine power as well as being a magic rite to secure fertility, though, curiously enough, in many of the confessions wrung from the girls accused of partaking in lunar Sabbaths, they describe congress with the "devil-divinity" as being cold and very hard, but never resulting in pregnancy, which would seem to indicate the use of some sort of linga.

One reason for the extraordinary persistence of the witches' Sabbaths, a persistence which survived massacre, burnings, and torturings, says Harding, was the fact "that the women who took part in them really believed the fertility of the countryside depended on their activities. Their religion had an extraordinary hold upon them. Its symbols must have sprung from a very deep level of the unconscious, for, as the records of the witch trials bear witness, they inspired hundreds of simple country women to face a horrible death without flinching."

Ritual sexuality to further the generative powers in the world is certainly comprehensible, though it may be surprising to find the performance could actually be effective!

But what of ritual castration?

So far none of the available explanations has come close to being satisfactory.

Gruppe, writing in the sixteenth century, supposed the self-emasculation of the Galli to have been for the purpose of securing chastity "in conformity with an ascetic desire to renounce the joys of the world." Fine, but so what?

Farnell thought the self-mutilation necessary for the attainment of the status of eunuch-priest may have arisen from "the ecstatic craving to assimilate oneself to the goddess and to charge oneself with her power, the female dress being thereupon assumed to complete the transformation." There is something in this; but again, why?

Frazer has pointed out that the assumption of women's garb by certain classes of effeminate priests—a custom curiously alive to this day—was widespread in antiquity: "These feminine deities required to receive from their male ministers, who personated the divine lovers, the means of discharging their beneficent functions: they had themselves to be impregnated by the life-giving energy before they could transmit it to the world." But this explanation gets us only a little further.

Ward is very interesting in his analogy of the goddess with the queen bee—and bees are curiously sacred to Venus—in which the queen, to be fertilized, is required to tear off the male member which remains buried inside her, so that one male, sacrificing himself, can insure the continuance of the species.

Briffault, on the other hand, accounts for the castration of eunuch priests by saying that "the true Great Goddesses," those who belonged to an era of the primitive matriarchal law of the free woman and who had no priest-husbands as the Gods had priestess-wives, and who, not recognizing the rule of any patriarchal husband, had to be served by men who were neither husbands nor lovers but who renounced their sex by assimiliating themselves to women. Another whole approach to the subject is to postulate a time on this planet when men were, for some reason or other, rendered temporarily sterile, and to get the ball rolling again some really drastic sacrifice was deemed to be in order.

Or was it the other way around! Was there, due to some outside aphrodisiac influence, a time on this planet when men and women were driven to wild excesses of intercourse, and priests, to exert some sort of control, resorted to the knife or the sharp sherd of pottery from Samos?

If the *hieros gamos* represented a heavenly mating, was there a castration in heaven as well?

11
THE GIRDLE OF ISHTAR

What could have caused a heavenly castration?

What could have brought about the seasons?

The seasons are conditioned by the tilt of the axis of the earth.

Was it ever so?

Perhaps not.

If not what caused the change?

The theories that a tilt came about through an agency on or within the earth—such as icecaps growing to a point where they shifted the earth's center of gravity—have been largely discredited.

What remains is a power outside the earth.

The wrath of God? The mounting sins of humanity? We'll leave that for the future.

But there is one theory—based on careful study of the past—which goes a long way towards solving almost every one of the questions raised. It accounts for the tilt of the earth, for the loss of the Golden Age, for the birth of Venus from Jupiter, and for the roles in all of this of Isis and Osiris, or of Ishtar and Tammuz.

In the past, according to Immanuel Velikovsky, but in historic times, not more than 3,500 years ago, the planet Venus, formerly a comet, having exploded from the body of Zeus-Jupiter and wandered off its course, whizzed too *close* to earth, disturbing the latter's equipose; this cataclysmic event was then followed, according to Velikovsky's data, by a brush between Venus and Mars, as recently as the eighth century B.C.

To support these theories, Velikovsky has adduced several volumes of fascinating data which stirred up academic hornets into stinging but generally sterile rebuttal.

But before analyzing the identity of the dying god, his metamorphosis, castration, death and resurrection in the light of Velikovsky's fascinating data which goes a long way to providing a solution to the problem in terms of the nature and movement of heavenly bodies, there are earlier postulated cataclysms in the history of this planet which have a bearing on the subject.

According to the thesis of the Viennese cosmologist Hans Hoerbiger, as supported by the English mythologist H. S. Bellamy, a tilt in the earth's axis was brought about by the capture out of space of our present satellite Luna, as recently as eleven to twelve thousand years before Christ.

It was then, say Hoerbiger and Bellamy, that our moon,

a small planet whose orbit lay between the earth and Mars, spiraling closer to the sun, began to trespass in the immediate gravitational realm of the earth. After numerous unsuccessful conjunctions—in their estimate about 13,500 years ago—the favorable conjunction occurred, and "henceforth the planet Luna was the Satellite of Earth."

Were our moon in fact to have been captured out of space—in a manner to be detailed in a moment, it most certainly could have, in one catastrophic stroke, shifted the axis of the earth, caused—for half the year—a sudden emasculation of the sun, unleashed the deluge, sunk in great tidal waves large parts of the antidiluvian world; brought on the seasons and their effect on plants, animals, and women; caused, with its revolutions, the present tides and tempests; cut up the tranquil solar year into our months and weeks; dominated, with a grim mixture of benignity and dread, all of life upon this planet.

Elaborating on Hoerbiger, H. S. Bellamy maintains that before the capture of Luna, the earth's axis was practically vertical to the ecliptic, the atmosphere was evenly distributed, making for an even climate everywhere, with no recurrence of seasons. "Because of the heating of the subcrustal layers of the earth during the cataclysmic age," says Bellamy, "both through the ingestion of satellic material and the association of the water which had penetrated the magnetic layer, it was also generally warmer on Earth."

In such a world living would have extended practically to the poles, which would not have been in their present location, and the earth would have been luxuriantly covered with plants, animals and man.

"Man," says Bellamy, "very definitely lived through the Tertiary period, and fully as *Homo sapiens.*"

The myths of all peoples tell of a Golden Age that ended in a Deluge. So abundant and universal are these myths that it would take another volume to quote from them at length.

The biblical tale is clear enough.

Hesiod's description, though a trifle Edenic, revives the flavor of a time when "men lived like gods, without vices or passions, vexation or toil. In happy companionship with divine beings, they passed their days in tranquillity and joy, living together in perfect equality, united by mutual confidence and love. The earth was more beautiful than now, and spontaneously yielded an abundant variety of fruits. Human beings and animals spoke the same language and conversed with each other. Men were considered mere boys at a hundred years old. They had none of the infirmities of age to trouble them, and when they passed to regions of superior life, it was in a gentle slumber."

Plato's description of the Golden Age and of the Deluge is one in which a great empire—stretching from Peru to Egypt and from Etruria to the Mississippi—lived by agriculture and commerce, building temples, ships, and canals. It is a tale "devoid of marvels, gods, gorgons, or hobgoblins," the tale of a flourishing empire which perished in a day as the result of a cataclysmic inundation.

According to the modern English geographer Egerton Sykes, the only agencies that could have moved about the amount of water required for the descriptions of the Noachian and Atlantean floods is the tilting of the axis of the earth by the acquisition of the planet Luna as our present moon, or a combination of both these factors together.

This would account for *that* deluge; but the evidence points to a whole series of such disasters, for which, up to the development of the theories of Hoerbiger and Velikovsky "no branch of science could supply the mythologists with a likely or possible cause. . . ."

Hoerbiger's theory, extrapolating data from the present and past movement of heavenly bodies, and known as the theory of ice, is based on a dualism of cosmic matter (glowing stellar material and ice) and of power (collective gravitation and distributive explosion) creating ever new tensions, engendering the primordial chaos, ordering it into a solar system, and finally bringing about its end.

Though there is now some doubt about the validity of his ice theory—into which the Russians have reportedly been checking with their space probes—this does not necessarily impair his theory of earth satellites.

According to Hoerbiger this earth has had a series of satellites over a period of millions of years, each of which was captured out of space and eventually crashed onto the earth, the last such disintegration being the satellite which, in his opinion, brought the Andes and most of North and South America out of the water and instituted the millennia of the "Golden" asatellic age.

The capture of Luna, according to these scientists, affected the earth's atmosphere, hydrosphere and lithosphere—its air, water and rock structure. The gravitational pull rearranged the earth's atmosphere, drawing away great quantities of the air coat from the polar and temperate zones, piling them so high in an equatorial ring that a good deal of it escaped, and was lost to the earth. "The air blanket," says Bellamy, "having thus become threadbare at the poles and in the higher altitudes, it was no longer able to protect these regions from spatial cold. Quite suddenly, certainly in a matter of weeks, extreme 'arctic' conditions began to prevail in those areas: the great Klimasturz, the catastrophic climatic breakdown, had come about."

As for the waters, says Bellamy, the gravitational pull of the new satellite drew the terrestrial oceans more toward the tropics which resulted in the submergence of extensive land areas. The result was a sudden flood which buried whole continents and changed the outline of those which remained. Rivers were diverted, ancient lakes disappeared, new ones formed.

Bellamy's description has the ring of an epic saga.

The greatest continental catastrophe, says he, was the sudden draining of the Mongolian Sea. "This gigantic inland sea, a landlocked ocean almost of greater area probably than the Mediterranean and certainly of much greater volume, once filled most of that remarkable, vast depression in the interior of the Mongolian Plateau. Where now the sand-waves of Han-han, the Dry Sea, the marvelously plastic Chinese name of the Desert of Gobi or Shamo, slowly wander, there rolled once the wide waters of this Mediasiatic Sea. The richly sculptured coast of this huge expanse of water was the home of a teeming population of many nations, that lived in abundance in an almost subtropical paradise enjoying an equable climate. There lay one of the 'Cradles of Mankind.'

"At the advent of our present Moon this paradise was lost.

"The capture deformations laid a broad breach in the western dam of this Mediasiatic Sea, the Khaptagai Mountains, situated between the Tian Shan and the Altai systems. Then its waves surged out in a mighty flood between the Dzungarian Alatau and the Jair and Barluk (Orkochuk) Ranges. A bankless river of unimaginable dimensions, soon thirty miles and more broad at its 'source,' 4000 feet or more deep, rushed down into the western lowlands, with terrific speed. If we connect the lakes of Turkestan—Telli-nor, Ebi-nor, Ala-kul, Sasyk-kul—with Lake Balkhash, we have traced the 'channel' of this deluge-river very fairly. In the Balkhash region the waters of the Asiatic deluge expanded into the dimensions of a sea, which reached from the northern ranges of the Celestial Mountains into Siberia. Then the way to the west was found and this Sea of Turkestan drained down into the Aralo-Caspian depression. Over the Famine Steppe the waters reached the Aral Basin. The southern spurs of the Ural Mountains and the northern chains of the Iranian system narrowed the vast sheet of water and caused it to flow west with a great volume and vehemence. The Caspian depression was now filled up, with the Ust-Urt Plateau as an island, probably. Then the waters found their way farther west through the Manych Depression down into the lower Don valley, the Sea of Azov, and the Black Sea. Again the waters were dammed up, till the Bosporus-Marmora-Dardanelles gate was forced and the Mediterranean valley was filled.

"The Mediterranean was not in existence at that time. In its place there were a number of small seas or huge lakes, probably three. The easternmost was the Levantine Sea, which, above all, the River Nile drained. The central basin was filled with the Ionian Sea into which the 'Adriatic River' flowed. The Balearic Sea was the farthest west and was chiefly fed by the Rhone.

"When the Mongolian waters found their way beyond the Bosporus they swept down into the Aegean valleys, and submerged all the land, except the mountain tops. Thus the 'Archipelago' (the broad-cast islands of the Aegean; the 'Kingdom of the Sea,' as its literal translation is) was formed as the Levantine Sea filled up. Then the waters flowed over into the Ionian Sea and rose considerably, hindered from a further westward spread by the Sicily-Malta-Tunis-Tripoli bar; in addition the valley of the Adriatic swallowed up a considerable volume of water. The ancient and high civilizations which fringed the Levantine-Ionian basins then met their doom. Only a small percentage of the inhabitants of those regions survived. . . ."

Bellamy then traces the flow of waters past the Pillars of Hercules into the Atlantic. With the capture of Luna, he says, Atlantis met its sudden end; Lemuria—the land of which Easter Island is the lone and enigmatic remainder—was lost beneath the sea.

In the vast basin of what is now the Mediterranean whole peoples were wiped out.

All over the earth there was a great setback in progress and culture, and everywhere man retrogressed, says Bellamy, often to the toolless state.

Whatever the historical truth may be, there seems to be no tribe that does not remember a great water catastrophe in its distant past.

To Bellamy these cosmic myths are faithful reports of actual events which happened, "at the beginning of things."

According to the Book of Enoch the axis of the earth was tilted at the time of the Flood. "In those days Noah saw that the earth became inclined, and that destruction approached." According to one of the Jewish myths all the trees of the Garden of Eden which had been evergreen before, shed their leaves from the day "the serpent successfully tempted Eve."

All peoples, says Bellamy, consider the Flood as the most important event in memory, forming so definite a caesura in the course of their existence as a community that most of them record their "Beginnings" from the time of the Deluge.

During the Golden Age, says Bellamy, man was a comparatively leisurely gatherer of abundantly growing semi-tropical fruit. He was forced to become a hardworking laborer only after Luna had made her devastating influence felt on earth, "wrenching poor harvests in the sweat of his face from a soil that had become stubborn."

The rich tropical plants of the "garden," says Bellamy, perished from the cold, dying as if the ground had been cursed; whereas the weeds, ever hardy and resourceful, continued to flourish, and "thorns and thistles" grew everywhere. Instead of the sweet luscious fruits, the only food now available was the herb of the field, which, according to Daniel, "the starving people devoured like oxen."

"They sought for food everywhere," it reads in the fourth chapter of the book of Adam and Eve. For nine days they roamed about, but they found no such food as they had eaten in "paradise."

It was then, says Bellamy, that men started to eat meat.

In an equable warm climate where plenty of easily gatherable plant food was available, man was naturally a vegetarian as in Genesis 1:29: ". . . every tree, in the which is the fruit of a tree yielding seed; to you it shall be for meat." But with the sudden cold and roaming for food, more calories, says Bellamy, became peremptory, and the solution was found in animal food.

It was then, says he, that fires were lit both for warmth and to propitiate the gods for the sacrilege of eating one's fellow creatures, animal, and possibly human.

As clothes had become essential with the sudden cold, animals served the dual role of both food and clothing; fires a dual role—for cooking and keeping warm.

With the arrival of the first serious winter, men might well have wondered if the sun would ever return.

What rejoicings there must have been after the first winter solstice when the sun appeared to move slowly back onto its warm, generative course.

Certainly, in a world depleted of human beings, of animals, and of a once plentiful supply of food, who can wonder at religious ceremonies of an orgiastic promiscuous nature, designed, by the most expedient of methods, to replenish the world, and as quickly as possible.

Such was the emergency that even Methodius, that early Father of the Church who is most rapturous in his praise of virginity and sexual purity, considered promiscuous intercourse and even incest permissible in order to replenish the planet. Not till the world was again "overflowing with countless numbers" did he consider that God took thought "how men might make progress and advance further on the road to heaven" by espousing the "science of virginity." To Methodius the proper progression was from incestuous intercourse, to marrying wives from other families, to the abandonment of multiple marriage "as though men were born merely for intercourse," to the abandonment of adultery, to an advance into continence, and, finally, to virginity and a state in which men and women "train themselves to despise the flesh and come to anchor unafraid in the peaceful heaven of immortality." But that is getting ahead of the story.

The Book of Genesis, according to Bellamy, does not tell the story of Creation, but of Re-Creation, and has only been turned to the former purpose partly by a redactor, or group of redactors, "but chiefly by illiterate or squeamish commentators or expositors."

The account of the Deluge, says Bellamy, should preceed the story of Creation, and part of the myth of Lot even that of the Deluge.

It is Bellamy's contention that parts of the Book of Genesis describe not Creation, but the reorganization of life on this planet after the cataclysm known as the Deluge —a contention supported by many another scholar.

The first eleven chapters of Genesis are, as Bellamy points out, readily separable from the rest of the book by their mythological tenor.

The mythological material which really counts in the third chapter of Genesis is that which describes a certain profound and sudden physical change which took place in our world. Such physical change—he and several other eminent scientists believe—could be brought about only by an extraterrestrial influence: not through phenomena within the earth, nor divine, nor human agency.

The Book of Revelation, called "the despair of theology" and the "nightmare of the exegete," contains, according to Bellamy, a magnificent series of powerful mythological reports of two great cosmic and terrestrial convolutions: the breakup of our former satellite, and the capture of the present satellite, Luna, at the end of an asatellic Golden Age.

Bellamy also draws a fantastic and fascinating picture

in very great detail of the various phenomena that accompanied this postulated capture of Luna.

For one thing, immediately after the capture, he theorizes on the basis of Hoerbiger that the new satellite developed a long tail of ice particles which followed it in its whirling course around the earth, much in the shape of a great tailed dragon.

From this he deduces the myths of the Great Cosmic serpent, though, as will be seen from Velikovsky's works, this appears to be but one of several.

With the tilting of the earth's axis, says Bellamy, the panoply of stars was shaken and left askew, and Luna, as an apple hanging on the tree of heaven, falling toward earth, would be "a most graphic description of the optic impression which was gained by the witness of the sudden approach of the planet Luna."

It is practically certain, says Bellamy, that John did not understand the true meaning of the myths he used; however, his treatment of the material "shows he was fully aware they constituted sacred traditions handed down from remote times. He neither added nor took away from that which came to his hand and he sends forth the work he has compiled, beseeching future generations to rival him in his reverence and care."

Certainly the arrival of such a powerful cosmic being as the moon, claiming half the heaven as its domain, "The mysterious night with its hosts of stars, during which the sun is quite powerless" would have had the greatest effect on the minds and imaginations of human beings alive at the time.

Worship of the moon as such would be likely to date from its arrival, though, depending on its previous orbit and behavior, it might already have been venerated along with other planets. But why "venerated" and not "lunarated"?

Bellamy suggests that the rise of the usurping moon-god or goddess would have excited the jealousy of the sun-god or its worshipers "or at least of his priests." And he adduces the lines in Revelation to this effect. "If any man worship the beast and his image, and receive his mark on his forehead or his hand, the same shall drink of the wine of the wrath of God. . . ."

What worship would the capture of the moon have displaced or altered? The available data on antediluvians indicate they were monotheistic worshipers of one god symbolized by a solar orb, and that they brought as offerings, not human or animal sacrifices, but fruit and flowers.

Interestingly enough, Bellamy suggests that at the disintegration of the previous satellite, eons earlier, the worshipers of that satellite, as opposed to worshipers of the sun—respectively shore dwellers and mountain dwellers—had marks tattooed on their hands and foreheads. The custom is indeed very ancient on this planet.

The initiates of Attis, says Bellamy, bore distinctive tattoo-marks on their foreheads, made with glowing needles; though their form, says he, was unknown. Lucian, in his De Dea Syria says it was the universal practice at Hierapolis to make punctures in honor of the gods, some in their hands, others in the neck; "and hence it is that all the Assyrians are marked in that manner." In the Etymologicum Magnum it says that the evergreen pine was sacred to Attis and that his eunuch priests were tattooed with "the ivy leaves sacred to Dionysus." And ivy, says Frazer, was sacred to Osiris because it was always green.

For those interested in tracing the history on this planet of the satellites previous to Luna, some of which are said to have become fixed—one of them over what is now Abyssinia, causing the great rift valley—and eventually disintegrated, changing the face of the earth, suddenly trapping and fossilizing all kinds of vegetation, animal and human remains, Mr. Bellamy has produced a variety of books, all of them eminently readable: *In the Beginning God; The Book of Revelation Is History; Man, Moon and Myths; A Life History of Our Earth;* and *Built Before the Flood*, the latter a fascinating exposition (in conjunction with Hoerbiger's theory) of the great calendar at Tiahuanaco in the Andes which he recently followed by a more detailed second volume.

"Myths," says Bellamy, agreeing with the Abbé Banier, "are history in disguise." The realm of mythology is not fableland. Myths, says he, are primeval lore, holy lore, the "science" of unknown, unsuspected forefathers living in the dark days far beyond our earliest history.

The cosmogonic myths of the Bible, and of all peoples, says Bellamy, are the traditionally handed-down reports of eyewitnesses concerning happenings in the remote past.

With this last conceit no one would be likely to agree more than Immanuel Velikovsky, a man much maligned for his painstaking research in the field, and who, with two of his main theories, brings much additional material to the subject of a heavenly castration.

12
HEAVENLY BODIES

If Ishtar were the moon and Tammuz the sun, as so many mythologists have claimed, the arrival of the moon, the tilting of the earth's axis, the loss of the equable climate of the golden age, the banishment of the castrated sun to the lower world for half the year, would all be fitting analogy.

A tendency to propitiate such a divinity as the Moon would not be very surprising; at springtime her wedding with the resurrected sun would be a joyous festival; and orgies of promiscuous intercourse in a depopulated world would become the most sensible and proper sort of rite.

But why—just because the sun was castrated—would a priest be required to do likewise?

Would the earth really refuse to bring forth without the spilled blood or the bleeding phallus of the king-priest?

Why was Noah, the prototype of flood survivors, castrated in the scriptures? And why the repeated association of Noah with Saturn?

Might there be a key to all of this in the very act of "veneration"?

Shifting from Bellamy's postulated rape of the moon, to the earth's intercourse with Venus, as described by Velikovsky, we again hear of cosmic battles, of the earth being deluged with water, scorched by fire, bombarded by celestial matter, knocked from its regular orbit, plagued by vermin; again mountains are pushed up, continents submerged, polar icecaps melted, temperate zones covered with layers of ice; this time the sun, accompanied by the moon, is said to stand still, the planets and stars to move backwards in their courses!

According to Velikovsky, about the middle of the second millennium before our era, what is now the planet Venus, having sprung from Jupiter in the form of a comet, whirled off in an elliptical orbit round the sun, bore down on the earth, entangled its tail in our planet, shot off once more, returned again in about fifty years.

The picture Velikovsky paints of these events is as broad and bold as if Rubens had been let loose with a Mitchell camera.

On a colossal screen he unrolls a saga of hurricanes of global magnitude, of forests burning and swept away, of dust, stones, fire, and ashes falling from the sky, of mountains melting like wax, of lava flowing from riven ground, of boiling seas, of bituminous rain, of shaking ground and destroyed cities, of humans seeking refuge in caverns and fissures of the rock in the mountains—all curiously sacred to Venus! —of oceans upheaved and falling on the land, of tidal waves moving toward the poles and back, of land becoming sea by submersion and the expanse of sea turning into desert, islands born and others drowned, mountain ridges leveled and others rising, of crowds of rivers seeking new beds, of sources that disappeared and others that became bitter, of great destructions of the animal kingdom, of decimated mankind, of migrations, of heavy clouds of dust covering the face of the earth for decades, of magnetic disturbances, of changed climates, of displaced cardinal points and altered latitudes, of disrupted calendars, and of sundials and water clocks that point to changed length of day, month, and year, of a new polar star.

If this *was* seen by an eyewitness on earth the heavenly pageant which brought it about must indeed have taken on the aspect of a gigantic battle. Sure enough, mythology tells of just such a battle between an evil monster in the form of a serpent, and a light god—who engaged the monster and saved the world.

Descriptions of the battle between Zeus and Typhon follow the same pattern and have the same details as the battle between Marduk and Tiamat the dragon, between Isis and Seth, Vishnu and the serpent, Krishna and the serpent, Ormuzd and Ahriman, even of the Archangel Michael and the fallen angel Lucifer.

These postulated events even found their way into history.

Pliny, in his *Natural History* says: "A terrible comet was seen by the people of Ethiopia and Egypt, to which Typhon, the king of that period, gave his name; it had a fiery appearance and was twisted like a coil, and it was very grim to behold: it was not really a star so much as what might be called a ball of fire."

In Apollodorus' tale, Typhon "out-topped all the mountains, and his head often brushed the stars. One of his hands reached out to the west and the other to the east, and from them projected a hundred dragons' heads. From the thighs downward he had huge coils of vipers which . . . emitted a long hissing. . . . His body was all winged . . . and fire flashed from his eyes. Such and so great was Typhon; when, hurling kindled rocks, he made for the very heaven with hissing and shouts, spouting a great jet of fire from his mouth. . . ."

One of the first visible signs of the encounter with the comet, says Velikovsky, was a reddening of the earth's surface by a fine dust of rusty pigment. "In sea, lake, and river, this pigment gave a bloody coloring to the water."

Apollodorus relates the tradition of the Thracians that the summit of mountainous Thrace was called "Haemus" because of the "stream of blood which gushed out of the mountain," when the heavenly battle was fought between Zeus and Typhon, when Typhon, cut at close quarters by an adamantine sickle, was struck down by a thunderbolt.

It is really nothing but chance that at the spring festival when the Galli castrated themselves, the river Sangrarius (whether through their efforts or some natural phenomenon) was said to run blood red—an event associated with the great castration of Attis? A castration which is said to have taken place with a sickle at the hands of a wild and heavenly boar, and Typhon is the equivalent of boar!

According to Velikovsky, after the first brush and after an interval of about six weeks, the comet again approached the earth, this time shrouded in a dark column of gases like a pillar of smoke by day and like fire by night. At this conjunction, says Velikovsky, the earth passed through the comet at the neck, with the result that violent electrical charges shot between the atmosphere of the tail and the terrestrial atmosphere.

Great discharges of interplanetary force are commemorated in the traditions, legends and mythology of all people on this planet.

The Zeus of the Greeks, the Odin of the Icelanders, the Ukko of the Finns, the Perun of the Russian pagans, the Wotan of the Germans, the Mazda of the Persians, the Marduk of the Babylonians, the Shiva of the Hindus, are all pictured with lightning in their hands and described as the god "who threw his thunderbolt at a world overwhelmed with water and fire."

Emerging from the struggle, says Velikovsky, the earth seems to have changed the direction of its rotation, to have had its orbit removed farther from the sun and its polar regions displaced. With the axis on which the earth rotates now pointed in a different direction, the seasons would have changed, calendars would have had to be modified.

Of this too there is corroborative evidence in mythology.

American Indians, and Polynesians too, say the sky was pushed up, the weather changed, and the sun, after being stopped on its way across the firmament "became small, and small it remained. . . ."

In a narrative of the Pawnee Indians it was the planet Venus which established the present order on the earth and placed the north and south polar stars in their present position.

In the Pacific Islands, Eskimos tell of the birth of the planet Venus, that a blazing star disrupted the visible movement of the sun, caused a world conflagration, and became the Morning-Evening Star.

In the mythologies of all peoples it is the planet Venus which is born, not Jupiter or Mars or Saturn.

In Greece, says Velikovsky, the goddess who suddenly appeared in the sky was Pallas Athene, who sprang from the head of Zeus-Jupiter. In another legend she was the daughter of the monster Pallas-Typhon who attacked her and whom she battled and killed. The relation between Typhon and the modern typhoon needs no etymological elaboration.

It was to Athene, "the glorious goddess, virgin, Tritogeneia" that Homer dedicated his hymns. When she was born the sky was said to "reel horribly . . . the earth roundabout cried fearfully . . . the sea was removed and tossed with dark waves, while foam burst forth suddenly, and the sun stood still for a while."

Throughout the Aegean the story of Phaëton tells how the son of Helios yoked his father's chariot, but because he was unable to drive it burned up all that was on the earth and perished by a thunderbolt.

Phaëton—"the blazing one" according to Hesiod—became the Morning Star.

Pythagoras taught that Venus was a planet that had been a comet.

Plato, on the authority of Egyptian sages, pointed to the planets as the cause of periodic catastrophes, and ascribed the deluge and its concomitant conflagration of the world to the action of a celestial body which, changing its path, passed close to the earth.

In mythologies the world over it is Isis, Ishtar, Astarte or the Great Mother who is said to have been responsible for the Deluge and to have saved a remnant of mankind.

Augustine quotes Varro to the effect that Venus, called Vesperugo by Plautus, changed its color, size, shape and course, which never happened before or since.

According to C. Bezold, Ishtar was at first considered a male planet, and only subsequently female.

Most interesting of all, Velikovsky says that in early times Ishtar was definitely the Assyrian-Babylonian name for the planet Jupiter, but was later transferred to Venus, while Jupiter retained the name Marduk.

Could Jupiter's changing into Venus afford the simplest explanation of her priests unmanning themselves and putting on female garb? And what of the extraordinary portrayal of Jupiter as androgynous?

Baal, in the male form, and Belith in the female, which became the name of the planet Venus, had previously been applied to Jupiter, and earlier still apparently to Saturn.

Venus had been called "the star that joins the great stars" and "the far-darting one."

It was in its orbit as a comet, and not yet a planet, that Venus was the "far-darting."

For about eight centuries, says Velikovsky, Venus, as a comet, traveled in a wide and irregular elliptic around the sun. During this period it appeared to have a tail, or hair, or to be on fire.

In the Vedas it says that Venus looked like fire with smoke. The Talmud says "Fire is hanging from the planet Venus."

By the Chaldeans Venus was said to have a beard—and was thus incongruously sculpted.

The Mexicans called Venus a "smoking star" or the star with the "mane"; their ancient records tell of a snakelike body being transformed into a great star, with the name Quetzalcoatl, or Venus. When the Spaniards arrived they reported the natives still held Venus in great veneration and that "so exact was the book-record of the day when it appeared and when it concealed itself, that they never made any mistakes."

Peruvians called Venus the "wavy-haired." The Incas of Peru and the Mayas and Toltecs of central America all observed the synodical revolution of Venus in which five Venus years equaled eight solar years.

Mexican texts also preserve the tradition that fifty years separated two great catastrophes attributable to Venus.

Every half century, according to these legends, the people would congregate to await the repetition of the approach of Venus: "When the night of this ceremony arrived all the people were seized with fear and anxiety."

Afraid the sun might never rise again, "they watched for the appearance of the planet Venus, and when on the feared day no catastrophe occurred, the people of Maya rejoiced. They brought human sacrifices and offered the hearts of prisoners to the fearful crowds, thankful that a new period of grace had been granted and a new Venus cycle had started."

Thereafter, says Velikovsky, so long as Venus returned at regular intervals, fear of the planet was kept within bounds. But when Venus began to move irregularly, fear grew intense.

The fifty-two-year period was related to Venus by both Mayas and Aztecs. According to G. A. Dorsey, the old Mexican custom of sacrificing to the Morning Star survived in human sacrifices of the Skide Pawnee of Nebraska in years when the Morning Star "appeared especially bright, or in years when there was a comet in the sky."

In Polynesia, up till very recently, human sacrifices were offered to Venus, the Morning Star.

In modern times the Arabs still sacrificed boys and girls to the Morning Star; and even today, according to Julius Wellhausen, Arabs seek the aid of Venus.

In the Syrian city of Ugarit, according to C. Virolleaud, a poem was recently found dedicated to the planet-goddess Anat "who massacred the population of the Levant and who exchanged dawns and the position of the stars."

Velikovsky considers the earlier catastrophe—our brush with Venus—coincident to the time of the Exodus.

In his book *Ages in Chaos* he goes into detail of the grave and ominous signs which preceded the Exodus—clouds which darkened the sky, dust which tore wounds in the skin, plagues of vermin and reptiles, swarms of locusts, hailstones and blasts of cinders—fitting them in with the data available from other sources.

When the Israelites, pursued by the army of the Egyptians, were trapped between mountains and the sea, amidst dreadful hurricanes, and a cleft appeared in the waters, Velikovsky surmises that it was the then comet Venus, passing by the earth, which first held the waters high, then, with a discharge of electricity, let the waters fall back, sweeping the Egyptians to their doom.

By the time of the second encounter with the comet, about six weeks later, the surviving fugitives, according to Velikovsky, were on Mt. Sinai. During the years in the wilderness the sun appears to have been clouded and the earth covered in darkness. According to Midrashic literature the sun and moon were only seen by the survivors at the end of forty years' wandering.

According to the Iranian book of Bundahish, "the blight was diffused over the vegetation, and it withered away."

In the traditions of other peoples it is told that "when the sky was shattered, the day became dark, and the earth teemed with noxious creatures. For a long time there was no green thing seen; seeds would not germinate in a sunless world, and it took many years for the earth to bring forth vegetation."

Is this not reminiscent of the mourning for Ishtar when the earth's generative powers were impaired?

During Ishtar's search for Tammuz in the underworld it is told that a terrible depression and despair fell upon the earth: during her absence nothing could be conceived: neither man nor beast nor plants nor trees could propagate, and, worse, "did not seem to want to." As recorded in one hymn: "The bull mounted not the cow, the ass impregnated not the she-ass, the strong man impregnated not the maid in the highway . . ."

According to American sources, the regeneration of the world took place under a veil of gloomy shadows which lasted the better part of a whole generation.

Conversely, in relation to the biblical data of pestilence and horrors, Velikovsky has a fascinating theory that the internal heat developed by the earth and by the scorching gases of the passing comet may have been cause enough for the sudden propagation of vermin on earth at a feverish rate; he believes that some of the plagues, like that of the frogs and the locusts may be ascribable to such causes.

Anyone in North America who has seen a sudden cloud of black flies materialize in late October just because the temperature has risen to 100° will not find this hard to believe.

Velikovsky adds that when a hot, electrically charged sirocco blows from the African desert, villages begin to teem with vermin, and he believes that a change in atmospheric conditions can cause galloping germination among insects.

The question arises, says Velikovsky, whether the comet Venus may have infested the earth with vermin carried in its trailing atmosphere in the form of larvae together with stones and gases. It is significant, says he, that all around the world peoples have associated the planet Venus with flies (and their lord Beelzebub) and that Venus is the reputed home of both bees and ants.

The ability of many small insects and their larvae to endure great cold and heat and live in an atmosphere devoid of oxygen renders not entirely improbable the hypothesis, says Velikovsky, that Venus, and also Jupiter, from which Venus sprang, may be populated with vermin!

Is it just chance, one might ask—though Velikovsky avoids the subject—that venereal disease is attributed to Venus? Was circumcision practiced because it was considered a help in preventing the spread of venereal disease? Or was it the spread of venery?

What accounts for the extraordinary practice of "castrating," not only males but females—and in a manner far more brutal than anything practiced by the Skoptsi?

What primordial power could motivate old men in Australia to prepare a long roll of emu feathers with a loop of hair at the end, thrust it into the vagina of a young girl, leave it there for several days, then pull it out, tearing away a great part of the womb, after which what remained of it was cut horizontally and vertically with a small stone knife? This to be followed, as soon as the wound was healed, by a form of female circumcision, after which the girl was turned over for compulsory intercourse with a number of young men, the resultant bloody semen being collected and drunk by feeble tribesmen as a strength-giving tonic!

And what could be more elaborate than the system of female circumcision practiced by the inhabitants of Rio-Real and D'Andra who, having plugged the vagina with a piece of wood, placed a colony of ants on the vulva of young girls "till they had devoured the clitoris, the small lips and the soft part of the large ones."

Yet such are the details given by anthropologists, who describe the resulting girls as anomalous hermaphrodites having only slightly developed lips, breasts and *mons veneris*, and with some hairs growing on the chin.

Could Aphrodite—or the comet Venus—in a hot embrace with Terra, so madden humans that they were forced to extirpate their organs?

William Whiston, the English mathematician and theologian, who was a deputy to Isaac Newton, not only propounded the idea that the earth had been created from the atmosphere of a comet, but fancied that it had been deluged by the tail of another.

Heat, thought Whiston, so excited the whole antediluvian population, men and animals alike, to "sin," that they were all drowned in the deluge, excepting fish "whose passions were apparently less violent."

If Dr. Wilhelm Reich's theories of "heavenly superimposition" are applied to such a circumstance as the mating of Venus and Earth the amount of "orgone" energy generated in the air could well have made the fleshly lustings of St. Jerome pale to insignificance, or, in the favorite phrase of the Chilean metaphysical painter Matta—blown everybody's fuses!

But this is getting away from Velikovsky. The other phenomena of procreation that may have resulted from the intercourse of earth with Venus are of greater importance still.

Indian tales indicate that these cosmic events resulted not only in a change in the order of celestial bodies, but in extraordinary changes among animals—along the order of mutations.

Ovid, incidentally, says that it was thought that the people of Ethiopia had become black-skinned at this time because the blood was drawn to the surface of their bodies by the heat.

On this subject Dr. Velikovsky points out that during the last war in the bomb craters of London, new plants not previously known on the British Isles, "and possibly not known anywhere," were seen to sprout. From this he surmises that the thermal action of bomb explosions could be the cause of multiple metamorphoses in the genes of seeds and pollens.

To this he adds as evidence the results of the experiments of H. J. Muller, who, by subjecting the vinegar fly to X-rays, found that some chemicals at temperatures close to the limits that the insect organisms could endure, acted as mutation-provoking agents. Thus, says Velikovsky, the numerous catastrophes and bursts of effective radiation which have taken place in the past on this planet might have been the cause of radical changes in living forms on earth; many mutations simultaneously or in quick succession, says he, could have been capable of transforming an animal or plant into a new species—such as recorded by fossils embedded in lava.

From this it follows that increased radioactivity coming from outside the planet, or from the bowels of the earth, could be the cause of spontaneous origin of new species. The effect, says Velikovsky, of an interplanetary charge between the earth and another celestial body such as a planet, or planetoid, a trail of meteorites, or a charged cloud of gases, with possibly billions of volts of potential difference and nuclear fission or fusion, would be similar to that of an explosion of many hydrogen bombs with ensuing procreation of monstrosities and growth anomalies on a large scale.

One fascinating theory of Velikovsky's is his explanation of a phenomenon described in the Bible which has had me puzzled since Sunday school: the nature of manna.

According to the Old Testament, the Children of Israel wandering in the wilderness subsisted on a substance with an oily consistency and the taste of honey which fell from heaven, was found on the ground "like hoar-frost" by man and beast, was ground between stones and baked in pans into bread, and which, according to Haggadic literature, fell in such quantity every day that it could "nourish the people for two thousand years." A few hours after daybreak the heat was said to liquefy the grains of manna and volatilize them.

What on earth was this manna?

In Velikovsky's theory the tail of Venus contained great quantities of carbon and hydrogen in suspension which the earth captured when it passed through the tail, and that just as when the air is overcharged with vapor it causes rain, snow, hail or dew to come down, so particles of hydrocarbon descended onto the earth in the cool of the night. It came, says Velikovsky, in the shape of coriander seed, with the yellowish color of bdellium and the oily taste of a honeycomb.

As the Italians say: *"Se non è vero è ben trovato!"*

To support the biblical evidence Velikovsky adduces an Icelandic tradition which tells of a dark winter which endured many years when nothing would bud and when the morning dew served as food, and Greek mythology in which Hera, the earth, was veiled with ambrosia, the heavenly food, when she hurried from Mars to Jupiter.

So much for the effect of Venus on the earth. If the theories are true, is it any wonder that Sabian worship of the heavenly bodies should have been so widespread on this planet?

Velikovsky says there is no doubt that in both Judea and Israel planetary cult was the official cult of the priests and kings, and many of the prophets and of the people, too, at least till the eighth century, when a more spiritual monotheism seems to have developed throughout the eastern Mediterranean.

But if for eight centuries—between 1500 and about 700 B.C. – Venus, an angelic-demonic heavenly power dominated the minds of men, what brought about the change?

In the middle of the eighth century B.C., says Velikovsky, another series of cosmic upheavals took place at short intervals; he singles out the year 747 B.C. for one of the major upheavals.

During all this commotion the axis of the earth was once more shifted and tilted. The sunset was hastened by several hours.

This time, from a comparison of Hebrew historical, Chinese astronomical, and Latin ecclesiastical material, Velikovsky deduces that a heavenly body passed very close to earth, moving in the same direction as earth on its nocturnal side.

As a result, the orbit of the year became wider, the seasons changed, stones fell from heaven, as did brimstone and pitch, the earth was scorched by blasts of fire, the sun was darkened.

The cause: our planet Mars, wandering off its course.

What made it wander?

In its greatly elongated orbit the comet Venus, says Velikovsky, got entangled with Mars, causing a series of events which are described in the Talmud and kept alive in the traditions of people all over the world. The conflict between Mars and Venus, says he, was a spectacle which fills the pages of the *Iliad,* and it is interesting that the erudite Lucian should claim that it was the conjunction of Venus and Mars which created the poetry of Homer. "All that he [Homer] hath said of Venus and Mars his passion, is also manifestly composed from no other source than this science [astrology]."

Venus, says Velikovsky, was at that time moving at a lower elliptical velocity than when it first encountered the earth eight centuries earlier; but Mars, being only one-eighth the mass of Venus, was no match for her. It was therefore a notable achievement, says he, that Mars, "though thrown out of the ring, nevertheless was instrumental in bringing Venus from an elliptical to a nearly circular orbit. Looked at from the Earth, Venus was removed from a path that ran high to the zenith and over the zenith, to its present path in which it never retreats from the sun more than 48 hours."

Venus became a morning and an evening star that precedes the rising sun or follows the setting sun.

Up till then Venus still had a tail, considerably shortened since the time she was a comet, but still long enough to give the impression of a hanging flame, or smoke, or attached hair.

When Mars clashed with Venus, says Velikovsky, asteroids, meteorites, and gases were torn from this trailing part, and began a semi-independent existence, some following the orbit of Mars, some other paths.

The zodiacal light, or glow seen in the evening sky after sunset, stretching in the path of the sun and the planets, the mysterious origin of which has for a long time occupied the minds of astronomers, says Velikovsky, has been explained in recent years as the reflection of the solar light from two rings of dust particles, one following the orbit of Venus, the other an orbit between Mars and Jupiter, places where collisions of planets and a comet took place.

Nearly a century ago R. Proctor ascribed the origin of the so-called Jovian family of comets to eruptions from Jupiter, saying that "the near collision between major planets brought about the birth of comets," and N. Bobrovnikoff of the Perkins Observatory offered as an explanation of the origin of the asteroids that they were "remnants of a gigantic prehistoric comet." F. Whipple, calculating the orbits of asteroids, came to the conclusion that two collisions had occurred between these bodies and a comet, one 4700 years ago, and the second 1500 years ago.

Was there, at some earlier time, another comet or planet whose presence or disappearance could help unravel the telescoped mythology?

Was it in this struggle that Venus changed its sex, lost its queue?

Could the struggle of heavenly bodies have had the appearance on earth of a truly heavenly *hieros gamos* of entwined twisting powers in the throes of a great creative concourse? Or has this to do with an earlier event in which the myth and ritual of Venus and Adonis have their origin?

The sights which accompanied the most recent of these celestial spectacles must have been vividly etched on the minds of terrestrial viewers.

As Velikovsky recreates them, swarms of meteorites with their gaseous appendages flying in bands and taking various shapes made an uncanny impression. According to his estimates, they also ran along different orbits, grew quickly from small to giant size, and terrorized the peoples of earth. Such phenomena could at last explain the universal picture of witches flying through the air on broomsticks.

When, soon after the impact of Venus and Mars, says Velikovsky, Mars began to threaten the earth, the new comets, running very close to the earth must have added new terror, continually recalling the hour of peril.

Comets, says Velikovsky, just beginning to whirl, looked like revolving torches or writhing snakes; they assumed the form of spinning wheels, changing their forms they looked like horses racing along the sky, and again "like a host of warriors leaping, climbing, irresistible."

At last a glimmer as to the possible nature of the four horsemen of the Apocalypse!

Could this not explain Athene's shield with its paralyzing snakes? Tie in with the description of a sacrificial victim being stung by giant rays so as to be alive but petrified at the moment his heart was torn out.

Can any reader of mythology escape the obvious analogies?

Fantastic figures on the sky, chariots, running horses, marching warriors, the trembling earth, the reeling firmament, were not only visualized, says Velikovsky, but felt and feared all over the world.

It was no local display, but a display of cosmic forces in cosmic dimensions, as the "dreadful figures" scattered a hail of meteorites that bombarded walls with hot gravel turning cities into heaps of ruins.

But since the latter part of the eighth century B.C., according to these calculations, Venus has followed an orbit between Mercury and Earth, which it has maintained ever since: "the wild and dreaded comet became the regular and respectable planet Venus, the Morning and the Evening Star."

It was, says Velikovsky, the demise of this earlier heavenly force, which for eight centuries had kept terror alive on the planet, that inspired Isaiah to exclaim:

"How art thou fallen from heaven, O Lucifer, son of the morning! How art thou cut down to the ground, which didst weaken the nations."

To which Velikovsky adds that in both the Septuagint and the Vulgate, the Morning Star is translated as Lucifer.

As Venus had been the St. Michael of the Israelites who saved them at the time of the Passover, eight centuries later it was to be the Archangel Gabriel, in the form of the planet Mars, who was to save them by scorching to death their Assyrian enemies.

Among the wealth of evidence to support his dating the

two cataclysms at the time of Exodus and Isaiah, Velikovsky found that early Babylonian astronomy counted only four visible planets, excluding Venus, that in Hindu tables of the planets attributed to the year 3102 B.C. Venus was not shown.

More indicative still were various changes in ancient calendars necessitated by change in the celestial order.

For the period from about 1500 to 800 B.C. when Velikovsky says Venus was a comet, he has found all sorts of evidence to show that the earth had a year of 360 days divided into twelve lunar months of an even 30 days.

The Hindus, who were admittedly very ingenious in their geometric reckoning, had a year of 360 days thus evenly divided. They could not, says Velikovsky, have missed 5¼ extra days in a year. In fact, about the seventh century B.C., the Hindu year became 365¼ days long.

The Persians too added five days in the seventh century. The Babylonian year of 360 days recorded in cuneiform script added five days in the seventh century. The Assyrians, till they changed their calendar, had a year of 360 days and decades called *sarus* of 3,600. Had the year been its present length, how could they have accounted for an extra 54 days every decade?

The Egyptians officially added five days to their 360 day year in 238 B.C.

Plutarch says that the Romans in the time of Romulus in the eighth century B.C. had a year of 360 days.

The Mayan year consisted of 360 days. Later five days were added, and every fourth year another day.

The same applies to South America and to China.

But that is not all. There is evidence that at some point in the eighth century B.C., before Venus settled into its present orbit, the moon was farther away and there were ten months of thirty-five to thirty-six days. The Hindus, Persians, Egyptians, Chinese, Romans, and the Homeric Greeks, left records of a nine day week in ten months of thirty-six days.

Furthermore, says Velikovsky, this was not the first time the phenomenon occurred; it had been the case in a very much earlier phase of the world's history.

A dramatic piece of evidence to support a sudden shift of the poles was the discovery in recent years of the carcasses of mammoths—a mammal of the elephant family with 10-foot tusks, extinct some thousands of years—so well preserved that the sledge dogs of the discoverers, and, I am told, at least one human being, were able to eat the flesh "fibrous and marbled with fat" without ill effect.

As an indication of the suddenness with which they were killed, between their teeth and in their stomachs, leaves and twigs were found. Had they not been frozen and plunged into subfreezing temperatures, thereafter to be encased in snow and ice, it is generally agreed they would long since have decomposed.

Though Velikovsky is uncertain as to whether they met their death in the days of Isaiah twenty-six hundred years ago, or in the days of Exodus eight hundred years earlier, he supposes them to have been asphyxiated or electrocuted, or killed by a tempest of gases which accompanied a sudden and spontaneous lack of oxygen caused by fires raging high in the atmosphere at the moment of a cataclysm which suddenly shifted the poles.

Another interesting corroboration of the shift is to be seen in the fact that the foundations of Mediterranean temples which were built before the seventh century no longer face east, whereas the ones built *after* the time face properly east, as did the Temple of Solomon.

But how does all this fit in with Venus and Adonis? with Cybele and Attis, with Isis and Osiris—with the Virgin and the Eunuch?

As late as 1960, Sir Alan Gardiner, the eminent Egyptologist, admitted that "the origin of Osiris remains for me an insoluble mystery."

As has been noted, ancient writers such as Macrobius and Diodorus Siculus designated Isis as the moon and Osiris as the sun. In modern times this view, says Frazer, has been held by so many distinguished writers—based largely on the grounds that the death of Osiris fits better with the solar phenomena than with any other in nature—that it deserves examination. Whereupon, with one short sentence, he proceeds to administer to it the *coup de grace:* "If we enquire on what evidence Osiris has been identified with the sun or the sun-god, it will be found on analysis to be minute in quantity and dubious, where it is not absolutely worthless, in quality."

Yet even Frazer tantalizingly skirts the answer, and does not clearly assign an identity to Isis and Osiris.

Now at last the great veil is about to be rent. To Velikovsky the identities of Isis and Osiris are no longer a mystery: to him their stories describe actual events in history, celestial happenings which affected mankind and the earth, a detailed description of which forms the central theme of the next two volumes of his *Ages in Chaos.*

In his maple-shaded, gray stone house, overlooking Princeton's Lake Carnegie, Dr. Velikovsky gave me a glimpse into the results of many, many years of research on the mysteries of Isis and Osiris neatly catalogued in dozens of large black binders.

To Velikovsky, Osiris, Attis, Tammuz, Adonis are the names of one and the same celestial body: the planet Saturn. To him Isis and her namesakes refer first to the planet Jupiter, then, after the comet Venus was extruded from its body, to this second planet.

Part of the confusion, says he, is attributable to the fact that observers themselves were uncertain what was happening in the sky, uncertain which of the erupting bodies was Jupiter and which was Venus, a confusion which led to different interpretations, to different descriptions in different parts of the world, and to different namings which resulted in arguments and fights.

But his sequence of events is basic, and at last with this research the identity of the dying, castrated and reviving god has a pattern into which it can now be neatly fitted. Hesiod's chronology turns out to be basically correct: as Saturn (or Cronus) castrated Uranus in the more distant past, Jupiter in turn castrated Saturn and usurped his place as the principal planetary power in the sky.

These are not whimsical conceits, but wondrous heavenly pageants which caused indelible caesuras in the ages of man.

According to Velikovsky, his descriptions of cataclysms in the first and second millennia B.C., which formed the substance of *Worlds in Collision*, merely scratched the surface.

The third, fourth and fifth millennia are full of catastrophes, says he, and they go a long way to unraveling the mysteries of mythology.

Meanwhile, a careful look at Frazer's wealth of material on the king-hero Saturn and the rituals and ceremonies of the Saturnalia commemorating a Saturnine age of plenty under the benign influence of Saturn provide the missing clue to the phenomenon of the earthly castration, putting to death and resurrection of the Dying God.

"When we remember," says Frazer, "that the liberty allowed to slaves at this festival season was supposed to be in imitation of the state of society in Saturn's time, and that in general the Saturnalia passed for nothing more or less than a temporary revival and restoration of the reign of that merry monarch, we are tempted to surmise that the mock king who presided over the revels may have originally represented Saturn himself."

And then: "Since the custom of putting a mock king to death as a representative of a god cannot have grown out of a practice of appointing him to preside over a holiday revel, whereas the reverse may very well have happened, we are justified in assuming that in an earlier and more barbarous age it was the universal practice in ancient Italy, wherever the worship of Saturn prevailed, to choose a man who played the part and enjoyed all the traditional privileges of Saturn for a season, and then died, whether by his own hand or another's hand, whether by the knife or the fire or on the gallows-tree, in the character of the good god who gave his life for the world."

At last, says Frazer, "the good god, the kindly king, vanished suddenly; but his memory was cherished to distant ages, shrines were reared in his honor, and many hills and high places in Italy bore his name. Yet the bright tradition of his reign was crossed by a dark shadow: his altars are said to have been stained with the blood of human victims, for whom a more merciful age afterwards substituted effigies."

In the end, of course, men grew to realize that the

planets and the moon, though spectacular in their heavenly antics and dreadful in their effect upon the earth, were, in fact, subsidiary bodies to the sun, the central power of this system on whom they depended, in whom they most likely had their origin, and to whom, in the end, they would return.

And beyond the solar system lay the nebulous world of the stars, the void of the cosmos, within it the void of the atom, in both of which a mysterious serpentine power seemed at play, and to deal with which even more fundamental symbols were required: the snake around the egg, the ovum and the sperm, energy and matter, the Pistis Sophia and the Logos, chaos and reason, the circle and the cross.

Beyond the complex of mythology—even when its symbols are arranged into a clear and simple story—and beyond the pageant of heavenly bodies, with whom, for better or for worse, we are so intimately linked, lurked another great drama to which the research that has gone before stands but as a proscenium.

Having traced the Eunuch and the Virgin into the mist and myth of the antediluvian world, the quest for the origin of castration now leads into the twilight of poetry and psychology, and beyond it, into the rarefied ether of the pneumatologist and mystic.

13
THE CRUX OF THE MATTER

If some twentieth-century scientist—with all the proper degrees, with years of academic training, years of testing in laboratories, a psychiatrist, sociologist, biologist, and physicist—were suddenly to proclaim the discovery of a hitherto unknown or unidentified form of energy, a non-nuclear, nonelectric, nonelectromagnetic, mass-free, all-pervasive cosmic energy, sun-radiated, present in the atmosphere, congealed into sand and earth, demonstrable visibly, thermically, electroscopically and with a Geiger-Mueller counter, do you think the world would listen to him?

Of course not. They'd laugh at him as they did at

Galileo, or lock him up, as they did Giordano Bruno, who, incidentally, had the same idea some centuries earlier.

Unfortunately it is now difficult to reproduce the experiments of such a scientist because of a Federal judge, who, in 1954, ordered his laboratory equipment dismantled, and the literature pertaining to his experiments destroyed—this in the sovereign state of Maine.

Luckily they haven't yet burned the Library of Congress, or put its books on the Index—though many a rare and important volume does somehow manage to disappear.

The scientist, a pupil of Freud by the name of Wilhelm Reich, might well have been "mad"—indeed that's what many once said of Freud—but how can one junk a man's lifework, without at least a glance at it, if only to re-establish the principle that one's reading, in this republic, cannot be done for one by "higher authority."

No matter how terrible were the experiments of Dr. Reich, or wild his claims, they did not cause any Hiroshimas or permanently stunted unborn children. His claim, indeed, was the very opposite: that he had discovered an energy which might well be capable of combating the toxic effects of nuclear fission, and of freeing man from centuries of stunting by neurosis.

This energy, to which Dr. Reich applied the name of Orgone, has some extraordinary yet hauntingly familiar attributes: filling a cosmic continuum, it obeys, as he describes it, a generally valid natural law; as freely moving energy it is transformed, by a process of slowing and cooling, into hardening matter; akin to fire it moves in snakelike undulations; in man, woman and beast it arouses sexuality; it is excited by the friction of coitus; it is a color from blue to bluish-gray—accounting for the blue in the sky, the blue in the ocean, the blue in thunder-clouds, and, when added to the resinous yellow of leaves, the green they become in springtime.

It is energy, says Reich, which is capable of charging nonconductive substances, such as wood.

Which was the divinity that lurked in wood? To whom was fire sacred? Who was the azure goddess?

There is more to come.

Plant chlorophyll, which is related to the iron-containing protein of animal blood, contains orgone, says Reich, which it takes directly from the atmosphere and the radiations of the sun. Red corpuscles, in Reich's experiments, at a magnification of over 2000X, showed a bluish glimmer; they are, says he, vesicles charged with orgone energy which they transport from the lungs to the body tissue. Strange, those ancient rites of drinking blood, which have survived to this day!

Living organisms, says Reich, contain orgone energy in every cell and keep charging themselves from the atmosphere by breathing. In the realm of living matter, orgone energy functions as "biological energy," as the energy of emotions, the later being, says he, manifestations of biological energy, something basically different from the sensations caused by electric shock, by X ray, or by electromagnetic fields, the last of which affects no more than radio.

In his experiments the movement of biological energy took the form of slow undulations, reminiscent of the movements of an intestine or a snake.

Is it just by chance that in the Mysteries of the ancients the serpent-symbol should have played such an impressive part?

It was, says Mead, the glyph of the creative power, and in its lowest form was debased into a phallic emblem.

Physical procreation and processes of conception, says he, are lower manifestations of the energizing of the creative will and the evolutionary world-process, "but the one is as far removed from the other, as man's body is from the body of the universe, as man's animal desire from the divine will or deity."

As the serpent was the glyph of the "Divine Will, the Divine Reason, the Mind of Deity, the Logos," says Mead, so the egg was "the Thought, the Conception, the Mother of All."

To the ancients the "germinal universe" was figured as a circle with a serpent lying diagonally along its field, or twined a certain number of times around it. "This serpentine force," says Mead, "fashioned the universe, and fashioned man. It created him; and yet he in his turn could use it for creation."

But here Mead parts from Reich. Reich makes no puritan distinction between anything but the life force and neurotic pornography. To him the sexual orgasm is a vital function of being. Mead is of the school of sexual sublimators. To Mead, man's greatest fling at creation comes only when he can *cease from generation*. In the flowery language of the Gnostics: "The Caduceus, or Rod of Mercury," says he, "and the Thyrsus in the Greek Mysteries, which conducted the soul from life to death, and from death to life, figured forth the serpentine power in man, and the path whereby it could carry the 'man' aloft to the height, if he would but 'cause the waters of the Jordan to flow upwards.' "

What a strange poetic wonder is this serpent, as much the glyph for sperm as for the wavelike power of cosmic, of atomic and of subatomic universes!

To Reich, the function of energy was the same in the

human being as in the sun: to him the energy which governs the growth of living substances, the movements of animals, and the movements of the heavenly bodies is one and the same. And the membranes of living matter, says he, are nothing but frozen orgone energy.

All gonad cells, says Reich, all protozoa, and cancer cells, consist of orgone-charged bluish energy vesicles; these bions, as he calls them—microscopic vesicles produced from organic and inorganic material by a process of disintegration and swelling—he claims to have produced in the laboratory, by heating and swelling particles of earth and ocean sand, which, as he sees it, are nothing but solidified sun energy.

The bions, says he, are not complete living beings, but only carriers of biological energy, forms of transition from the nonliving to living, yet they propagate like bacteria.

The prime mover of the heavenly bodies, as Reich postulates it, is a cosmic flow of this energy. All planets, says he, swing in a common galactic orgone stream; each planet possesses a disclike envelope of concentrated orgone, which rotates faster than the globe; the creation of galactic systems is due to what he calls the "superimposition" of two cosmic orgone streams.

Most "spiral galaxies," he points out, show two or more arms which unite toward the "core" of the total system, a spiral which is clearly shown in photographs.

In Reich's system when two cosmic orgone energy streams approach, they "superimpose," merge, and fuse at the core, a superimposition, says he, which runs from the subatomic, microscopic level, in which matter is formed in the progressively hardening core, to the macrocosmic level as the galaxy itself emerges.

What a truly heavenly *hieros gamos!*

The same system, of course, would apply on a planetary level!

To pursue the analogy with what has been noted in previous chapters, Reich maintains that hurricanes, tidal waves, and major weather phenomena (as well as sunspot cycles and the aurora borealis), are expressions of the interplay of two or more orgone energy streams.

The hurricane, says he, is a natural cataclysm, due to the superimposition and merger of two orgone energy streams, which, on a photographic plate, look like whirling swastikas.

To tie in with the rain-making king-priests of yore, Reich describes in detail several experiments made by him in the State of Maine, in which, by directing hollow tubes to one side of a thunder cloud he was able to increase its charge of orgone and thus its size, or, by pointing the tubes directly *at* the clouds, cause them to ground their orgone energy, and dissipate the molecules of water vapor.

These experiments are described in scientific detail in a booklet of the Orgone Institute Press.

When lightning, which is a phenomenon of orgone energy, says Reich, strikes the earth, the flow is from the smaller to the greater charge. Were it electrical, rather than orgone energy, says he, the flow would move from the earth, with its higher potential, *up* to the cloud in the sky!

This is interesting in terms of Velikovsky's postulated brush between Earth and Venus, in which Venus would have been the lesser charged of the two bodies.

What would the effect of "orgone energy" be on human beings?

It is a commonplace by now that human beings react

peculiarly to thunderstorms. It is also established that moon and sun have an increasing effect on generation as they move in conjunction.

Reich's theory, in brief, is that sexual energy, or orgone energy, building up in the human being, cries for release.

What affords the release is the orgasm.

To Reich, the orgasm, with its cycle of mechanical tension, bio-electric charge, bio-electric discharge, and mechanical relaxation, is the very formula of life, the method by which cells grow and generate.

In the human orgasm, says he, the whole protoplasmic body behaves like a single cell.

The orgastic function, together with the known effects of the sun on living organisms, is one of the phenomena, says Reich, which shows that the living organism is part of nonliving nature.

In human terms, the orgasm duplicates the superimposition of heavenly bodies in the macrocosmic, and of atomic bodies, in the microscopic.

At the acme of excitation, says Reich, two human orgone systems which have become one, discharge their energy in clonic convulsions. In this process, as he elaborates it, highly charged substances (including the sperm cells) are discharged, which in turn continue the function of superimposition, penetration and fusion.

What a fantastic progression: from the formless ether, to stars, to planets, to human beings, to semen, to living protoplasm, to bion vesicles, *and back again!*

No matter how "mad" Dr. Reich may have been considered, such ideas could not be discarded without at least a mention.

And apropos of madness, following Freud—who attested to the sexual origin of neurosis—Reich maintains categorically that all neurosis is the result of dammed-up sexual energy.

If somatic sexual excitation is barred from perception and discharge, says he, it is converted into anxiety.

By a sort of hardening process, this anxiety is transformed into what he calls "Character Armor"—layers of solidified energy which he compares to geological and archeological strata within the human being, or solidified history. The whole experiential world of the past, says Reich, is alive in the present in the form of character attitudes. Conflicts which have been active in the past leave traces in the character, in the form of a rigidity. These function automatically, and are difficult to eliminate. All of which is thoroughly corroborated by other schools of psychiatric investigators.

The rub comes with the cure.

It was with his therapy rather than his theory that Reich ran into opposition. To him, the cure for aberrated man was to change the neurotic character back into what he called a "genital" character, capable of an uninhibited release of dammed-up energy through a full and proper orgasm.

And where Dr. Reich got into trouble was with what he called his "orgone accumulator."

An ordinary metal-lined box—as he describes it in his experiments—it somehow managed spontaneously to accumulate orgone energy, which, once manifested (as a bluish light), could not be removed even though the box itself were dismantled.

The resemblance between such a simple metal box and the one so celebrated in antiquity which *always* contained a mysterious living symbol of divinity, described by so many authorities as phallic or generative—the ark—is too striking to avoid.

The *Encyclopedia of Religion and Ethics* says quite plainly "the god contained in the Ark was regarded as the god of fertility, Attis, Adonis, Osiris." And what of the ritual ascribed to Egyptian hermetic adepts of lying daily in a metal ark or "coffin" in order thereby to be "rejuvenated"!

Nor is it easy to avoid a further biblical analogy from later experiments of Dr. Reich—which he describes in another volume—with the wandering of the Israelites in the wilderness. When infinitesimal amounts of radioactive nuclear material were placed in an orgone accumulator in his laboratories in northern Maine there developed what Reich called a "Deadly Orgone" which caused black and toxic clouds to appear in the skies above them—very much like the ones described in the Bible and attributed by Velikovsky to a brush with Venus.

But these were later developments. To begin with Reich's orgone accumulators, which were manufactured in several sizes, appeared to have the therapeutic effect on human beings of raising their natural energy, tanning them, and, according to *vox populi,* helping their genital potency.

Inevitably, this led to cries of scandal. And the greater the scandal the further it wandered from Reich's attempts to keep it scientific.

To Reich, the genitally potent have no more to do with the satyr or the nymph than with the sex-starved spinster or the impotent martinet, all of whom he considered equally neurotic and incapable of surrender to a natural flow of biological energy.

Yet more and more he came to consider that what is called "bad" was in fact neurotic—a false encumbrance foisted onto a naturally ethical creature.

His description of ideal intercourse is of an aesthetic and poetic quality rarely to be found in the works of medical doctors. His idea of morality, far from being a distorted patriarchal imposition of compulsive attitudes, is one in which self-determined individuals freely choose their mates on the basis of mutual attraction. To Reich nothing appeared more obscene than the squalor of the brothel, than the husband having his way with his wife not by love but by *law,* than the rape and horror of the modern world.

But this is an area where officials dread to tread. Better look the other way.

Humanity, says Reich. has for millennia been so forced to act against its fundamental biological law that it has acquired a second nature which is "*counter-nature*" and cannot help but "go into an irrational frenzy when it tries to restore the fundamental biological function, *and at the same time is afraid of it!*"

No doubt neurosis is a damming of life energy; certainly no human being should be denied arbitrarily the natural development of his capacity for a full and proper orgasm, especially by an implanted distortion of values in his tender years.

But once this ideal is achieved, is it said that such a discharge is the only point and purpose of the energy?

Even Reich admitted that the self-regulated individual can withdraw the energy from a desire which cannot be satisfied, by transferring the energy to other goals or partners.

Other schools have ventured further, into other solutions, involving sublimation or regeneration. And here we get to the crux of the matter, and back to castration.

If only from the evidence of evolution, one could reasonably deduce that man, having come this far, still has some progress to make, that the present is *not* the *ne plus ultra.*

Indeed it is from man's present condition that theologians were led to conclude the race must have fallen to begin with: that some primeval "moral" catastrophe must have affected all of mankind.

Catholics are taught that man's fall resulted from a concupiscence which alienated him from God, with a resulting loss of immortality and bliss. In the words of St. Paul: "As by one man sin entered into this world and by sin death; so death passed to all men."

It is extraordinary the number of texts which ascribe the appearance of death to the appearance of sex.

If this were taken as an analogy of the evolution of the cell originally reproducing an identical and equally ageless daughter by dividing itself in half, the idea would be valid enough, as it was with the development of sexual reproduction that the excess unfertilized cells were allowed to die off.

Commenting on the mythology of the arrival on this planet of sex and death, Joseph Campbell points out that without the latter the former, unhindered, might prove worse than a blessing, that in their rites the early planters well understood the necessity for killing and eating to maintain a happy continuance of all that grows. To the modern world, in which drugs and druggers appear to have stayed the sickle of death, the risk—worse than pestilence and war—appears to be oversurvival.

Could death—as the ancients pictured it—be as salutary a divinity as life?

Is death, in the form of a temporary doffing of sheaths, also required for the "growth" of the soul?

Whence came sin? What is the matter with sex? How and why should sex be involved with sin? Or was it once all right, and did it somehow get bitched?

To Cardinal Newman, Original Sin, which Pascal called "the master key to the intricacies and perplexities of the human race," is absolutely basic: "If there be a God," says Cardinal Newman; "and since there is a God, the human race is implicated in some terrible aboriginal calamity. It is out of joint with the purpose of its Creator. This is a fact, a fact as true as the fact of existence; and thus the doctrine of what is theologically called original sin becomes to me almost as certain as that the world exists, and as the existence of God."

The 1545-63 Council of Trent considered the "fall" to have caused man the loss of his primitive holiness and justice; that to all Adam's descendants had been transmitted "both bodily death and sin, which is the death of the soul."

How sin is transmitted has also remained a mystery, though the modern discoveries of dianetics and scientology may throw some interesting light on the problem, as well as on what is known as the Oedipus complex.

To the early fathers original sin was passed to succeeding generations by the act of generation, which led to a controversy with the Pelasgians who maintained that "If the soul is created in a state of sin, as you Catholics contend, God must be the author of the sin." A doctrine naturally considered blasphemous by its opponents.

Yet how and why Original Sin should be associated with the genitalia is nowhere spelled out.

The Biblical Commission of 1919 decreed that the preternatural qualities of Adam before his fall included along with immortality, what is known as integrity, or a total absence of concupiscence. In modern English, concupiscence is generally understood to apply only to fleshly desires; in theological parlance it indicates any motion or impulse of "the lower nature" which is not under the perfect rule and dominion of his higher faculties, reason and will.

Of the faculties, says the Church, even the lowest are from God; it is their use, by the exercise of free will, which constitutes the test; this would make of original sin not so much an act of sexual indulgence as an act of rebellion.

In fact, in the eyes of Catholic theologians, *before* his "sin," Adam was by no means denied the enjoyment of what they call "the pleasures of a sensitive life." St. Thomas teaches that in his state of innocence Adam enjoyed these delights *even more,* since his natural faculties "were purer and therefore keener."

Pythagoras—who as early as 540 B.C. taught that the sun was the center of our little system and that the planets revolved around it, making night and day—postulated that it must have been the guilt of the soul in a higher state which caused its separation from the divine and its imprisonment in the body, through one or several existences. But was there sex and sexual differentiation in this "higher state?"

Plato and the Orphists maintained that the soul expiated in the prison of the body sins it had committed in a previous existence, an idea with which both Philo and Origen agreed.

This leads to the conceit of a duality in the universe and of a contest between man's spiritual nature and a grosser material substance which would tend to degrade him, whereas the spirit's function would be to illumine, enliven, quicken, irradiate matter.

Plotinus, in an exposition of the descent of an evolving soul, or consciousness, attributed the "Fall" to mind and emotions being attracted by the desires and sensations of phenomenal existence—in which context Reich describes sensation as the sieve through which all inner and outer stimuli are perceived.

Plotinus, postulating that man, through the "Fall," exchanged a blissful state of passive receptivity for a condition of active responsibility, becoming thereby a moral being involved in the struggle between good and evil, asks: "Why then does the soul descend and lose knowledge of its unity with the whole? For the choice is better to remain above."

The error, says Plotinus, lies in self-will, "The soul desires to be its own, and so ventures forth to birth, and takes upon itself the ordering of a body which it appropriates, or rather which appropriates it, so far as that is possible. Thus the soul, although it does not really belong to this body, yet energises in relation to it, and in a manner becomes a partial soul in separation from the whole."

In the Gnostic system, whose sources preceded, and whose main exponents succeeded, Plato and Plotinus, doubt itself was regarded as a motivator downward on the path to even more dense and gross states of existence than physical; whereas prayer and aspiration led upward to a more rarefied, heavenly world.

The very emotion of fear, said the Gnostics, contracts and densifies the aura or subtle envelope of man—a phenomenon easily manifested by what is vulgarly known as the "lie-detector." To the Gnostics, the psychic plane was already a densification of the mental, as the material was of the psychic.

Interestingly enough it was the Great Mother herself whom they considered to be the original fallen wisdom, a prime substance, chaotically moved by four great impulses, her primal "afflictions" or "passions"—a Mater Dolorosa!

To the Gnostic, says Mead, this cosmic substance was so fine and rare and subtle that it transcended all the substance we know of; indeed, says he, the mother-substance of cosmos was of so marvelous a nature that the Gnostics called it Wisdom herself, Sophia, the highest vesture with which the spirit could be clothed.

The dwelling of Sophia, according to the Gnostics, was in between the upper and purely spiritual worlds, and the lower psychic and material worlds. Resting on seven spheres of psychic substance, "The Seven Pillars of Wisdom," it acted as the mediatrix between the upper and lower spaces.

Why, says Mead, Wisdom, who was originally a pneumatic or spiritual essence, should be in the Middle Space, an exile from her true Dwelling, was the great mystery which the Gnostics endeavored to solve.

Unfortunately only fragments of the Gnostic philosophy are yet available, and, as Mead has pointed out, anyone trying to make a concordance of the names alone in Gnosticism "may think himself lucky to escape a lunatic asylum."

The Ariadne's thread which takes one out of the maze, says he, is spun, not of names but of ideas. "He who seeks the idea behind the name finds himself in a realm of great beauty and harmony of thought. . . . Men like the Gnostics have ever had intuitions of a real state of being, or definite and precise realms of consciousness; yet each has caught but a glimpse of the reality, as all men must so long as they are imprisoned in a body."

If the physicist today has a hard enough time with his instruments and mathematical symbols to convey the realities of nature, how much more difficult must it have been to convey the ideas of metaphysics, dealing with realms of the invisible and the intangible!

Yet the intuition of antiquity and the most recent discoveries of modern science may be coming closer day by day.

In a recent lecture on the philosophical problems of atomic physics, Werner Heisenberg, one of the founders of quantum mechanics, had to admit that modern physics kept moving closer to the postulates of Plato. Not only, said Heisenberg, is energy the force that keeps the "all" in continuous motion, but "it is also—like fire in the philosophy of Heraclitus—the fundamental substance of which the world is made. Matter originates when the substance energy is converted into the form of an elementary particle. Like the regular elementary bodies of Plato's philosophy, the elementary particles of modern physics are defined by mathematical conditions of symmetry."

To Pythagoras, Platonists, and Indian philosophers the dodecahedron was the symbol of the material universe, and, as Mead has noted, psychic clairvoyants maintain that the field of activity of the atom is contained in a rhombic dodecahedron.

For those who have the inclination, a comparison between the conceits of modern physics with those of the Gnostics—in which, through their symbolism, they attempt to convey to physical consciousness some idea of the modes, not only of superphysical existence, but also of what was definitely stated to be a suprarational being—may well prove rewarding.

To the Gnostic too there was a fall of the soul, whether cosmic or individual, from original purity, which involved suffering and misery, and in the course of which the material mind was to be purified so as to be one with the spiritual mind.

As Mead put it: "In the nomenclature of the Gnostic this was dramatized in the redemption of the Sophia by the Christ, who delivered her from her ignorance and sufferings."

The Logos, in the Gnostic system, as summarized by Mead, "takes a body, and His body is the cosmos. The Heavenly Man is thus crucified in space. But the crucifixion is no shame, no disgrace; the cross is the body of the Heavenly Man, the universe; and the symbol which was chosen for that mystery was the figure of the Heavenly Man with arms outstretched pouring His life and love and light into His creatures, the source of all good to the universe, the perpetual self-sacrifice."

Interestingly enough, it appears that the figure of Christ with a pained expression—of the type so pleasing to Spaniards—was quite a late development, virtually unknown before the fifth century after the historical death.

It is as if light, to create form, had to be crucified into matter. Interesting in terms of Reich's theory that form is frozen motion, and that matter is frozen sunlight, which, as the form disintegrates, is once more liberated!

In one interpretation of the Creed, Christ is said to "endure a dense sea" and to be "crucified on the cross of physical matter" in which he is described as being dead and buried.

In a nutshell: the spirit, to take form, must solidify; each solidification is a crucifixion, from which release is obtained by death which amounts to a rebirth.

Lower in the scale of being, says Mead, there was another crucifixion, when the spirit was incarnated into the plane where there is male and female, and is thus cut off from the great life of motion in the world of life and light, beyond time and space, or, as Mead calls it, "the undecaying heart of the eternities."

But if that is the way down, what is the way up?

To the Gnostics, the way up and out was through Christ, who, they said, had preached a universal doctrine, a new revelation of the Good God, the Father of all.

They claimed—in a manner bound to get them tarred as heretics—that they alone understood what Jesus really meant, that they, with their libraries, "were heirs to a universal revelation," not just a Christian one.

To them the "in order that it might be fulfilled" school of biblical writers had adulterated and garbled the original sayings of the Lord, the universal glad tidings, by "unintelligent and erroneous glosses they had woven into their collection of teachings."

It certainly stands to reason that if Jesus were the adept he is claimed by Christians to have been, it is mystifying that the body of his teachings, as canonized by the Church, should be so subject to varied and confusing interpretations. One would have expected such a mind incarnate to have left a lucid, clear-cut gospel.

If there is anything to Sabinus' and Pappas' descriptions of how the canon was selected, one need hardly wonder at the results.

Sabinus, the contemporary bishop of Heracles, though perhaps a little partisan, describes the bishops who constituted the Council of Nicaea as being, with the exception of Constantine, the Emperor, and Eusebius Pamphili, "a set of illiterate, simple creatures, who understood nothing." And Pappas, in his Synodicon, thus describes the selection: "Having promiscuously put all the books that were referred to the Council for determination under a communion-table in a church, they (the bishops) besought the Lord that the inspired writings might get up on the table, while the spurious ones remained underneath, and it happened accordingly."

As Robert Graves puts it: "All the available evidence goes to show that the original Nazarene Gospel was terse, factually accurate, intellectually satisfying to those chosen students of the Law and the prophets for whom it was primarily intended. But Gentile heretics pirated it, mistranslated it into pedestrian Greek, recast it, and then subjected it to a century-long process of emendation and manipulation."

To this he adds, "The glamor of the early Jacobean prose in which the gospels are now clothed, and their judicial authority, are most deceptive. Judged by Greek literary standards, they are poor, by historical standards, unreliable; and their doctrine is confused and contradictory."

To the Gnostics there was a redeemer from heaven who

gave to those by nature capable of salvation, the knowledge which *was* salvation.

The Gnostic, says Mead, "knew himself as a spiritual being, whence he had fallen, and wither he will return." The Gnostic's mysterious grades of purification were steps "whereby the man rises to higher grades of consciousness, by the purity of his inner vehicles, which correspond with certain states or regions."

To the theosophists the mystery-institutions were founded as the most efficient means of giving humanity instruction in "higher things." In their view the mysteries were conducted by adepts who had a knowledge of nature-powers which was "the acquisition of a prior perfected humanity not necessarily earth-born." Eventually, says Mead, the mysteries were committed to the care of the most advanced pupils of humanity, who had to substitute symbols and devices, dreams and scenic representations for what had previously been revealed by higher means."

According to the Gnostic version of the initiation of the disciples on the Mount, Jesus had his disciples "soar aloft into the aerial regions" where he instructed them on the "nature of this space and its rulers."

The mysteries into which he initiated them were to bring them into "the regions of Truth and righteousness, into the region of the Holy of Holies, into the region where there is neither female or male, nor form in that region, but only Light, unceasing, ineffable."

When, according to this gospel, the disciples asked to be instructed in the Life of the Father, Jesus answered that they must purify their souls from all earthly stain, "making them to become the Race of the Mind, so that they may be filled with understanding, and by His teaching perfect themselves, and be saved from the Rulers of this world and its endless snares. Let them hasten to receive the Gnosis He is to impart—His Word—for He is free from all stain of the world."

When, according to the same source, the disciples asked to be instructed in the nature of ignorance, the opposite of gnosis, Jesus told them that to understand this great mystery they must first "put on His virginity and righteousness."

Unfortunately, when it comes to further details, the text of what follows is missing in the versions that have so far been discovered, or made public.

In the end, however, still according to the Gnostic testaments, when the disciples have received the proper mysteries and understood them, they will go out of the body, "they will become pure light and soar upwards into the Light-Treasure."

St. Paul himself speaks of people being in and out of their bodies, and tells of how at one point he was raised to "the third heaven."

One Gnostic sect, the Naassenes, believed the primal being to have been both male and female, and that it was to a similar state that human beings aspired. They considered sexual intercourse an error because it represented "man's fatal effort to become one without recognizing that the only real unity is spiritual."

Man's true goal, in their view, was to reach a state like that of "the first creation" where the creature was "both male and female." To do so, man must cast off his physical body and become one being. "By casting off the fleshly garments, men recognize that the kingdom is within."

Known as rigid ascetics, the Naassenes are said to have been initiated into the Mysteries of the Great Mother, "because they found in these rites the teaching of the whole mystery of rebirth."

The gospels, they said, contained "psychic teaching" which could only be correctly interpreted by those who knew the secret traditions and the gospels considered apocryphal.

It is noteworthy, of course, that apocryphal originally did not have the present pejorative connotations, but meant containing esoteric knowledge not to be lightly revealed to the uninitiate.

In saying number 23 of their Gospel according to Thomas, a collection of more than a hundred sayings of Jesus, which its declared author Didymus Judas Thomas claimed to be the "secret words which Jesus the Living" spoke to him and he carefully wrote down, Jesus tells the disciples that they will go into the Kingdom of Heaven "when you make the two one, and make the inside like the outside, and the outside like the inside, and the upper side like the under side, and that you make the man and the woman a single one, in order that the man is not man and the woman is not woman."

Here, no doubt, the male-female problem is being dealt with on more than one level.

It is a curious idea that the soul should be considered female, and that whether cosmic or individual, it should have fallen from an original purity, involving suffering and misery, from which it has to be redeemed and purified by spiritual "self-analyzing reflection" of mind, by the Christ, or the Logos, male, yet virginal.

Oddly enough, Reich once said that "in the act of thought, the living grasps itself."

In verse 112 of the Thomas gospel when Simon Peter

wants to send away Mariham because "women are not worthy of life," Jesus is said to have rebuked him with the words: "Lo, I will draw her so that I will make her a man, so that she too may become a living spirit which is like you men; for every woman who makes herself a man will enter into the kingdom of heaven."

Some trace of such gospels must no doubt have been alive among the Skoptsi, and they may have had a point when they claimed further references had been cut from the gospels.

In the canonical gospels there is an overt reference to the subject when Jesus is tested by the Pharisees with the conundrum about the widow who married and had sexual intercourse with seven brothers in succession, and is asked to whom she would belong in heaven.

Mark quotes Jesus as answering: "When they rise from the dead, men and women do not marry; they are like angels in heaven." A quotation corroborated by Matthew, to which Luke adds that though the men and women of this world marry, those who have been judged worthy of a place in the world of the resurrection do not marry because "they are not subject to death any longer."

One of the rare remaining references in the early Church writings is in 2 Clement 12: "When the Lord was asked by someone when his kingdom would come, he said, when the two will be one, and the outside like the inside, and the male with the female neither male or female."

The reference appears to be to the gospel of the Egyptians where the same dialogue is reported at greater length, and the interlocutor of Jesus is a woman called Salome.

To Mead, treading on the vesture of shame means to

rise above animal nature. To Jungian psychologists, "When the two become one, and male with female neither male or female" means an inner marriage between the male and female parts of the psyche, through which marriage the individual would once more become whole. This, they say, would give rise to "an inner child whose birth brings release from the power of death."

How entwined are these threads of Ariadne in this baffling labyrinth!

One might even add the thread of the astrologists who maintain that before there can be what they call "regeneration" the sexual power of Scorpio must be taken from that sign and transferred to Taurus, or, as someone else explained it: "That the generative force of sex organs must be transmuted and raised to the throat, where it can find expression in the Word as a manifestation of the mind's creative power."

In another word: to overcome death one must overcome the power of the sexual organs, and sexual passion!

Here the Gnostics, who considered themselves true Christians, were not far from some of their more orthodox brethren who considered them heretics.

In what a Jesuit has called "perhaps the most beautiful symbolic prose poem of the early patristic period" in which "its noblest thoughts were to become the permanent heritage of Christian asceticism and mysticism," St. Methodius, discussing the place of celibacy in Christian life, calls it nothing less than the perfect practice of Christian virtue "without which we cannot enter heaven."

"This is the reason," says Methodius, "why Our Lord, in that passage in the Gospels in which he instructs us in the various ways in which men have become eunuchs, promises that all who make themselves virgins will enter the Kingdom of Heaven."

In his Symposion—an imitation of Plato's dialogues to be used as a manual of Christian doctrine—Methodius maintains that virginity "becomes a means of achieving the Platonic ascent of the soul, whereby the chaste rise to behold the heavenly realities, of which the doctrines of the Church here below are but the image."

In answer to the question why there was no mention in Jewish scriptures of the advantages of virginity, Methodius says that "it was reserved for the Lord alone to be the first to exalt this doctrine, just as He alone, coming into the world, taught men how to draw near to God. It was only fitting that he who was Archpriest, Archprophet, and Archangel, should also be called Archvirgin."

Interpreting the gospel through the mouths of ten virgins, Methodius has one of them say: "Now I think I perceive quite clearly that of all the means offered to men to guide us to the eternal life, nothing is superior to chastity in its power to restore mankind to Paradise, reconcile them with God and transform them into a state of incorruptibility."

What he means by incorruptibility he makes clear with an analogy which though it may sound strange in the mouth of one of his virgins, is certainly pungent enough: "Just as the bloody fluids of meat and all the elements which make for putrefaction are drawn off by salting it, so too all the irrational desires of the body are banished from a maiden by the pious instruction she receives. It is inevitable that the soul that has not been salted with Christ's words should begin to smell and breed worms." Not as ethereal perhaps as the language of the Gnostics, but who knows for what audience it was designed.

In the end, to both Christian and Gnostic, it was Jesus who triumphed over the weaker power of generation at the expense of his own body, which he handed to death—a manifestation of the God of generation.

But the Gnostics were of a mind that man too could so perfect himself that he became a conscious worker with the Logos; all those who did so, became "Christs" and as such were Saviors, but not in the sense of being the Logos Himself.

The neophyte, on receiving "baptism," that is on reaching a certain state of interior purification or enlightenment, was said to "rise from the dead"; thereafter he "never grew old and became immortal," or, as modern psychologists interpret it, "obtained possession of the unbroken consciousness of his spiritual ego."

To the Gnostic, the divine creative spark in man can either express itself in the creation of a human child, or alternatively "be assimilated into the individual himself, creating in him a spirit which is immortal."

The Gnostics were especially opposed to the materialistic doctrine of the resurrection of the body, and with this the Patristic writers were especially at odds.

To Catholic theologians, the Gnostic philosophies recognized in human nature no moral solidarity between soul and body, considering the body but a prison, the doors of which had to be broken open, the object of asceticism being to annihilate the flesh.

Christianity, in general, regards the body as the soul's companion, a rebellious companion, but one to be mastered and subdued by mortification to transform it into an instrument of merit and salvation, which, after death, "will rise again to share with the soul in the reward or penalty which it has merited along with the soul."

Doubtless there is some confusion as to the meaning of "body," though to enter into its subtle attributes might prove no more profitable than the discussion around the extra "i" in homoiousian.

In any case, there are scientists and theologians who maintain there are several layers of physical-psychic bodies, some of which are bound to be destroyed.

One such body could be the "armored" monster of Dr. Reich, built up by unnaturally inhibited sex, to the destruction of which his whole therapy was devoted. It is a body strangely akin to the "flesh" of St. Paul, which he also wished to dispose of.

But in all this discourse on bodies, and the making of the female into male, how was it that the split came about to begin with?

Many scholars have pointed out that Adam is a generic term for an early "human being," more likely androgynous from whose "thigh" a female was derived. Bellamy says that the translation by non-Jews of the Hebrew word *tsela* as "rib" has been the cause of some misunderstanding. "Its severely literal meaning," says Bellamy, "is flank, or 'side,' or 'loin.' That is: it should read, 'He took of his loin.' " But the person upon whom the operation is described in verse 21, says he, "must have been a woman."

Both Plato and Philo subscribe to the theory of the androgynous origin of the human race, maintaining that the separate sexes were a later evolution.

The opinion that Adam and Eve were hermaphrodites was revived in the thirteenth century by Amaury de Chartres, who also held that at the end of the world both sexes would be reunited in a single person. For this and other opinions he was condemned as heretical by Innocent III.

William Law, in his *A Call to Holy Life*, believed that

the first human being was a creature containing both sexes in its own perfect nature.

To Paracelsus man and woman were originally one, but man having become separated from the woman in him, lost his true substance, and now seeks the woman outside of his true self.

In the mythology of the Marind-anim and West Ceramese there were in the very beginning, presexual, premortal ancestral beings who lived in innocence until some extraordinary event brought a transformation of all things, "whereupon death and sex came into the world as the correlates of temporality."

In the Kabala it is stated that only when, from a potential androgyne, man had become separated into male and female, could he be endowed with the conscious, rational, individual soul or Monas, "the principle or intelligence of the Elohim" to receive which he had to eat of the fruit of Knowledge from the Tree of Good and Evil.

But the clearest and most detailed description of the process of the division of the sexes comes from the Book of Dyzan, the oriental source of wisdom translated and commentated by H. P. Blavatsky, where it is stated that originally every class and family of living species was hermaphrodite.

In a more recent comment on this body of philosophy, M. S. Yewdale says that nothing is clearer than that modern man and modern woman evolved from a bisexual species, and that in the far distant past the species split in two, the parts eventually becoming predominantly male and female.

What's more, according to Blavatsky and Yewdale, we are heading back toward a sexless more spiritual future.

In general, says Yewdale, the body of the modern woman still possesses all the evidence that it once was bisexual, and the body even of modern man still contains the vestigial evidence of its bisexual inheritance.

According to the Book of Dzyan, earlier races of humans procreated differently: in a manner somewhat similar to that first enacted on the London and New York stage by Bernard Shaw in his *Back to Methuselah.*

The very earliest progenitors of man, according to the Book of Dzyan, eons ago, reproduced by budding, by exudation, then by eggs from an androgynous parent, but nourished by cosmic forces. These early races were first sexless, then hermaphrodite, then bisexual; among the latter, one sex began to predominate over the other.

However, says Blavatsky, these early races would hardly be recognized in modern times as humans, and the continents on which they lived have, for the most part, been sunk beneath the waves.

The history of the human species as we know it, says Blavatsky, begins properly with the Third Race after it had separated into two sexes. "Yet," she adds, "from a mass of data, which remains to this day in the form of ancient written records, pictures, sculptures, and fossils, we can reconstruct a picture of the preceding period, when all forms of life were bisexual, and when not only human beings, but animals, birds, fishes, trees, plants, and all other living things were of gigantic proportions."

There is, of course a great wealth of data on gigantic human beings, gigantic animals and vegetation, and in this respect H. S. Bellamy's chronology of the history of this planet gives some very plausible explanations for their coming and going.

A rabbinical belief asserted that before Adam's sin he stretched from heaven to earth but that when he sinned his height diminished!

Yewdale's reconstruction of the development of human beings from the Book of Dzyan reads like science fiction, but if it were to be taken merely as a mythological analogy of the development of what passes for "scientific" evolution, it would still be very well worth reporting.

The oviparous creatures of the third race—meaning those producing eggs hatched outside the body rather than ovoviviparously, inside the body—were, says Yewdale, though of giant size, undoubtedly formed on the order of humans, but without breasts or mammary glands, and with only a single opening in the lower part of the body, through which the nuclei could be extruded, in the manner of birds laying eggs. It is not impossible, says he, that the young were hatched from unfertilized eggs; that is, by parthenogenesis, as with some birds.

From the oviparous state to the ovoviviparous, millions of years apparently elapsed. When the Third Race had reached that stage, outwardly the creatures now had breasts with active glands, and a second opening had appeared in the lower part of the body, the urogenital. Inwardly the reproductive system was developed to a point where the eggs were fertilized and hatched inside the body, but without placental attachment or direct connection with the blood vessels of the parent. The progeny were born alive—emerging from the second bodily opening and having to be nourished at the breast.

This process was a kind of internal incubation, but not a true gestation or pregnancy. Like the marsupials, which in general are oviviparous, the creatures of the Third Race at this stage, says Yewdale, had no uterus. In marsupials, in fact, the oviducts do not unite to form a uterus.

When, after millions of years, the Third Race reached the latter part of the ovoviviparous stage, its reproductive system became more definitely developed, including not only ovaries, but testes, phallus, and uterus as well, all of which were completely inside the body.

Thus, says he, the ovoviviparous creatures possessed all the reproductive organs necessary to the generation of the species, and, by immaculate conception and birth, continued through eons of time to bring forth progeny of their own kind.

It was then, says Blavatsky, that came one of the most momentous phenomena in the history of life on earth: the splitting up of all bisexual forms, both human and animal, and the ultimate evolution into separate male and female entities. When procreation resulted from cohabitation, speech is supposed to have developed.

With the awakening of the mind, which also resulted from the separation of the bisexuals into sexes, says Blavatsky, true speech was born; that is, when the reasoning faculties were born, language came into being.

Before that, says Blavatsky, communication was by thought transference; guidance in everyday life was gained by clairvoyance, clair-audience, dreams, divination, and similar means.

So far as their outer physical formation was concerned, the bisexual human beings were female in appearance, says Yewdale. Inwardly they were female and male, the double-sexed reproductive organs being closely associated in a unitary system and situated at the entrance of a canal which had its terminus in the second bodily opening. It was with the forming of this canal that evolution initiated the first move in the separation of the sexes; for it was through this canal that the reproductive organs descended and eventually formed the two sexes.

From the bisexual beings evolved women, and from women evolved man. The bisexual beings, by an extraordinary change in their reproductive system, says Yewdale, were transformed into females; later some of the females, by a further change in their reproductive systems, were transformed into males.

To evolve into males the second group had to undergo a more radical change. Not only did the phallus have to continue its descent until it had emerged from the body, but the testes likewise descended and rejoined the phallus; furthermore, the uterus also descended, and, greatly reduced in size, took position at the base of the phallus. The ovaries, left alone in the body, eventually atrophied and practically vanished. The breasts at this time were still developed and functional; but gradually they were reduced and finally became functionless. Thus, says Yewdale, evolved the males who were to become the fathers of the future races. Also, thus did the Third Race reach the viviparous stage at which the race was separated into two sexes and in which the young were brought forth alive, having maintained before birth a "vascular vital connection with the body of the parent until they were born in a comparatively advanced stage of development."

Medical dictionaries indeed indicate an organ in the male analogous to the uterus of the female, called the *uterus masculinus* "a small vestigial blind pouch situated at the middle of the highest portion of the crest of the urethra."

According to the Book of Dzyan the first sexually differentiated humans, though still gigantic, were smaller than their bisexual ancestors; with the progress of evolution, which little by little developed the brain, the size of the body decreased.

As all the important work of the race during this period, says Yewdale, was the perpetuation and care of the species, Nature impressed the women into her service, and women in turn impressed the men into their service. The result was a system of matriarchy, in which the women ruled, and with their more primitive energy and strength, not only brought up and guarded the children, but did all the hard work necessary for the support of the men.

These women, say Blavatsky and Yewdale, were stronger and more energetic; their intuitive mind "acting inevitably and in harmony with Nature" guided them in their undertakings without drawing greatly upon their physical strength or weakening it. The men, so they say, though originally possessing great physical strength, gradually lost much of it through lack of use, and because part of it became transformed into mental energy, through the increase in use of the rational mind.

Over a period of millennia they developed a high civilization, says Blavatsky, and Greek and Roman and even Egyptian civilizations were nothing as compared to that of the Third Race, after its separation: their home, a gigantic continent, Lemuria, now buried beneath the Pacific Ocean, reportedly stretched eastward as far as the two Americas, and west to the Indian Ocean and Africa: "Australia was a portion of it, and the numerous islands dotted over the great ocean are the mountain tops of that ancient land." Easter Island, says Blavatsky, belongs to the earliest civilization of the Third Race.

Under the guidance of their "divine rulers" they are

said to have built large cities, cultivated arts and sciences, known astronomy, architecture, and mathematics to perfection.

The remains of Cyclopean walls, says Blavatsky, were the handiwork of the Lemurians of the last subrace, which accounts for the stone relics on Easter Island being "very much like the walls of the Temple of Pachaomac or the ruins of Tiahuanaco in Peru."

Between the first city built and final evolution, many hundreds of thousands of years are supposed to have passed. Then, "inner fires, volcanic eruptions, and subterranean explosions began to shatter the great continent, beginning nearly at the Arctic Circle; and at a period far preceding the Tertiary Age of the Third Race, Lemuria sank beneath the waves."

On a surviving portion of land, in mid-Atlantic, according to this doctrine, a body of North Lemurians were saved and from them, as a nucleus, the Fourth Race of Atlanteans developed.

The famous island of Plato, says Blavatsky, was but a fragment of this great continent, which once extended from the coast of Venezuela, across the Atlantic, to the Canary Islands and North Africa, and from Newfoundland to the coast of France.

On this vast continent a great civilization was born and developed, of which traces, says Blavatsky, remain in many parts of the world. Though smaller than the Lemurians, the Atlanteans were supposed to be quite gigantic. The Book of Dzyan tells how "They built great images 27 feet high, the size of their bodies."

Before they too were submerged in a great deluge, they are said to have developed a fascinating civilization.

After the deluge, according to Blavatsky, a few men

remained: some yellow, some brown and black, and some red, but "the Moon-colored were gone forever."

We, today, would be members of the Fifth Race, a race which, according to the Book of Dzyan, "will not die, but survive for a while, overlapping a new [sixth] Race for many hundred thousands of years to come" to be transformed with (but more slowly than) its new successor, and getting entirely altered in mentality, physique and stature.

Mankind, says Blavatsky, will not again grow into giant bodies. The Fourth Race, says she, "touched the very bottom of materiality in its physical development."

The present race, according to this rare but not unpleasant doctrine, is on an ascending arc: the Sixth is to rapidly grow out of the bonds of matter, and even flesh.

In the higher stages of *yoga,* of course, it is said that after the particles of the body have been entirely refined by a process of ascetic living, a body of a higher grade of matter can be gradually substituted.

As for the Seventh, and the last race of the round, says Blavatsky, it "shall follow the laws of the Krita age of purity," i.e., be known as "the race of Buddhas, the Sons of God, *born of immaculate parents.*"

And so we are back with castration!

The fundamental symbol for rebirth, says Harding, speaking as a Yungian psychologist, is self-castration. "In self-castration the lower nature of man has to be slain so that the perfected being can rise triumphant from its dead sheath."

Furthermore, she adds, Immaculate Conception has served as a universal symbol of the coming into expression in the human individual of what has variously been called the higher self, the Christ within, the spirit. "In this aspect," says Harding, "the idea of virgin birth shows explicitly that only in the body of a virgin, of either sex, could the spirit come to fruition."

Buddha, Zoroaster, Sri Krishna, Lao-tze, Appolonius, Quetzalcoatl, Huitzilopochtly, Montezuma, Plato, Romulus and Remus, Servius Tullius, Julius Caesar, Alexander the Great, Cyrus of Persia, Genghis Khan, Karyala the Finnish hero, and Fo-hi, founder of the Chinese Empire, were all considered to have been born of virgin mothers, and the list could be further prolonged.

And here we are back to Isis and Osiris in a spiritualized form.

We are almost back to the Skoptsi!

And next come Isis and Osiris in a spiritualized form.

The outcome of the initiation to the Goddess, says Harding, "which for the priests involved actual castration and for the ordinary initiant probably some form of ritual castration not involving physical mutilation," was a sort of rebirth.

Christianity, she says, taught that every man must sacrifice himself mystically and spiritually as Christ did actually so that each of us could reach the Light, attain to Union with the Source of Being.

As Mead points out, there was a definite identity in the inner teachings of Gnostic Christianity with the tenets of the Mysteries—Phrygian, Eleusinian, Dionysian, Samothracian, Egyptian, and Assyrian.

Frazer says the ancients regarded initiation in the Eleusinian mysteries "as a key to unlock the gates of Paradise."

In the psychology of Harding, the initiate to the mysteries of the later centuries had to impersonate an ass "because it was considered the most lusty of creatures." In this form the initiate was to experience his own lustfulness until he could realize its inability to satisfy his human need. Thus, says Harding, "the truly human part of him, the spirit, was, as it were, killed by the domination of the Typhonic spirit, just as Osiris had been killed by Seth or Typhon. Then, and not till then, could the love of Isis and his longing for her regenerate him. By her power and grace, he was restored to life, not any longer as brute beast, but as man, redeemed from his own animal passions, a living spirit like unto the gods, assimilated to Osiris, governed no longer by lust, but by reason, or Logos, which Osiris symbolized. This rebirth, however, could only be achieved by lifting the veil of Isis. By recognizing, that is, that this worldly show is only the garment of the true, the real, which lives on a different plane." All of which may account for the eerie sensation one gets in reading *Pinocchio*—not as emasculated by the cartoonists, but in its original Tuscan—the story of a spirited young being locked in a piece of wood, metamorphosed into an ass, devoured by a whale, and resuscitated by an enchantress with sky-blue hair!

According to Harding, only when the postulant had passed through an ordeal, when he had fully experienced this life, and realized its hollowness and sterility, would he be able to find the goddess Isis, by accepting self-castration.

The Roses of Isis, Harding is saying, "are the flowers of pure passion, symbolizing love redeemed from lust."

Modern man, she adds, expects life to give him what he wants, to act as mother to him; but this very expectation robs him of his manhood. "It is, as the ancient myths put it, a castration to the mother."

But, says Harding, the blame should not fall on the actual flesh-and-blood woman who is his partner, but "on the Old Woman in himself, the anima, who, if she gains the upper hand will cause him to 'lose his manhood.' "

So long as all the son's attention is directed toward persuading the "mother" to give him what he wants, says Harding, he has no capacity to gain it for himself. His voluntary castration and death as son result in rebirth as a man.

To Harding, T.S. Eliot's *The Waste Land* deals with just such a problem and, says she, is indication that there may be a second deluge in the offing!

In a way, Harding's psychology may be a key to the whole subject. The essential requirement of the sacrifice of "desirousness," as she calls it, *must be a late initiation,* only to be attained by those who have *already* had experience of life and of their own nature.

If it is undertaken prematurely, says she, or as a childish evasion of the risks and hardships of life, it will only result in disillusion, in what the Freudians call loss of "libido" or "psychic energy."

Such an evasion, in their terms, is a false castration, a "childish clinging to the mother by which all emotional development is forestalled or frustrated."

By this yardstick man isn't grown up till he can treat "woman" as an independent self-determined creature, with her own prerogatives of virgin, mother, and sleeper-with-whom-*she*-pleases.

By the same yardstick, life might be considered a sort

of test: one in which the individual grows from childhood to manhood, and only when he has fulfilled the requirements of sex can he embark upon further progress—whether "spiritual" or extraterrestrial.

By the same token, failure could mean remaining embroiled in the world of flesh and desire—perhaps through a continuum of incarnations, maybe even on a descending scale: a situation like that of the offal eaters in one of the Gnostic realms who perpetuated their existence by the consumption of their own excrement!

Such conceits form the crux of many an oriental religion. Perhaps this is what the various rituals of self-castration intended to dramatize. Only with such a drastic and startling act could those who believed they had found the way indicate to others that there might be more to this world than met the eye. If so, some meaning would be given to the otherwise inexplicable gesture of the Corybantes, the Galli, the Skoptsi, the Indian ascetic, the theosophist, the poets, and Methodius' virgins.

The St. Johns, "the natural-born virgins untouched by woman," instead of being a neurotic anomaly, would then be the forerunners of a novel breed of men engendered without passion, of which the ideal prototype would be the mystical sempiternal Christ.

As an example of a sacrifice, what could be more striking than to brandish one's severed and bleeding genitals as an indication to the world not necessarily to imitate the gesture, but to learn that in the long run to "be saved" man must sacrifice his sex?

Yet the act of self-castration, in the eyes of the early fathers of the Church, destroyed the very purpose of the test. Abstinence alone, in their eyes, allowed for the development of man's capacity for choice, for the use of his own free will serving as a means of mastering his own imagination in order to become not a compulsive, but a self-determined, creature.

And here comes the rub.

In the patriarchal era there is no choice, at least not for the adolescent; and, once inhibited in childhood the choice is hard to recover in adulthood.

To Reich, this inhibiting of children and teenagers is what has led the world to its present sorry state. An extraordinary thesis; but worthy of analysis.

For what sociological reason, asks Reich, does society suppress sexuality and does the individual repress it?

The Church, says Reich, claims to do it for the sake of the soul in the hereafter. Actually, says Reich—whose early works are colored by years of analysis of the Marxist-oriented working classes of Europe—sexual suppression is an essential instrument in the production of economic enslavement. The formation of the authoritarian structure, says he, takes place through the anchoring of sexual inhibition and sexual anxiety.

The method imposed at first was castration, or the threat of castration; then circumcision, then the punishment of child and adolescent sexuality.

Freud has pointed out that when children learn about ritual circumcision they identify it with castration. "It is very interesting," says he in *Totem and Taboo,* "that among primitive men circumcision is combined with or replaced by the cutting of the hair and the drawing of the teeth, and that our children, who cannot know anything about this, really treat these operations as equivalents to castration when they display their fear of them."

As Frazer put it, "More expert examination of the history of the rite of circumcision seems to indicate it is a substitute for castration. . . . The practice is far older than the Jewish institution—it was prevalent throughout Ethiopia, Egypt, and Asia in prehistoric times."

The basic religious idea in all patriarchal religions, says Reich, is the negation of the sexual needs. The relationship between religion and sexuality changed with the advent of the patriarchy: while originally it was essentially a religion of sexuality, it turned into the enemy of sexuality.

In the early beginnings, human sex life, says Reich, followed the natural laws which laid the basis for a natural sociality. "Since then, the period of authoritarian patriarchy of the last four to six thousand years has, with the energy of the suppressed natural sexuality, created the secondary, perverse sexuality of the human today."

On the origin of the patriarchal system Reich does not elaborate, though poetically he uses the word "catastrophe." It would be interesting indeed if some heavenly catastrophe, in which the generative powers affecting the earth had been impaired, had also been attributed by priests to some "sin" on the part of mankind which caused mankind to lose its simple, happy life.

Dr. Velikovsky's new books may adduce some evidence.

In any case, says Reich, the common principle of sexuality and religion is "the sensation of nature in one's own organism," and when the sexual expressions of nature in the human animal were repressed, by the development of patriarchy "a sharp unbridgeable antithesis arose of sexuality as 'sin' and religion as 'an absolution from sin.' "

The "mechanist" and the "mystic," says Reich, are products of this contradiction, remain imprisoned in it, and reproduce the split in their children.

Originally and by nature, says Reich, sexual pleasure was that which was good, beautiful, happy; that which linked man with the whole of nature. With the splitting up of the sexual and the religious feelings, the sexual "became inevitably that which is evil and infernal."

The "god-given" genital embrace, says Reich, was turned into the "pornographic four-lettering male-female intercourse."

On the basis of years of clinical research and analysis Reich concluded that the suppression of infantile and adolescent sex life is the basic mechanism by which character structures supporting political, ideological, and economic serfdom are produced.

Suppression of the natural sexuality in the child, says Reich, particularly of its *genital* sexuality, makes the child apprehensive, shy, obedient, afraid of authority, "good" and "adjusted" in the authoritarian sense. Furthermore, says Reich, the sexual inhibition of the average adolescent blocks his way to rational thinking and feeling. Who has not witnessed, in despair, the moods and follies of the adolescent!

In brief, says Reich, the goal of sexual suppression is that of producing an individual who is adjusted to the authoritarian order and who will submit to it in spite of all misery and degradation.

The authoritarian family fixation presupposes, in Reich's theory, the inhibition of sensual sexuality. Without exception, all children in any patriarchal society, he says, are exposed to this inhibition. No matter how "free" and "uninhibited" later sexual activities may be, he adds, they cannot hide this deep-seated inhibition. More than that, the pathological manifestations in sexual life, such as promiscuity, sexual restlessness, perversions, etc., are in his opinion the direct result of the inhibition of the capacity for orgastic experience.

The result of this process is fear of freedom, and a conservative, reactionary mentality: the more so in what he calls "red fascist Russia," even than in the West.

The suppression of natural sexual gratification leads to various kinds of substitute gratifications, says Reich. Natural aggression, for example, becomes "brutal sadism which then is an essential mass-psychological factor in imperialistic wars."

Sexual inhibition alters the structure of the economically suppressed individual, says Reich, in such a manner that he "thinks, feels, and acts against his own material interests."

Sexual weakness, he adds, undermines self-control; for the maintenance of sexual repression leads to the development of compulsive, emotionally highly charged ideas of honor, duty, courage, and self-control.

With this conceit, Freud also concurred: "My general impression," he wrote in the 1930's, "is that sexual abstinence does not help to build up energetic, independent men of action, original thinkers, bold advocates of freedom and reform, but rather good weaklings who become merged later in the great mass which follow, though reluctantly, the impulses emanating from strong personalities."

As early as Hitler's advent to power, Reich wrote of the middle class that it is "an enormous social power, a power far beyond its economic importance. It is that stratum which keeps alive several thousand years of patriarchy with all its contradictions."

Under lower-middle-class influence, he added, the women develop an attitude of resignation which covers up repressed sexual rebellion while the sons develop, in addition to a submissive attitude toward authority, "a strong identification with the father which later becomes identification with any kind of authority."

The genitally gratified individual, on the other hand, says Reich, "is honest, conscientious, courageous and self-controlled, without making any fuss about it."

But for thousands of years a tremendously powerful organization, says he, preached that pleasure in the genital union is sinful. "And man believed it, no longer felt his own body, did not trust his own sense, neglected his very origin and lost the key to his fecundity."

None of the authors he came across, says Reich, hit upon the idea that the sexual misery of youth is basically a *social* problem, that it would not exist but for the demand for sexual abstinence made by conservative society.

What is more, says he, the moral regulation gained a reason for its existence the moment when that which it produced actually began to endanger social life. "Sexual abstinence for children and adolescents creates the very chaos it professes to control."

In Robert Briffault he would have found an ally. "The patristic and Puritan Christian plan for eliminating from life the disturbing factor of sex," says Briffault, "has had the effect of greatly increasing the evil which it was intended to abolish. . . . To stamp out life from the face of the earth would be a comparatively easy task. To stamp out the primeval biological force which actuates life is not possible . . . organic impulses are, like water, incompressible, and whenever pressure is exercised upon them, their power becomes thereby concentrated and increased, and they inevitably spurt forth in another direction."

He then wrapped up his point in an analogical nutshell:

"The suppression of the natural gratification of hunger led to theft; this in turn necessitated the moral condemnation of theft." The same, says, he, applies to adolescent sexuality.

With this, one of his principal theses, Reich ran head on into the sublimationists and the "regenerationists" whose proponents maintain that it is only by preserving and not "wasting" sperm that it can be transmuted into psychic or brain power—and thus "culture."

Also, with this thesis Reich parted company with Freud, whose philosophical standpoint remained that "culture" owed its existence to instinctual repression and renunciation, that cultural achievements are the result of sublimated sexual energy. To Reich the only thing that was correct about such a theory was that sexual suppression *did* form the mass-psychological basis for a *specific* culture: the patriarchal, authoritarian one.

To be fair, Freud too was specific on this point in his *Modern Sexual Morality and Modern Nervousness* when he said that "the task of checking an urge as powerful as the sexual urge by other means than its natural gratification is one that consumes all the energy a man is capable of." To which he added, "Checking it by sublimating it, that is by deflecting the sexual instinct from its sexual aim and towards loftier cultural aims succeeds in a few cases, but only temporarily; the task is especially arduous in the fiery period of youth."

What Reich was attacking was primarily the inhibition of *infantile* and *adolescent* sexuality which had the dual effect not only of inhibiting the youth but of inhibiting him later in life. That the adolescent has no choice, is patent: unless it be the choice between abstinence and masturbation.

And it is nonsense to maintain that abstinence makes for culture in the adolescent. On the contrary, it is the guilt attached to his secretive sex life and its inhibition which actually make him neurotic.

No one can have suffered the pangs of adolescence without having realized that something was wrong with a system in which children are reduced to such a choice, or to whoring: a system in which they are schooled often by neurotic spinsters or crabbed and pederastic masters.

The schoolboy with his mind on the problem of inhibited sex—and who cannot remember the problem—has to read a page several times before its doubtful content is absorbed, and then to what purpose? To pave his way to slavery in some mechanistic monster of society!

What becomes of life, nature, beauty, love, and creative wonder?

From the books one is given in his teens most of the life has been removed by pedestrian pedagogues. So the teenager falls for pornography, just as for lack of nourishing food he will stuff himself on poisonous candy which only makes him the hungrier.

To believe that teenagers with the opportunity for sexual expression with willing and unafraid partners their own age become either dangerously promiscuous or libertine is the folly of those who have never had the chance of experience. The moment a teenager's sex life is satisfied he is more than likely to run for relief to the monastic privacy of some cell barred to the opposite sex, where, instead of wasting time and money on liquor and prurient pastimes, he can study in peace and quiet.

And as for those who think they can force a youngster into sublimation by the cane, by passages in Latin of a dullness nowhere to be equaled in literature, by the football stadium or the ballet class, they are merely avenging on others the sins perpetrated on them in their own youth.

Reich may well have bared a basic aberration in man. But whether he was right or wrong, it takes no savant or seer to realize the world is off the rails, so much so that to grasp at any straw may be worth the effort.

In my own buffeted youth I used to dream of an ideal society in which at puberty the boys and girls discovered sex; in their twenties paired off to bear children; in their thirties built and explored (while the grandparents watched the issue); in their forties, grandparents themselves, divided their time between philosophy and policy; in their fifties, retired to a world of the mind from which to foray on occasion into gardening or communing with the grandchildren, ready, when the moment came, for a tranquil passage to the next dimension.

Is that not what Hesiod describes as the Golden Age of Saturn—except that the life span was longer?

Is that not what Malinowski found among the inhabitants of the Trobriand Islands where there was no sexual repression among the children and no sexual secrecy, where their sex life was allowed to develop naturally and freely, unhampered through each stage of life, and with full satisfaction?

The result, says Reich, was that among the Trobrianders there was "no promiscuity," that the socially accepted form of sexual life was "spontaneous monogamy without compulsion, a relationship which can be dissolved without difficulties."

The only exceptions were among girls specially kept "virgin" because they were earmarked for a foreign market!

Even more indicative was the fact that on a nearby island where the patriarchal authoritarian family organization prevailed, Malinowski found the natives showed "all the traits of the European neurotic, such as distrust, anxiety, neurosis, perversion, suicide, etc."

As early as 1926, Malinowski rejected the concept of the biological nature of the sexual child-parent conflict discovered by Freud, the Oedipus complex. He points out, correctly, says Reich, that the child-parent relationship changes with social processes, that it is of a sociological, not biological nature.

As a result, says Reich, the condition of the love life of a population is the determining factor in their mental health.

To the objection that teenage love would merely compound an already ominous population explosion, Reich answers that contraception is the only sensible solution.

And as for the church's stand, his rebuttal could hardly be simpler:

"The church," says he, "contends that the use of contraceptives, like any interference with natural procreation, is against nature. Now, if nature is so strict and wise, why has it created a sexual apparatus which impels to sexual intercourse not only when one wants children, but on an average of two to three thousand times in the period of adult lifetime?"

On this point Freud also took his stand, saying "man's sexual instinct is not at all primarily meant to serve purposes of reproduction but is intended to furnish certain forms of gratification."

A rebuttal to this rebuttal might be that Original Sin consisted in the willful change by man of his procreative function into one of sexual indulgence: a sin compounded by willful contraception, taking creation right out of the hands of providence.

Somehow there *is* something basically unnatural about contraception.

Until we know, understand, and can match the biological wonder of sperm and ova producing men and women, can we safely afford to tinker with the process?

Yet soberly analyzed, at this stage in the game the problem of contraception does appear to have become fundamental to the plight of the world.

Some stand must be taken, else, while we ponder, the *ronde* of "sin" and "absolution" will continue, with more and more humans progressively available to compound the medley, threatening—if the statisticians are reliable—to swamp us in a sea of flesh.

A good, safe, and effective contraceptive might well fulfill several essential requirements: it could eliminate or drastically reduce the population explosion, rid the world of a great deal of sex-engendered neurosis, put a stop to the horrors of abortion, go a long way towards eliminating venereal disease, do away with the problem of unwanted children along with enforced and incompatible marriages.

Without the fear of impregnation, teenagers could relieve their tensions to their heart's content. When they do want children—and what young people don't?—they could go about it with intent, cherishing the forthcoming creature from conception—thus avoiding whole chain reactions of aberration in future generations.

Sexually uninhibited, teenagers might prove a good deal less neurotic; males could concentrate more on their work and their sport instead of drinking and smoking, hanging around dance halls and bars, driving cars at breakneck speeds; whereas girls might be a help around the house—even learn to cook and dance and sing!

How much shoeleather has been consumed by poor males hopelessly in search of willing and unafraid females! And no doubt vice versa.

Sexually satisfied, the young male might be more amenable to doing chores around the house or farm, or help build and improve property (for his own enjoyment) instead of compulsively being unable to indulge in any pastime other than perhaps gambling—which for very good reason was the favorite sport of the eunuch, being the only tolerable substitute exhaust for the pent-up energy caused by the lack of women.

Less neurotically aggressive, the males would be more conservative of property, less willing to rush off—largely in the hope of finding women—to an endless series of sadistic wars.

Attachments between teenagers could be based on companionship and compatibility of mutual interests rather than on the hook of sex.

Once attached, couples might lead, like the Trobriand Islanders, happily monogamous lives, without compulsive philandering, which, in any case, without fear of offspring, would be less damaging.

Finding mates by mutual agreement and satisfaction might produce unions with the most sensation: hence, in Reich's terms, the optimum orgasm with the optimum flow of *elan vital.*

My own conclusion, which seems to coincide with the view of the ancients, is that sex must be freer first, and only *once* it is free can men and women choose to sublimate it.

And in all of this, one thing stands out as categorically anathema: the imposition on others, especially on the innocent, of puritanical creeds by inhibited, covertly sex-starved, neurotic persons, as often as not in uniforms—political, military, or clerical—and as likely as not to be merely forbidding to others that which they themselves are afraid or incapable of doing.

If any man believes he has seen a brighter truth, let him proselytize his fellows by the only truly admissible and effective method of compulsion: by his own example.

Who will dispute the attraction of an uninhibited, clear-eyed, genitally potent man, shining with an aureola of power, as opposed to the foggy-eyed, twitching, bad-tempered, impotent neurotic. At the same time what is more disgusting than the old man with tinted hair and painted jowl, still leching after nymphets, unless it be the gimlet-eyed inquisitor standing by the stake!

And do not for one minute think that the stake is no longer with us. If anything, the methods of torture have been refined, especially since Pavlov. Castration is no matter of the past. Nor is it likely to become so until a conscientious effort is made on the part of free citizens to ban it.

In the 1920's and 30's several European countries emulated the example of the United States and introduced legislation permitting the castration not only of males but of females, the latter operation being accomplished with the added subtlety of an overdose of X-ray.

In Nazi Germany castration became a weapon in the hands of the judge who could use it as an additional penalty for men over twenty-one—so much so that the Nazi sexologist Wilhelm Meiwerk was emboldened to say of the law that it raised castration "to a social measure in the service of the community"; to which he added the incredible statement: "All writers are agreed that most castrated men are satisfied with their fate."

In some countries the law was, and is, such that the police chief could and can order the operation in the case of sex offenders "at the request of a curator." Here the sophistry lies in the fact that "the curator" is "a guardian appointed when the question of castration arises."

In Norway, during the Nazi occupation, anyone declared insane could be castrated and "police support could be demanded" to perform the operation against the victim's will.

That the operations performed in such countries as Denmark, Norway, Iceland, Finland, Sweden, and Nazi Germany were on "willing" patients was easily discredited by the Swiss psychiatrist Charles Wolf, who pointed out that when the victims "face the alternatives of detention on the one hand and castration-postponement-liberty on the other . . . they almost invariably choose castration, not to be cured but to regain freedom." To which the Swedish doctor Olof Kinberg added significantly: "It is questionable whether there is any penal measure, besides death sentence and life imprisonment, which is so effective as a crime preventive."

Castration was called for in these penal codes even for such offenses as "indecent intercourse" or "indecent acts and indecent behavior." Indecent intercourse comprised not only normal coition, but coitus *inter femora* or *in anum.*

Exhibitionism and similiar offenses and "violation of decency by indecent words" were described as indecent behavior.

Anyone who cares to read the nauseating record in the

detailed case histories of some 250 human beings castrated in Scandinavia as recently as the 1950's will find that most of those operated on for "sexual offenses" were admittedly only classifiable as "troublesome" rather than "dangerous," and that "in the majority of the cases the situation was such that the offended or their relatives threatened to notify the police if 'nothing was done.' "

The elementary conclusion, so obvious to Reich, that a sexual pervert, or criminal, can be cured of his pathological impulses only if he finds his way into a biologically normal sex life, appears to have evaded the castrators, and some of the reasons given for the castrations are almost beyond belief: "homosexual tendencies exhibited more and more frequently—to protect the other patients, castration is desired," or "visited young wives with offer of marriage—accosted girls on the road," or "sexual approaches to the wife of his guardian," or "castration is resorted to as an expedient—a presumably harmless operation that makes legal proceedings superfluous."

Of the women, most of whom were "castrated" very young, some under twenty, one as young as fifteen, and two thirds below twenty-five, some suffered the ordeal for such reasons as "castrated for promiscuity," or "disturbed behavior during menstruation," or "proved to be sexually excited and 'mad about men,' " or "boasted of her sexual life and caused offense by her obscene talk to children."

The simplest means of resorting to castration, of course, is to maintain that the victim is crazy.

That these accused persons are sick and need help seems not to enter people's minds. Nor will people face the fact, self-evident on the slightest reflection, that no man has the right to judge of the sanity of another: otherwise any genius may risk being classed as insane.

The most that society can safely afford is to segregate a man after due process of law as a danger to himself or the community. But so long as the laws of the several states do not prohibit the tampering with human beings by drugs, electric shock, and other modern means of torture, and so long as the asylums and prisons are not improved and made accessible to the public and the press—the methods are at hand for removing from under our noses our hard-gained freedoms.

How many citizens realize, I wonder, that today a man or woman can be delivered to the experimental torture chambers of the psychiatric ward on the say-so of two political appointees who receive as little as $5 for their opinion, that habeas corpus, in the case of those labeled insane, becomes a dead letter, and that, once drugged or electric shocked, or otherwise subtly tortured or brainwashed, *any* person can be made to look or act crazy in a court of law!

All this was supposed to have gone out with the demise of the Sick Man of Europe, with the end of Imperial China, with the advent of the Russian Revolution, with the opening of the Dark Continent, with the probing of the even darker continent of the "unconscious." But it hasn't. We had Hitler and World War II, and Hungary and the Bay of Pigs. And on and on it goes.

Somewhere, something is definitely wrong, if only to judge by the madhouses, the dope fiends, the drunks, the strutting fascists, the self-emasculated communists, the politicians clamoring for war, the police persecuting for the sake of a doubtful security, the white-slavers, brothel keepers, pornographers, and builders of bigger bombs.

Is not the gun, ever bigger, just a deadly substitute for the creative phallus?

Could it really be misdirected sexual energy, inhibited from its proper function by an imposed form of psychic castration which is the cause of all this cruelty and war? Yet what would we do were we to master war and famine and disease?

Procreate *ad infinitum,* and provide the wherewithal to sustain an ever-increasing population?

Colonize the other planets? Engender *Lebensraum* by scientific wonders, distill from space more matter on which to spawn more species? Learn by chemical perfection to change the world from rural into Ruhral?

Were we to spend on parks and cleaned-up rivers, on lakes and fountains, trees and flowers, and on distributing our excess food what we spend on military hardware, what a global garden we could make of this planet, on which to entertain each other with the lively arts.

Or is it all too late?

Are we too far gone to linger at play in a garden? Is it time for even the memory of the Golden Age to vanish? Is the turmoil of this world but a testing ground and preparation for another and more rarefied existence? Must we develop a finer being to cope in a realm or realms of finer beings—or drop like lead to the bottom of despair!

Or is there progress constantly at hand; is progress no more than the gradual elimination of faults till what is left is perfect?

Who knows!

In any case Frazer, who admitted that his *Golden Bough* raised more questions than it answered, was right when he concluded by saying that moral, intellectual, and material progress are bound up with the forces of science and that every obstacle placed in the way of scientific discovery is "a wrong to humanity."

Then, of course, quite wisely, he went on to warn that the generalizations of science are at bottom mere hypotheses devised to explain "that ever-shifting phantasmagoria of thought which we dignify with the high-sounding names of the world and the universe," that in the final analysis, magic, religion, and science are but theories of thought, and that, "as science has supplanted its predecessors, so it may hereafter be itself supplanted by some more perfect hypothesis, perhaps by some totally different way of looking at the phenomena—of registering the shadows on the screen—of which we in this generation form no idea."

Likening the history of thought to a web woven of three different threads—black for magic, red for religion, and white for science—with his final admonition and a conceit from the *The Tempest* Frazer set the problem in the terms of his own generation.

"In the ages to come man may be able to predict, perhaps to control, the wayward courses of the winds and clouds, but hardly will his puny hands have strength to speed afresh our slackening planet in its orbit or rekindle the dying fire of the sun. Yet the philosopher who trembles at the idea of such distant catastrophe may console himself by reflecting that these gloomy apprehensions, like the earth and the sun themselves, are only parts of that unsubstantial world which thought has conjured up out of the void, and that the phantoms which the subtle enchantress has evoked today she may ban tomorrow. They too, like so much that to common eyes seems solid, may melt into air, into thin air."

Now Freud, Frobenius, and Frazer all lie buried—dead within a year of each other and the beginning of World War II—and Reich, for his belief that space is filled with energy and that this universe need not run down—has died a martyr's death in a federal penitentiary.

Yet the world spins on. Velikovsky, himself a Freudian analyst, about to be vindicated by a series of discoveries made since his first works went to the printer, may yet rip a veil from Isis; and each day fresh genius springs from the source of life.

If a final word is needed on the negative side of the subject of this tome—castration—Ovid's is still the best: that it be done to those who do it.

And on the positive side perhaps the suggestion of the Greek anatomist Galen may find support as much among the fairer sex as with the men: that the testes are as precious as the heart, the latter being essential to living, the former to living well.

Who would now dispute the wisdom of Paré that they make for *la paix du ménage?* Or even that the universal prescription for hysteria recommended by Freud's great master at the Salpêtrière, Dr. Charcot, "Rx: *penis normalis, dosim repetitur,*" may not turn out in the end to be a good deal more than a clinical stab at humor.

Strange it is, is it not, that that which we most believe in, that which we call the "word of God," that which we swear to in a court, and that which we will, when we depart, should, each and all, be called a *testament*—a word whose origin is patent.